# The Iraq-Iran Conflict

# The Iraq-Iran Conflict

Éditions du Monde Arabe

First Edition 1981

I.S.B.N. 2-86584-002-6

# The Iraq-Iran Conflict

*Institute of Studies and Research*
*« Editions du Monde Arabe »*

**Editor-in-Chief:** NICOLA FIRZLI
**Editorial Director:** NASSIM KHOURY
**Art Director:** ELIAS DIB

# TABLE OF CONTENTS

9

# PREFACE

The present work, published in Paris in Arabic, French and English simultaneously, inaugurates a collection prepared by the Institute of Study and Research of "Editions du Monde Arabe" (E.M.A.). The books making up this collection will analyze important international issues. However, priority will essentially be given to the development of the Arab World and to the relations with its environment. The aim of "Editions du Monde Arabe" is to make the Arab cultural and political heritage better known. The simultaneous publication of its works in several different languages is intended to favor both communication and dialogue between the Arab people and other peoples of the world.

It is only natural that the choice of studies and research published by "Editions du Monde Arabe" is to be guided by objectivity and attention to scientific rigor. Presenting the reader with the facts just as they have occurred without distorting them is in perfect accordance with one of our major concerns, that is, to see the building of a more just world order by means of the development of an understanding between peoples and a better knowledge of their respective problems. Such information we hope will contribute to dissipate the ignorance of some and the selfishness of others, both of which attitudes unfortunately very often lead to the adoption of aggressive politics.

# INTRODUCTION

The Arab-Iranian conflict is as old as the history of this region of the world. The historian will not fail to call attention to the fact that the present-day war between Iraq and Iran has broken out between two peoples belonging to dissimilar civilizations, and whose origins date back to the ancient times of Arabia and Persia (1). As history amply demonstrates, the numerous divergences between these two countries are obvious from a purely geographical point of view as well as from the ethnic and cultural traits of their peoples.

The Iranian language is considered as one of the ancient Indo-European languages (2) along with Greek, German and Armenian, among others. The Arabic tongue belongs to the Semitic language group, in the same way as the Arabs would be included in the Semitic ethnic ensemble. Despite their geographical proximity, the differences between Iraq and Persia have always been greater than their similarities. Relations between the two countries were frankly hostile until the birth of Islam and the Arab conquest of Persia. Islam, carrying a novel message, brought about considerable changes in Persia and in its relations with the neighboring countries.

(1) In 1935, under the reign of Reza Khan, the name of Persia was changed to Iran.
(2) Cf. Course on French Linguistics of Professor Georges Matoré at the University of Paris IV - Sorbonne.

The Arabs settled in Mesopotamia before recorded history. There, they edified a brilliant civilization and marked this region with their cultural imprint. The Arabs left the Arabian Peninsula by successive waves in order to attain the Mediterranean Sea, where they became known under the name of Phoenicians, as well as reaching the fertile lands of Iraq. Among them, there were the Akkadians, the Assyrians, the Chaldeans and before them, perhaps, the Sumerians, whose origins still pose the historian problems. In any case, the experts agree on the fact that the Sumerians always inhabited Iraq, where they have left substantial traces. Some writers even claim that the men living in Mesopotamia were the first to use cuneiform writing (1).

The Arabs of contemporary Iraq thus inherited an illustrious civilization having benefitted from all those that were to flourish on Mesopotamian land over the centuries: Assyria, Babylonia, etc. Hence, Iraq must be considered as one of the richest regions of the world with respect to both its history and culture. The mountains of Zagros constitute a natural barrier to the east of this country. A new life and a new people are to be found on the other side of those mountains, that is, a people belonging to a civilization which differs from that of the Arabs: the Persians.

Persia, too, had known a specific cultural development. It had its own sciences, its own customs and its own religion, namely, Zoroastrianism. The historian J.M. Roberts writes that the central idea in the Persian religions was the affirmation of the divine nature of royalty. Moreover, "the doctrines in which they (the Persians) believed stressed the existence of a creature, Ahura

---

(1) Matoré G. *Ibid.*: "The Sumerians invented writing around 3500 B.C."

14

Mazda, whose viceroy on earth was the king." (1). He notes that their science, customs and religion were foreign to those of the Arabs.

With respect to military strategy, the Arabs and the Persians also had varying conceptions, as clearly shown by the battle of Qadisiyah. It is indeed at this site that the decisive battle took place, allowing the Arab Muslims led by Sa'ad bin Abi Waqqas under the Omar Bnul Khattab Caliphate to defeat the Persians headed by Rustam (2). This victory occurred on the last day of May or the first day of April 637 A.D. (3). The Arabs were surprised during the battle by the Persian army's use of elephants. Protected within small, wooden fortresses mounted on the backs of the elephants, the Persian archers succeeded in inflicting serious losses upon the Arab infantry and cavalry which were momentarily stunned by a war technique unknown to them. After the bitter defeat at Qadisiyah, having ended with the death of Rustam and the routing of the Sasanid army, the way was cleared for the Muslim conquests in Persia, India and other Asian countries.

The Arab conquest of Persia meant that this country would become part of the region governed by the Arabs, and thus marked the beginning of a history common to both peoples. The situation did not last long. Persia took advantage of the decline of the Abbasids (and thus, of Arab leadership) as well as the overthrow of the Caliphate by other Muslim peoples, namely, the Turks, in order to free itself from Arab control and to assert its independence. As for the Arabs, they found themselves under

---

(1) J.M. Roberts, *The Hutchinson History of the World.* Hutchinson Publishing Group Ltd. London, 1976, p. 356.
(2) Rustam was the head of King Chosroe's Persian army.
(3) Philippe Hitti, *History of the Arabs,* Macmillan Student Editions, 10th ed. London, 1974, p. 155.

15

Turkish rule for a long period that only ended with the First World War. In 1501, Persia retrieved its independence under Ismail, the founder of the Safawid dynasty (1). Historian Philippe Hitti considers the Safawid Kingdom as "one of the greatest and most glorious Persian Muslim states" (2).

The conflict was to again break out between Persia and Iraq (henceforth occupied by the Turks) in a way almost analogous to the pre-Islamic period. International agreements concluded between Persia and Iraq and to which specialists in international law refer in the debate over today's conflict, were in fact signed between Persia and the Ottoman Empire. The most significant treaties were those of Ard Roum (Erzeroum) in 1847 and the Constantinople Protocol of 1913. We have analyzed these conventions in the context of the developments that this book treats with regard to Arabistan and Shatt-al-Arab. To bring to light the true facts opposing Iraq and Iran today, the history of the relations between these two countries must be retraced and closely examined. It is for this reason that we have axed our discussion upon three main themes. First of all, we have recalled the direct causes of the war which broke out in September 1980 (Chapter 1). The historical roots of the Iraq-Iran conflict are then exposed through the geographical and historical development of the region from its origins to the present day (Chapters 2 and 3). The period subsequent to the Turkish occupation has been considered in detail because events which took place then were later to have important consequences (Chapters 4 and 5). The sixth and seventh chapters describe the turns taken by the war.

Even though this book is to be published at a moment when the war is still going on, we hope to have attained

---

(1) J.M. Roberts, *Ibid*. p. 430.
(2) Philippe K. Hitti, *History of the Arabs*. 5th edition, 1974, p. 797 (Arabic).

our goal of clarifying some of the ill-known aspects of the present conflict. It is also our hope that an objective presentation and analysis of its causes, both ancient and modern, will favor a better understanding of the realities behind this ferocious clash, whose theater is one of the most vulnerable and vital regions in the world.

---

NOTE:  For the needs of transliteration, we have adopted the most generally accepted spelling for the non-arabophone reader.

# CHAPTER 1

# TOWARDS WAR

## THE UNIVERSITY BOMBING

Tuesday, April 1st, 1980, thousands of students from all over the Arab world and Asia were assembled at Al-Mustansiriyah University (1) in Baghdad. They were awaiting the arrival of Tareq Aziz, Deputy Premier of Iraq and member of the Revolution Command Council (R.C.C.), who had been scheduled to inaugurate the International Economic Conference organized by the National Union of Iraqi students in collaboration with the Asiatic Student Committee. In the crowd, a young man was waiting - he was Iranian.

When Tareq Aziz made his entrance, greeted by peals of applause, the young Iranian threw a bomb in his direction. Seeing the danger, the President of the Student Union, Mohammed Dabdab, hurled himself toward Tareq Aziz, shouting: "Look out! There's a bomb!" Immediately the Deputy Premier flung himself to the ground, just missing the full force of the explosion. In the midst of the bellowing crowd the student leaders rushed towards Tareq Aziz to find him only very lightly injured.

As the ambulances were taking away the numerous wounded and dead, the Deputy Premier took control of

---

(1) Founded by the Ba'ath Party following the 8th February 1963 Revolution, and named after the Al-Mustansiriyah School created by Abbasid Caliph Al-Mustansir in 1234.

the situation and rapidly met with the student organizers of the conference. Together they took the decision to carry on the inaugural ceremony as planned. However, due to his state which required hospitalization, Tareq Aziz was unable to deliver the speech he had prepared. A second bomb was later discovered in the same area and defused in time. If it had exploded, this bomb would have slaughtered many students.

In the meantime, the President of Iraq, Saddam Hussein, was visiting the borderline province of Suwayra from which the Iranian summits can be seen. This visit was one of those that the President regularly paid throughout the country. Rarely a day would pass without his touring a city, a neighborhood, a school, a university or an industry, generally ending up each trip with a visit to an Iraqi home.

At the time of the bombing at the University, the Iraqi president was addressing the crowd that had gathered to welcome him to Suwayra. Especially intending his message for the Iranian neighbors, he strongly affirmed : " The Iraqi people does not wish to break off relations with any state unless some state so desires and believes it could endanger the sovereignty of our country or offend the honor and will of our nation... We proclaim to any state wanting to halt relations with Iraq and the Arab Nation that we are determined to combat its interference... We are not prepared to give way before our duty and the defense of our principles... "

The opening of the Student Conference at Al-Mustansiriyah went on without any further incident; the Deputy Premier's speech was read to the audience and won the success expected. News of the bombing was broadcast on the radio, and when the Iraqi president arrived in Baghdad that evening from Suwayra, he went directly to the hospital to visit those injured.

## THE OATH OF PRESIDENT SADDAM HUSSEIN

The next day, April 2nd, President Saddam Hussein went to the place where the bomb had exploded. Pain and sadness could be read on his face. Beginning to speak in the midst of a throng of students, he firmly summoned Iran not to intrude in the internal affairs of Iraq or the neighboring Arab countries. " Yesterday ", he said, " a miserable agent caused the very dear blood of young Al-Mustansiriyah students to be shed... " The President then vowed three times that this criminal act would not remain unpunished.

> The Iraqi people has become an unyielding mountain that they (the Iranians) are not capable of attaining with their bombs or by any other means. Fourteen-hundred years ago the Arabs took it upon themselves to accomplish a divine mission on this holy ground. It is still they who are the most apt to fulfill such a calling for the honor of the Arabs and in the interest of all humanity... Our people are ready to fight to defend their honor and sovereignty, as well as to maintain peace among the Arab nations... We shall pursue this vocation, in the service of the Arabs...

After the speech, the President's threefold oath was considerably commented by the crowd. Nevertheless, people's minds were soon occupied by the preparations for the celebration of the 33rd anniversary of the Ba'ath Party. Since the ninth summit held in Baghdad in November 1978 at the close of which the Camp David politics were condemned, and since the eight-principle national proclamation of the Head of State on February 8, 1980 (1) in which Iraq committed itself not to resort to force in its relations with the neighboring countries,

---

(1) Cf. Appendix I (p. 167) for the integral text of this proclamation.

except for cases of its own legitimate self-defense or that of the other Arab countries, Iraq has taken on a determining political role in the Middle East region. Indeed, this phenomenon has been commented upon by the French newspaper "Le Monde":

> Baghdad, which just a few years ago had the appearance of a modest, old-fashioned provincial capital, has become the rallying place of a steadily increasing number of presidents of small, unaligned countries and leaders of national liberation movements of Africa, Asia and Latin America.
>
> The oil revenues of Iraq have attained the record figure of 150 billion French Francs, allowing the regime not only to improve the standard of living of the population, but also to play a political rôle in the Arab region and in the Third World...
>
> Baghdad is getting ready to welcome in 1982 the Movement of Nonaligned Countries, the exercising president of which will be Saddam Hussein, succeeding Fidel Castro. (1)

## THE PERPETRATORS OF THE CRIME

An investigation brought to light the fact that the Iranian student who was responsible for the bombing at the University, was a member of the Daawat Al-Islam Organization whose headquarters are in Qom in Iran. Daawat Al-Islam (the "Call of Islam") is a small faction of religious inspiration adhering to the ideas of Khomeiny (2). This movement was organized in Iraq after the Revolution of 1958. It was then manipulated by the Shah in order to foment disorder in the surrounding countries. Even before the fall of the Shah, the Iraqi authorities had discovered ammunition dumps containing immense quantities of arms and propaganda (tracts, bro-

---

(1) *Le Monde,* September 21-22, 1980.

(2) *Le Monde,* September 20, 1980.

chures, etc...). The Iranian Revolution aided in the revival of Daawat Al-Islam, which reorganized its cells and proceeded to obtain financial and military assistance from Teheran. Thereafter, the authorities noticed a multiplication of the actions of this movement whose ties with Iran were confirmed after the University bombing.

Iraq's moderation following that attack gave way to more severity when another bomb was thrown from the window of an Iranian school (1) April 5, 1980, during the funeral of the victims of the University attack. An investigation of the Al-Daawat Party led to the discovery of several depots in which great amounts of money and weapons (especially bombs and guns with silencers) were found. In the same hiding-places there were tracts, pamphlets and printed matter of all kinds attacking the Iraqi leaders as well as the Ba'ath Party. Hence, the authorities decided to investigate the Iranians residing in the country. All Iranians having secretly entered Iraq, in particular, the adherents to the Al-Daawat movement and those having been found guilty of activities against the security of the State, were deported. Most of the persons in question were either shopowners or wealthy merchants.

On April 12, 1981, another attempt was made to assassinate a member of the Iraqi Government, this time Latif Nsaif Jassim, Minister of Culture and Information. The assailant was soon arrested and confessed his ties with the al-Daawat Party.

The Al-Mustansiriyah bomb was therefore part of a long series of incidents having begun long before April 1, 1980, the inevitable consequences of which increased the tension between Baghdad and Teheran to the point of

---

(1) According to an Iraqi-Iranian agreement, Iranian schools exist in Iraqi territory and vice versa.

23

rupture. Iran's President Bani Sadr himself openly recognized " that the state of tension between Baghdad and Teheran exists since the founding of the Islamic Republic..." (1) Furthermore, Dr. Saadoun Hammadi, Iraqi Minister of Foreign Affairs, had pointed out the gravity of the situation when he declared :

> The Arab nation, and especially Iraq, is linked to Iran by very close ties coming from their common geographic location, from the unity of their religion and from their both belonging to one and the same Islamic civilization... However, Iran, since the return of Khomeiny, has opted for fanaticism, and has again become as in the Shah's time a threat to the sovereignty and security of the neighboring Arab countries around the Gulf and Iraq in particular (2).

The positions taken by each capital confirm that Khomeiny's arrival at the top coincided with a multiplication of the incidents between Iraq and Iran. (3)

After the aggression at the University the crisis continued to deteriorate until September 4, 1980, the day Iran took the initiative to bombard several Iraqi cities and oil installations. This discreetly publicized attack by the Iranians fixed the real beginning of the war between these two countries. The University bombing is not an arbitrary reference point selected as the actual commencement of events ; it was chosen from the latter chiefly because of the oath taken by the Iraqi President on that occasion. Saddam Hussein repeated this pledge in his press conference of November 11, 1980 in asserting : " We set forth the truth of the situation to the Iranians and we took an oath that the blood shed at Mustansiriyah would not be an act without repercussions ".

---

(1) *Le Monde*, September, 19, 1980.

(2) Quoted from the declaration distributed to the Arab Ministers of Foreign Affairs at their meeting in Amman on November 21, 1980.

(3) Cf. Iraq-Iran Conflict-Documentary file, 1980 and "Why the Algiers agreement was nullified ", Paris 1980.

## STORMY RELATIONS BETWEEN IRAQ AND IRAN

● *The period when Khomeiny was still in Iraq*

When the Shah's regime tried to carry out reforms under the name of the White Revolution at the end of 1963, the Iranian Parliament met to ratify them. The amendments adopted partly undermined the privileges that the mollahs had acquired over the centuries. Imam Khomeiny voiced their opposition by denouncing the reforms decided upon by the Parliament. The Shah reacted by deporting the Ayatollah, who took refuge in Iraq at the beginning of 1964. Baghdad took the necessary precautions to guarantee his security. However, in order to avoid any incidents with Teheran, Iraq put some restrictions upon the political activities that Khomeiny would be able to exercise on Iraqi territory, and the Ayatollah promised to respect those conditions.

The Shah took offense at the welcome reserved the religious leader by Baghdad. On several occasions he requested that the latter be handed over. Expelling Khomeiny from Iraq was one of the basic conditions he attempted to impose before undertaking an official visit to that country. The Iraqi authorities refused this kind of pressure and continued to guarantee the safety of Khomeiny.

In January 1978, at the outbreak of incidents at Qom and Tabriz between the Iranian security forces and demonstrators from the opposition, the Ayatollah's followers obtained additional protection from Baghdad so as to eliminate any possibility of Khomeiny being assassinated by the Shah's agents. The Iranian Revolution brought about a movement of sympathy in Iraq that can be seen by reading the press. The latter defended the struggle of the Iranian people whose demands — takeover of the power by the masses and deposition of the Shah —

were in perfect agreement with the principles defended by Iraq, a democratic state intending to remain independent of all alignment with any foreign power whatsoever.  In this respect, the Imperial regime represented exactly the opposite option for the Ba'ath leaders : according to them, the reinforcement of the American presence in Iran was aimed at stifling the liberation movement in the Arab world.

At the end of 1978, the events in Iran acted as a spearhead in strengthening the position and influence of Khomeiny, who then became involved in activities which went well beyond the limits defined by the authorities and agreed to by him, besides violating Iraq's international obligations towards Iran.  Baghdad was to give the Ayatollah a choice, that is, greater discretion or his departure from the country.  Khomeiny thus decided to leave Iraq and to settle in France at Neauphle-le-Château in the Parisian suburbs.

In the atmosphere of collective exaltation then reigning in Iran, the news of Khomeiny's departure from Iraq raised a general outcry, and all the more so as certain collaborators of the Ayatollah misrepresented the real circumstances.  For example, it was said that Khomeiny had been placed under house arrest by the Ba'athist authorities.  The publication of this false information brought on mass demonstrations in front of the Iraqi Embassy in Teheran and its Consulate in Mohammarah (Khorramshahr).

● *Khomeiny's return to Iran and aggravation of the crisis*

After the return of Khomeiny to Iran in February 1979, relations between Baghdad and Teheran became more embittered, despite the support affirmed by the Iraqi leaders towards the Iranian Revolution on several occasions and their desire to see the ties between the two countries renewed. Baghdad's demonstrations of good will, however, were incapable of disarming the hostility of the Iranian leaders. When the former President of Iraq, Ahmed Hassan Al-Bakr, addressed a telegram of congratulations to Khomeiny on the occasion of the founding of the Iranian Republic, April 5, 1979, the Ayatollah had a response printed that largely exceeded the rules of courtesy existing between states. It represented " the incarnation of aggressivity itself... " "On two occasions Iraq invited Iranian Prime Minister Mehdi Bazargan to make an official visit to Iraq in order to clear up their divergences and create the basis for bilateral cooperation. These offers were never answered ".(1) Such initiatives had the effect of spreading the anti-Iraqi tendencies of Khomeiny and his partisans throughout the Iranian masses. Another instance was the appeal to overthrow the Iraqi regime as well as the attacks against the Arab Revolution broadcast by the Iranian media. This interminable campaign was soon transformed into more and more violent demonstrations outside the Embassy of Iraq, located on Mossadegh Avenue in Teheran. That Embassy also became the target of various aggressions and threats on the part of the demonstrators (such as arson and occupation of the premises) who returned each day before its walls to scan hateful slogans against Iraq, the Ba'ath and the Iraqi President, and entreating the people to revolt against the Iraqi regime. The walls of the Embassy were blackened by graffiti insulting the Ba'ath and the Iraqi Revolution. The Iraqi Ambassador himself became the object of a press campaign accusing him of spying, led chiefly by the newspaper "Joumhouri Islami ", organ of the Islamic

---

(1) Saadoun Hammadi - Cf. Appendix II (p. 171) for integral text of one of these invitations, addressed to Prime Minister Bazargan.

Republican Party, stronghold of the Iranian Revolution. In spite of repeated requests for the Iranian authorities to intervene in order to put an end to these acts of aggression, they did not react. At the end of 1979 the Iraqi Consulate in Mohammarah was attacked four times (October 11th and 26th, November 1st and 7th), the mobs breaking both the doors and the windows of the building, wounding the guard and civil servants. On October 7, 1979, Iran demanded that Iraq close its Consulate in Mohammarah within three months. Nevertheless, on January 11, 1980, before the expiry date, the Iranians attacked the Consulate. They seized diplomatic mail and other consular documents, tore up the Iraqi flag and portraits of President Saddam Hussein, before expelling the diplomatic corps they had already insulted and beaten. Iraq reacted by closing the two Iranian Consulates of Basra and Karbala.

## AGGRESSION AGAINST THE IRAQI CULTURAL INSTITUTIONS IN IRAN

The Iranian authorities refused to prolong the residence permit of the Iraqi teachers working at the Iraqi schools in Iran. Different methods were used against these institutions. The Revolutionary Guard beseiged several schools, threatened the students, ripped up Iraqi flags and multiplied its acts of provocation so as to find a reason for closing them down. In his press conference of November 11, 1980, the Iraqi Head of State incriminated the behavior of the Iranian state employees posted in the Iraqi schools in Iran and accused them of assisting in the preparation of attacks against these institutions. On this subject, Saddam Hussein was to explain that " these schools teach Arabic to our compatriots in Iran in the same way that the Iranian schools do for their citizens

28

residing in Iraq, in conformity with the agreement signed between the two countries ".

Subsequently, the Iranian authorities took their own decision to close all of these schools. The teachers were either deported or arrested for "concealing explosives", and only released after the Iraqi government protested energetically. Next, it was Iraq's turn to close the Iranian schools on its territory, because of subversive goings-on. Furthermore, the Iranian authorities arrested a considerable number of Iraqi citizens inhabiting the region of Arabistan.

## THE AGGRESSIVITY OF IRAN'S LEADERS

These demonstrations took on a new dimension once the Iranian leaders proved to be tacitly in agreement with the acts of aggression committed by the Revolutionary Guard against the Iraqi Embassy, consulates, schools and personnel. The stands taken by those leaders revolved around several main themes :

— Attack against the Iraqi regime and appeal to the Iraqi people to revolt against it.

— Provocative behavior toward the Arab regimes in the Gulf area, in particular, Bahrain, threatened by annexion.

— Refusal by the Iranian leaders to honor their agreements concerning withdrawal from the three islands (the Tumbs and Abu Musa) occupied by the Shah in 1971.

— Finally, profound animosity against Arab nationalism.

The accentuation of the revolutionary process in Iran, shown notably in the elimination of the army's higher echelons and the founding of the Islamic Republic, brought about an aggravation of the conflicts between the various ethnic, political or confessional groups in that country.

Rather than concentrating their efforts on bringing about internal unity and maintaining pacific relations with the neighboring countries, the Iranian leaders tried to export their revolution beyond the borderline.

## ATTACKS AGAINST ARAB NATIONALISM

Bani Sadr, at the time Minister of Finances and Economy, declared on December 23, 1979 to the Lebanese newspaper "An-Nahar" : "Arab nationalism presents the same features as Zionism. It is by no means in keeping with Islam". He explained in another interview that "Arab countries like Abu Dhabi, Qatar, Oman, Dubaï, Kuwait and Saudi Arabia constituted, in the eyes of Iran, states that are not independent ", before adding "that his country did not at all plan to evacuate the Tumb Islands nor Abu Musa"(1). This assertion was in contradiction with promises made beforehand by the leaders of the Iranian Revolution to give back those territories conquered by the Shah and to guarantee to respect the rights of all minorities.

On the same token, while on tour in the Gulf countries in May 1980, the Iranian Foreign Affairs Minister, Sadegh Ghotbzadeh, attempted to convince his counterparts to support the principles of the Iranian Revolution in overcoming their Arab national feelings. Several Arab leaders advised Ghotbzadeh not to exasperate Arab sensitivity by constantly defying it, and informed him of their conviction that the movement for Arab unity was perfectly compatible with that of Islam.

---

(1) *An-Nahar, Al Arabi Wa al-Dawli,* March 24, 1980, Paris.

## EXPORTING THE IRANIAN REVOLUTION

Iran's threats became more explicit when Khomeiny multiplied his declarations urging the Iranian Revolution to be "exported". This idea was very clearly stressed in the speech drafted by Khomeiny on March 31, 1980 and read for him by his son, in which the Ayatollah stated: "We are doing everything possible to export our revolution to other countries in the world". This declaration, in addition to the University bombing and the declarations of different Iranian leaders (notably the above-cited interview with Bani Sadr in the weekly "An-Nahar "), caused Baghdad to compose two letters of protest against the provocative acts of Teheran (1). These letters were sent April 2nd by the Iraqi Foreign Affairs Minister Saadoun Hammadi to Fidel Castro, in his capacity as President of the 6th Conference of Nonaligned Countries, and to Kurt Waldheim, Secretary General of the United Nations. In reply, on April 8, 1980, the Iranian Foreign Affairs Minister pretended that Aden and Baghdad composed two territories belonging to Persian sovereignty. The same day, Khomeiny declared that in the case in which Iraq would continue to demand the evacuation of the three Arab Islands, Iran would lay claim on Baghdad. He also addressed an appeal to sedition to the Iraqi people and army. On April 9, 1980, Ghotbzadeh exclaimed that the Iranian government meant to conquer Iraq.

---

(1) Cf. Appendices III and IV (p. 175, p. 179) for the integral text of both letters.

## APPEALS FOR AN "ISLAMIC REVOLUTION"
## IN IRAQ

On April 19, 1980, the Iranian newspaper "Joumhouri Islami" published an appeal of Khomeiny : "The Iraqi people must not fall into the hands of its aggressors. Its duty as well as that of the army is to overthrow the Ba'ath, that non-Islamic party".

April 18, 1980, at a meeting with the National Reserve Committee, Khomeiny declared : "The Iraqi government is not a real one, it doesn't even have a parliament ; it is a military clique which really holds power and does whatever it pleases. There are no ties nor communication between the power and the people... Saddam Hussein boasts of his Arabness... It is necessary that all Muslim nations know the real meaning of this notion. 'We are Arabs' is equivalent to saying 'We are not Muslims'... At a certain moment in their history the Arabs stood up against Islam. They want to revive the period of the Umayyads, or that of Jahiliyah, during which force and power were on the side of the Arabs..."

On April 23, 1980, Ghotbzadeh announced in a broadcast message that the duty of the Iranian people was to give its aid to the people of Iraq who were subjected to the repressive measures of a " criminal " regime. He also revealed that only the downfall of Saddam Hussein's regime would satisfy him.

With regard to the Iranian Chief of Staff, he claimed that his army was capable of occupying Iraq and that the population would welcome it with open arms. In addition, on April 23, 1980, Mollah Mohammed Chirazi made the following announcement :

We invite the whole nation to do its duty, that is, to resist by all possible means to and until the fall of the Ba'ath gang :

— Militate within the Islamic factions which offer military training !

— Print and diffuse tracts, books ! Intervene in the radio and television and in the newspapers ! Cover the walls with slogans !

— Arm the Iraqi people so as to help them resist against tyranny !

— Boycott everything that affects the Ba'ath in any way whatsoever !

## FALSE NEWS EMITTED BY IRAN : THE ASSASSINATION OF SADDAM HUSSEIN

During his trip through the Middle East, Sadegh Ghotbzadeh announced in Damascus that President Saddam Hussein had been assassinated during an alleged military coup. He also confirmed his government's support of the Iraqi opposition. Furthermore, the Iranian Foreign Affairs Minister gave a press conference on April 28, 1980 in Hazmieh (in the outskirts of Beirut) during which he revealed : "We uphold the Iraqi people so that it can free itself of its criminal regime". Then, replying to a question raised about the possibility of war between Iran and Iraq, he declared that "anything can happen".

## ETHNIC AGITATION IN IRAN

Besides the Persians, the Iranian territory includes other ethnic communities, such as those of Arabistan, Baluchistan, Kurdistan and Azerbaidjan. Throughout history and more particularly during the reign of Shah

33

Mohammed Reza Pahlavi, these communities suffered the immoderate  domination of the Persian occupants. However, each of the attempts to bring about their "Persianization" remained unfruitful; these ethnic groups conserved their specificity. During the revolution, their attitude eased Ayatollah Khomeiny's victory. The different ethnic communities started to rebel against the Shah's power and in fact supported the Iranian Revolution in the hope that Khomeiny would grant them certain rights. In reality, not only did the Ayatollah fail to answer their expectations, but pursued the harsh methods of the Shah in trying to subdue them. Ayatollah Sadegh Khalkhali, head of the revolutionary courts of justice in Teheran and leader of the Fidaiyou-Islami Party, declared: "The Iranian government is opposed to non-Persian minorities claiming the right to autonomy" (1). This policy rapidly created troubles within the various ethnic communities whose hopes for relative autonomy were dashed. However, as soon as a bomb exploded in Baluchistan, Arabistan, Kurdistan or Azerbaidjan, or whenever arms were discovered anywhere in Iran, Iraq was immediately accused by the authorities in Teheran.

## CLAIMS UPON BAHRAIN AND THE ARAB COUNTRIES OF THE GULF

During an interview at Radio Monte-Carlo, April 30, 1980, Minister Ghotbzadeh indicated that "all the countries in the Gulf are historically a part of Iranian territory."

---

(1) *Al-Mostakbal*, December 15, 1979, and the text of the new Iranian Constitution (Cf. Iranian review *Kayhan* April 28, 1979).

● *Bahrain*

April 18, 1980, Sadegh Rouhani, politically close to Ayatollah Khomeiny and one of the leaders of the Islamic Revolution, stated that :

Iran would again lay claim to Bahrain if Iraq continued to demand its retreat from the three islands in the Gulf conquered by the Shah in 1971. The decision of the Shah's Parliament to give up Iranian claims on Bahrain is not binding because it emanated from an organism to which we deny any legitimacy.

On June 15th, Sadegh Rouhani returned to the question, declaring during a press conference :

Bahrain is an integral part of the Iranian territory. According to the new constitution of Iran, Bahrain constitutes the fourteenth department of Iran. In the Algiers agreements the dethroned Shah made too many territorial concessions to Iraq. Today, we feel there is a need to elucidate Iran's position on Bahrain due to the claims formulated by certain Arab countries, notably Iraq, regarding the three islands in the Gulf.

● *The Tumb Islands and Abu Musa*

On April 19, 1980, the radio of Riyadh broadcast a declaration of Bani Sadr in which he once again affirmed Iran's will to maintain its occupation of the Tumb Islands and Abu Musa.

## THE REACTIONS OF IRAQ

In July 1980, the international press agencies cited Iraqi information in announcing an Iranian military reinforcement of the border with Iraq. Border incidents between Iraq and Iran had multiplied since January 1980, becoming almost daily by July. During a major press conference held before several hundred international

35

journalists in July 1980, Saddam Hussein once again raised the problem of Iraq-Iran relations :

> Iraq publicly declared to the new Iranian authorities that it wished to establish relations of cooperation and neighborliness with Iran, based upon a mutual respect and non-interference in the other's internal affairs, but our good intentions came up against the hate of the arrogant, racist leaders of Teheran. Khomeiny should therefore not expect us to be friendly in his regard. We shall not bend before one who has revealed himself a mere assassin in his own country. We do not want war, but if he provokes us, we shall know how to react - we shall not remain arms folded... (1)

\*
\* \*

One question arises : What is the reason for Iran's interference in the internal affairs of neighboring Arab countries and its incessant attacks against Iraq ? Several explanations have been proposed ; in principle, two must be recalled : according to the first, war with Iraq would offer the means to end the conflict opposing the diverse factions in Iran, thus creating the unity which would guarantee that a regime whose economic and social accomplishments are negligible would be kept in place. The second explanation deals with the historical causes of the conflict, the Iraq-Iran war simply representing another episode of Persia's perennial undertaking to annex Arab lands, notably those of Iraq, Shatt-al-Arab and Arabistan. Consequently, the events only expose one aspect of the clash between Iraq and Iran. To better understand the various elements, it is necessary to recall the history of this region to provide a key to the present confrontation over Shatt-al-Arab.

---

(1) *Le Monde*, July 21, 22, 1980.

# CHAPTER 2

# THE GEOGRAPHICAL
# AND HISTORICAL BACKGROUND

Since long ago the region of Shatt-al-Arab has constituted an exceedingly controversial subject between Iraq
and Iran. Despite all attempts at reconciliation, the
conflict has only grown worse: expansionist Iran has persisted in trying to annex this area, whereas Iraq has tena-
ciously tried to conserve what it considers as a blessing
bequeathed by history. A superficial analysis would
attribute this conflict to mainly economic and geographical causes, but in fact it is more complex, translating a
real confrontation between two profoundly different peoples, the Arabs and the Persians. Citing historical rights
must take us back into the past in order to locate the roots
of the conflict along with the political pretentions that are
at odds in this part of the world. Only then shall we
know the real meaning of the present war.

This investigation will essentially deal with the history
of Arabistan, which is at the heart of the conflict. The
Shatt-al-Arab will also be included for it has always been
Arab and Iraqi, with respect to both its profound reality
and the political powers that have ruled it. How can the
Shatt-al-Arab always have been both Arab and Iraqi?
Before replying, we must take a glimpse at the geography
of this region.

## GEOGRAPHICAL OUTLINE

Before speaking of its history and the definition of Iraqi rights over Arabistan, these territories must be situated in their geographical context. From the Iranian border on the Gulf to Sharm-el-Sheikh or Ras-Sinai on the Red Sea, there are several strategic areas such as the Strait of Hormuz and Bab-al-Mandab which enclose the Arabian Peninsula. Sovereignty over one or the other of these will be reflected in a minutely calculated regional equilibrium. It is thus that the Straits of Hormuz and Bab-al-Mandab, which constitute two strategic spots at the entrance of the Arabian Gulf and the Red Sea, are Arab, whereas the islands facing the Arabian Peninsula, namely, Lesser and Greater Tumbs as well as Abu Musa, were occupied in 1971 by the armed forces of the Shah. They were not surrendered by the Iran of Ayatollah Khomeiny. It is even the case that some of these islands have fallen under the direct control of the great world powers, as are Masirah and Socotra. The latter was recently transformed into a Soviet military base.

The geographical and strategic makeup of the Arabian Gulf resembles that of the Red Sea : there, the Island of Perim controls the southern entry of this sea; it too is in an Arab zone, while Sharm-el-Sheikh has undergone Israeli occupation, implying a threat to navigation and to all the states bordering on that sea. In any case, it is the study in depth of the Shatt-al-Arab that directly interests our analysis. We shall successively treat the region of Shatt-al-Arab, the Strait of Hormuz, Arabistan and the three islands (Lesser and Greater Tumbs, Abu Musa), without forgetting that though they are presented separately, these regions form a whole: a single strategic entity and a unique source of wealth constantly envied by the Persians.


## SHATT-AL-ARAB

It is made up of a delta in the Arabian Gulf created by the Tigris and Euphrates Rivers, and is situated 47 miles north of Basra, stretching over a distance of 136 miles between Al-Qurnah and the Gulf, into which it empties close to the port of Al-Faw.   Its width varies according to the region, from approximately 1/4 to 3/4 mile.  Waters coming from Hawizah close to Al-Qurnah empty into the Shatt-al-Arab, like those rivers originating in Karmat-Ali and irrigating the orchards of Basra; lastly, the Karun joins it at the entrance to the city of Mohammarah to the south of Basra.  A great number of affluents and waterways irrigate the two banks of the Shatt-al-Arab and form a homogeneous hydrographic network, naturally connecting the plains of Basra to those of Arabistan.   None of these waters ever dry up because the ebb and flow of the tide maintains a permanent irrigation.   Aside from its hydraulic potential, this earth is one of the most fertile in the world.   It lends itself particularly well to the organization of its agricultural and maritime resources (1).

When one comes to realize that 635 waterways bathe this region, crossing rich plains which begin at Basra and continuing along both banks of the delta where the palm groves contain over 14 million palm trees, it becomes easier to conceive the evocative power of these areas often recalled in Arab literature and painting.

---

(1) The waters around Al-Faw are well known for the quality of its fish.

The Shatt-al-Arab constitutes the only maritime outlet of Iraq. It is the waterway connecting Iraq to the Gulf and beyond it, the oceans. A mere glance at a map will show that Iraq, locked inland between Turkey, the An-Nafud Desert to the south and the Zagros Mountains to the west, has but this narrow passage to the sea. Consequently, this region is vital for Iraq, as it links the south of the country to the north. That is why any state occupying the bank of Shatt-al-Arab isolates Iraq by cutting off this natural access to the Gulf from its southern part. This region is of primary importance to the country's economy, notably with regard to its privileged position in international commercial relations. It also goes without saying that the Shatt-al-Arab is the only natural waterway allowing vessels to reach the port of Basra. For this reason, too, Iran wishes to control the navigation in this region.

Before enumerating the various points of contention in this zone, two regions should also be treated, the Strait of Hormuz and Arabistan:

> That muddy delta...barren landscape inhabited by skeletal brush, beneath a humid sky at the gates of the Orient. This time...the Shatt-al-Arab constitutes the battlefield. Tributary of the Tigris and the Euphrates, cradle of ancient Mesopotamia, this delta, opening upon the Arabian Gulf, is the jugular vein of Arabistan and the oil fields... (1).

---

(1) *Le Point*, nº 419, September 24, 1980.

## STRAIT OF HORMUZ

A point of communication where the waters of the Gulf merge with those of the Indian Ocean, it derives its strategic importance from this situation. The power controlling it has at the same time supervision of the jugular feeding the world economy in petroleum. It is through this channel, whose width never exceeds 60 km, that boats navigate at a rhythm of one oil tanker every ten minutes, equivalent to 62% of the oil transit intended for world consumption distributed in the following way: 90% of Japan's energy needs, 70% of the Common Market's consumption and 50% of the American needs. The Strait of Hormuz is the sole passageway out of the Gulf for the coastal states: Iraq, Iran, Kuwait, Saudi Arabia, Qatar, Bahrain, Oman and the United Arab Emirates.

It is indeed this key position that in the course of history and its fierce battles was at stake. It is known that this region is inhabited by Arab tribes. Still today, it can be seen what the Arab civilization at the Bedouin era was like from the customs and characteristic features of these populations. The Strait of Hormuz was regained by the Arabs in the beginning of the 20th century. It had always been a place of combat and contestation between the World Powers, and hence, was occupied from the end of the 15th century by the Ottomans, the Persians and the Portugese successively, and at the beginning of the 16th century by the English. Throughout history, the region of Hormuz knew a strategic importance which only increased with the discovery of oil. The economic weight of the Strait of Hormuz pushed the Shah of Iran into preventing the implantation of any foreign power along the banks of the straits, notably on the coast of Oman. Iran therefore fought against the revolution in Dhufar which opposed the regime of Oman. Furthermore, the Shah carried on a policy of hegemony in this area. He organized a military expedition to overthrow the islands in the straits so as to build bases. The Shah made of Chah Bahar a naval base with ultra-modern equipment able to shelter submarines.

The Shah spent billions of dollars on American technical assistance and equipment. As soon as the English evacuated the Gulf, November 30, 1971, he grasped the islands located near the straits. His troops took over the Lesser and Greater Tumbs and Abu Musa. After the revolution, Iran conserved its control over the straits and in 1980, the Iranian fleet pursued its military operations there. Moreover, the Iranian patrol boats based on the Island of Bandar Abbas escort to this day the tankers going through the straits.

Due to the specific character of the Khomeiny revolution, the mutual apprehension of the United States and U.S.S.R. was stirred. Reacting to Iranian threats, Moscow and Washington sent their fleets toward the Gulf where, from then on, they have remained stationed and in a state of alert, not far from the entrance to the Strait of Hormuz. If the straits are vital to this region, they are all the more so to the entire world. Hence, the preoccupation of the Western powers at the outbreak of war between Iraq and Iran. Immediately after Iran had threatened to bomb the straits in case of foreign intervention in that conflict, the United States emitted a communiqué dated September 20, 1980, proposing the calling of a six-member conference - United States, Great Britain, France, West Germany, Japan and Italy - with the security of the straits on its agenda:

> We have consulted a certain number of friendly countries about the conditions of oil supplies and international navigation in the Gulf. Given the importance of reducing the economic consequences of the conflict between Iraq and

> Iran upon international navigation and the world petro-
> leum markets, the United States indicated that they may
> hold a meeting to discuss this problem if necessa-
> ry. However, no meeting of this kind was decided. (1)

Whatever the nature of this Iranian threat, and despite the narrowness of the straits, the affirmations indicating that the mere sinking of a boat would block them are obviously false. Actually, there is a sizeable distance between the coasts, the maritime lines traced on the maps and the truly navigable space. In principle, a maximal margin of security is accounted for in the strait's naviga-bility: it is thus that the basis for any cargo is a draft of 20 meters while in reality the half is more than suffi-cient. Weighing this observation, the distance actually navigable in the straits extends over 50 km.

Nevertheless, fear of seeing the straits closed down because of the Iranian Revolution remains strong (2). Such an act would provoke the economic collapse of numerous states, especially those with an industrial structure. The event could even provoke a world war.

---

(1) *Le Monde*, September 30, 1980.

(2) Between March 1979 and November 1980, Iran reiterated its threat to block the access to the Strait of Hormuz 14 times.

## THE ISLANDS OF THE TWO TUMBS AND ABU MUSA

In spite of its limited area, the Arabian Gulf is very deep, which has facilitated the formation of a multitude of small islands. These islands were created by natural phenomena, for instance, river alluvium (Bubiyan and Warbah Rivers), or by the action of waves and marine currents carried by the wind toward the coasts, or else by coral rising to the surface of the sea found all along the coasts of Qatar and Bahrain. The majority of these islands are saline, namely, those of Larak, Henqam, Tumb, Abu Musa, Forur, Sirri, Halul and others that have immerged.

● *Abu Musa*

Abu Musa is a rectangular island situated 24 miles from the city of Sharjah along the coast of Oman and 44 miles from the Iranian coast. It is low land covered with sand plains studded with greenery and palm groves crowded around wells of drinking water. Several volcanic hills are to be seen, the altitude of which does not go beyond a hundred meters. Approximately one thousand people live there; they belong to two Arab tribes originating from Sharjah. The island's economy is based on raising livestock, fishing and agriculture. Immediately after the Iranian conquest, efforts were made to somewhat modernize the island.

● *Greater Tumb*

Greater Tumb is located at the entrance to Bab-al-Salam in the Strait of Hormuz, 19 miles from the Emirate of Ras-al-Khaimah. Its area is 35 sq. miles. It is inhabited by about 800 people of Arab origin and was under the administrative control of the Ras-al-Khaimah Emirate. Its inhabitants live from fishing and tending animals.

● Finally, Lesser Tumb is to be found in the Strait of Hormuz about 6 miles to the west of Grand Tumb islet. A little over half a mile long and less than half a mile wide, it is made up of deep-colored hills attaining 40 m. The only life on this islet is Arab fishermen and shepherds.

Due to their proximity to the Strait of Hormuz, these islands hold a considerable interest, comparable to that of Gibraltar at the entrance to the Mediterranean, or that of Aden at the entrance to the Red Sea.

Back-to-back with the coasts of the Emirates, these three islands constitute observation posts for the coastlines of the Gulf countries : United Arab Emirates, Qatar, Bahrain, Saudi Arabia, Kuwait, Iraq and Iran.(1)

Any power possessing these islands reinforces its position in the Strait of Hormuz and thus controls the entire region militarily, politically and commercially. From a strategic point of view, the Strait of Hormuz and the three islands are complementary. Aside from this, these islands are rich in minerals. The English company Alwan Al Wadi Azahabi(2) possesses, in exchange for annual dues of approximately $ 250,000, a monopoly that was granted at the beginning of the century by Salem Ben Sultan, the uncle of the Sheikh now in power at Sharjah. This company continues today to exploit the iron oxide deposits. Abu Musa is also well known for its red earth from which cosmetic products (for example, lipstick) can be manufactured. The abundance of the maritime resources around this island allows a fisherman with "traditional" equipment to earn 150 Rials a day

---

(1) *Le Monde*, September 25, 1980.
(2) Meaning "the colors of the golden valley".

(about $45). Oil drillings have been undertaken in its territorial waters, leading to the discovery of deposits that have not yet been tapped because of rivalries between the English and American oil companies.

The history of these three islands is closely tied with that of Oman. These territories have had a common fate over the centuries. From the 18th to the beginning of the 19th centuries, Oman was prosperous. The Arab tribes called Al-Kawassem, who have the same origin as all those settled around the Gulf, transferred their ancient capital of Ras-al-Khaimah to Sharjah under Sultan Ben Sakr (1803-1856). (1) These Al-Kawassem tribes opposed a fierce resistance against the English penetration. Great Britain was finally successful in reducing them and occupied Ras-al-Khaimah along with all other Al-Kawassem forts. London then imposed several conventions, signed successively between 1820 and 1853. Following the English occupation and the decline of the Al-Kawassem, particularly after the loss of its fleet, Iran started to extend its control over this region. It is hence that in Lanja in 1887, the Iranians overthrew the Arab government led by the Al-Kawassem and occupied Sirri which is found to the west of Abu Musa and was dependent on the Emirate of Sharjah. Afterwards, they occupied Henqam, which belonged to the Bani-Yass Arab tribe. Despite the extension of its influence to the west of the Arabian Gulf, Iran never pretended to hold sovereignty over the islets of the two Tumbs nor Abu Musa. The Emir of Sharjah, on which Ras-al-Khaimah depended, maintained control of these three islands. All existing sources attest the sovereignty of Sharjah over these islets. Lorimer, who was given the task of making up a "guide to the Gulf" by the Indian government, indi-

---

(1) Abed, S.A., *The Role of Al-Kawassem in the Arabian Gulf,* Baghdad, 1976, p. 114 on. (Arabic).

cated that these three islands were under the power of the Sheikh of Sharjah "who sojourns on them at moments of great heat".(1) In his research this author was able to consult secret documents placed at his disposal by the government of India, but which were only made public in 1960.

At the beginning of the 20th century, as an effect of the Persian occupation, trade in the port of Lanja declined and was finally ruined after the emigration of the Arab tradesmen toward the coast of Oman. In the meantime, the Arabs developed the Island of Abu Musa and transformed it into a commercial center used for the exportation of their merchandise. They requested that the British shipping companies include this islet among their mooring ports while awaiting the creation of a free zone. Abu Musa quickly rivaled with the Iranian ports.

In 1904, a Persian ship, the "Muzafiri", dropped anchor at Abu Musa. On board, there was a high-ranking British official taking care of customs for these islands, who lowered the flag of Sharjah to replace it by the Persian flag. An Iranian customs administration was then established on the island. This act of aggression caused the Sheikh of Sharjah to write a letter of protestation to the British agent in the Gulf. Great Britain backed out and thus obtained the withdrawal of the Iranians from that island. Sharjah was then able to restore its former prerogatives, after an Iranian occupation which had lasted three months.

Iran, having renounced this territory against its will, made further attempts to occupy the three islands. Great Britain, reticent at the thought of seeing Iran control these strategic areas that are rich in natural resources, threat-

---

(1) Lorimer, J.G., *Gazette of the Persian Gulf, Oman and Central Arabia,* Calcutta, 2 volumes, 1908.

ened to question Iran's occupation of the Arab islands of Sirri and Henqam. From then on, the status quo was maintained up to the middle of the 20th century. The departure of the English from the Gulf in 1971 made things easier for the Shah. The latter accepted to drop his claims to Bahrain but succeeded in getting the approval of the World Powers for his plan to occupy the three islands, taking advantage of the ceremonies on the occasion of the 2500th anniversary of the Persian Empire to assure himself the tacit support of those powers.(1)

Among themselves the Arab countries of the Gulf had planned to create a federation. Realizing the danger, the Shah threatened to occupy the islands, and then did just that on November 31, 1971, on the eve of the proclamation of this union.

## ARABISTAN

The Iraq-Iran conflict principally concerns this area. All throughout its history and even though it makes up a territory that is naturally Arab, Arabistan had been annexed, occupied or shared by different foreign powers. It is located southeast of Iraq and is bounded on the north and east by mountains of the Zagros chain. These mountains stretch over a distance of 620 miles and are 120 miles wide; their altitude varies from 1100 to 1700 meters. Rising up behind Arabistan, they seem to be a natural barrier separating this region from Iran. To the west, Arabistan reaches the two Iraqi departments of Basra and Missan, while to the south it is bordered by the Arabian Gulf. The surface area of Arabistan is about 71,430 sq. miles, with 263 miles in length

---

(1) Brière, Claire and Blanchet, Pierre, *Iran, Revolution in the Name of God,* Seuil, Paris, 1979, pp. 9-10.

and 238 miles in width. In 1936, Iran amputated 9,800 sq. miles by annexing them to its southernmost department. The population of Arabistan numbers 3.5 million, *composed of Arab tribes having come in successive waves from the Arabian Peninsula well before Islam.*

This region is known in Arabic under the name "Ahwaz", plural of the name "Hawz" and derived from the verb "Haza Yahuz", which means appropriation. This name simply designates the right a person actually exercises over a territory. It dates back to the period when Alexander the Great conquered Persia and divided it into provinces. The Arabs of this region reassembled themselves in an independent department they called "Ahwaz", in reference to the properties owned by the various tribes therein.(1) Subsequently, the Persians were to call this territory Ahwaz with an unvoiced "h", which takes away its meaning ; in fact, the Arab alphabet contains two letters which correspond, first, to the unvoiced "h" and, second, to the voiced "h". This phonetic shade of difference does not exist in Persian, both letters being confounded in one unvoiced "h", whereas to confuse these two phenomena in Arabic would modify the meaning of a word or make it incomprehensible, as with "Ahwaz". When this word became current in Persia, it lost its etymological meaning by the transformation of its voiced "h" into an unvoiced one.(2)

Later on, the Persians named this region Khuzestan, that is to say, the "land of combats and forts", for the Arabs had constructed military fortifications there which were to serve as bases of operations in their expansion

---

(1) Hamawy, Yakout, *Encyclopedia of the World,* I, p. 380 (Arabic).

(2) Le Strange, L., *The Land of the Eastern Caliphate.* Cambridge 1905, p. 267.
Baghdadi Safi-el-Din. *Observation Post of Places and their Names,* I. Cairo, 1954,
p. 135. (Arabic).

towards Persia and India. Under the Safawid Dynasty, this region was known under the name of Arabistan rather than Khuzestan, in reference to its inhabitants (1). The term Arabistan, which indicates the Arab nature of a people or territory, is the word used by all non-Arab populations of the region to designate the Arab lands situated on their frontiers; it is thus that the Turks called Syria, and even today, the Persians say "Saudi Arabistan" for the Kingdom of Saudi Arabia (2).

## THE CITIES OF ARABISTAN

In former times, the cities of Arabistan could be grouped into two zones, those in the north and those in the south, but with the discovery of oil in 1908 at Masjed Soleyman, a third zone was constituted to the west. During history, these cities changed names several times according to circumstances and to the power administrating them. For this reason, it is necessary to give some details on the most important cities of Arabistan.

● *Abadan*

This city is also known under the name of the island on which it lies : Khodr Island ; in Persian, it is called Abadan. Located 18 km to the south of the city of Mohammarah, today it is above all a port through which the oil of Arabistan transits. An imposing petroleum refinery is also found there. Built upon an island running north-south, surrounded by the waters of the Shatt-al-Arab, this very ancient locality was visited by many famous travel-

---

(1) The references are numerous; we shall limit ourselves to citing:
— Ibn Hawkal, *Image of the Earth*. Al-Hayatt Library. 1968, p. 225 on. (Arabic).
— Aboul-Fida, *The Reform of Lands*, p. 311 on. (Arabic).
— Dairat Al-Maarif, Al-Islamiyah, *Encyclopedia of Islam* IX, ch. 1. Baghdad, p. 37. (Arabic).
— Al-Istikhri, M. *Al-Masalek, Wal-Mamalek* (Routes and Countries), I. Cairo, 1961, p. 62. (Arabic).
(2) Sarkis, Yaakoub, *Geographical Research,* I. Baghdad, 1948, p. 237. (Arabic).

ers.  All the historians of the first Islamic times cited it as belonging to the department of Basra.  Abadan never experienced an exceptional development ; however, at certain periods its duties were in the order of 441,000 dinars, a relatively high sum paid to the treasury of Basra where the region's central administration was located.  In the past, this city was thought of as an Iraqi borderline city.  Its location gave rise to an Iraqi saying: "There are no villages beyond Abadan" (1).

## ● *Al-Mohammarah*

It is called Khorramshahr in Persian and is found at the outlet of the Karun River in the Shatt-al-Arab.  It is an important port the economy of which is closely dependent on the region of Basra.  Hajj Youssef Ben Mardaw, a Sheikh of the Arab tribe of Bou-Kasseb, was responsible for its construction in 1812. Hajj Youssef and his men made it their capital, calling it Al-Mohammarah (2).  This name designates the color red in Arabic, and was probably given to this city because of the color of the earth — red sand — carried by the Karun all the way to its mouth.  Today, Mohammarah is one of the most important ports of Arabistan.  Recent works to expand it now permit the largest vessels to use this port.

## ● *Al-Ahwaz*

It is called Al-Ahwaz in Persian (see above for the phonetic variation between these two words). This city is found along the Karun River in the center of Arabistan.  Long ago it was the capital of this emirate, but suffered enormously during the revolts of the Zanjs.

---

(1) Haidary F., *The Title of Glory: Baghdad, Basra, and Najd.* Baghdad, 1962, pp. 179-81. (Arabic).

(2) Hourani, Georges, *The Arabs and Navigation in the Indian Ocean,* Cairo, 1958, p. 44. (Arabic).

● *Al-Hawizah*

It takes the name Dasht-Mishan in Persian and is situated on the Karkheh River to the northeast of Mohammarah near the Iraqi department of Missan. It is the place where the Bani Tarf tribes resided. Later on, during the Mongol period, the Arab state of the Moucha'chi'ins made it their capital (in 1441).

● *Dezful*

The Persians named this city built among the hills Kantaret Kaz or Kantaret Al-Kala'a. It is located in the north of Arabistan. To the southwest of this locality, ruins of the city of Al-Shush are to be found, where French archeologists discovered in 1901-1902 the famous ziggurat (stela) of Hammurabi.

● *Felihiyah*

This city, known as Chawkan in Persian, is inhabited by the Bani-Kaab tribes. It was the capital of the Arab emirs of Arabistan before being supplanted by al-Mohammarah.

● *Tustar*

Finally, this city called Shushter by the Persians, with its perennial springs, is considered as the heart of the fertile valley of Arabistan.

All of these localities with their original Arab name and the way they have more recently been called in Persian, bring us to an analysis of the complex identity of Arabistan as seen through this ambivalence. Beyond its two banks, the Shatt-al-Arab forms a plain of constant fertility where the climatic and vegetal conditions attest to its unity. Enclosed by two mountain chains, Arabistan runs toward an opening upon the Gulf in its southern part : "The plain of Arabistan", writes Donald Wilber, "is a prolongation of the low plain found in the south of Iraq" (1). This plain is composed of lime deposited by the waterways flowing in this region and more especially by the two greatest of them, the Karun and the Karkheh. There was a time when Arabistan and a part of the Iraqi department of an-Nasiriyah were flooded over with water. Arnold Wilson claims that Arabistan was constituted at the same time as the other countries in the low region found in between the Tigris and Euphrates Rivers. All these lands have a geographical unity that brought prosperity to Mesopotamia and the Chaldeans. Later, it came under Arab control, whose domination spread throughout Persia and beyond (2). All these territories formed by the accumulation of lime are exceptionally rich in oil. The potential of the oil layer in this region is 68 billion barrels ; presently, it produces between 3 and 4 million barrels per year.

Louis Massignon considered this region as an Arab territory and described it as follows:

> We find ourselves in the middle of the Shatt-al-Arab delta, but this delta, compared to that of the Nile, the Ganges or the Chinese rivers, clearly appears dissymetric, and curiously so. It occupies a part of the floor of the gulf having subsided and which it has filled, forming on its southwest extremity the Arabian plateau with its appearance of an Indo-African peneplain, while on the northeast side more recent Persian plications are found.
>
> In sum, on its left, the delta has the desert which is barely higher, and Basra is the first oasis behind its canals; to the right, it is punctuated by a system of faults and subsidings

---

(1) Wilber, Donald N., *Iran, Past and Present*, Princeton University Press, 1956, p. 12.

(2) Wilson, Sir Arnold, *Southwest Persia, A Political Officer's Diary, 1907-14*, Oxford, 1941, p. 93.

which, with its aligned oil fields, prolongs the gulf up to the great bluish, pale arcs and parallel folds of the Arabistan and Fars mountains. On this side the waters of the delta are so abundant that they annex the Karun and its basin...

Recent surveys have shown that beneath the Shatt, 30 or 40 meters below the ground, a subterranean shatt flows, produced by infiltrations from the first and to which are owed the fresh water sources found in the gulf area (1).

The region of Arabistan and the south of Iraq have an identical climate, at the same time desert-like and Mediterranean. There is no clear separation between seasons. However, in Arabistan as in Basra, summer and winter are more marked, while autumn and spring last only shortly.

The Iraq-Iran conflict has revived the problem of to whom Arabistan belongs. This territory constitutes a national problem in the Arab mind. Examination of the past appears to be the best instrument for analyzing the identity of this territory and its population. Thus, a recollection of the events which brought about the separation of Arabistan from the Arab lands would now seem appropriate.

---

(1) Massignon, L. "Mohammarah", *Journal of the Muslim World*, No. 11, Year II, November, 1908, p. 385.

CHAPTER 3

# HISTORICAL CAUSES
# OF THE CONFLICT:
# THE ANCIENT PERIOD

Three thousand years before Christ the lands of Arabistan emerged from the sea (1). A Semitic population settled there, and later on, Arab tribes called the Bani al-'Am. Amidst the Bani al-'Am existed an important branch, the Bani Tamim, whose descendants still inhabit the south of Arabistan today.

The Akkadian kingdom, located in Iraq, had submitted these populations to its authority. This region was then subjected to the aggressions of the Elameans (2) having come from the East. The Babylonians ended these attacks under the reign of Hammurabi, who conquered the aggressors. Afterwards, the Assyrian State was created which, despite its emphemeral duration, safeguarded the independence of the region till the arrival of the Chaldeans. It was then the Chaldeans who underwent aggressions from the outside, that is, from the Ahminid Kingdom having appeared around 550 B.C. Notwithstanding these attacks, the Chaldeans preserved their autonomy and their laws inherited from Babylonia. The country endured another attack in 241 A.D., when the Sasanid Dynasty of Persian origin attempted to conquer Arabistan. The resistance of the population

---

(1) Parrot, A., in *Mesopotamian Archeology in Stages*, Paris, 1946.
   Butten, M., *Babylonia*, Paris, 1948.
(2) Elam was an ancient state adjacent to Chaldea.

55

was such that the Sasanids finally gave up.   Realizing the strength of these tribes, they came to a compromise with them and recognized the independent principalities composing the region.

In spite of many attempts on the part of the Sasanids to subject this region, it kept its Arab character until the beginning of the 4th century A.D.   This Arabness involved customs, practices and a way of life that are specific to the Arab bedouin culture.   All researchers specialized in ancient history and who have visited the region concur in recognizing its Arab character.   They consider that with lower Mesopotamia, modern Arabistan forms a geographical and cultural unity.   This region successively withstood several ancient civilizations, namely, the Sumerians, the Akkadians and the Babylonians.

From its birth, the Arab civilization assimilated the bases of all the preceding ones before more profoundly taking root in its Arab specificity.   This process went on until the emergence of Islam which gained Persia and then spread abroad (1).   Jacqueline Berryne has written the following on the Arabian Gulf:

> The Arabs have remained the masters of the Arabian Gulf coastline.   The Persian Kings were afraid of the sea and never became its masters.   They found it quite intolerable that the Arabs assert themselves on that coast (2).

Sir Percy Sykes, a well known historian on Persia, explained the cause of the inaptitude of the Persian navigator:

> Nothing better exemplifies the influence of natural phenomena upon the character and behavior of a people than

---

(1) Berryne, J., *The Discovery of the Arabian Peninsula* (V.A.) Beirut, 1963, p. 98.
(2) Berryne, J., *Ibid.* p. 166.

the repulsion of the Persians for the sea, from which they
are separated by gigantic mountains (1).

This demonstrates that there is a clear difference
between Arabia and Persia with regard to their relationship with the marine element. The fact that the Arab is
attracted by water is directly connected to the severe
conditions of life in the bedouin environment, to dryness,
and to life in the desert. It is for this reason that he
desperately seeks water. He does not give up for fear of
any danger and tries to see the freshness of a spring in the
salt water of the sea. He has forever lived in a desert
surrounded by the sea. His history is therefore that of a
flight from the desert towards water. The migrations of
the Arab tribes of the south towards the northern coasts
were thus related to an instinct of conservation. And so
the attachment of the Arabs to Arabistan can be explained
throughout the first phase of their history: this region was
indeed reputed for its fertility.

Climatic conditions in Persia were not the same.
Even though some regions of Persia have a desertic climate, this country is watered by both streams and rivers,
which explains the slight attraction of the Persians
towards the sea. Thus, it remained a universe unknown
to them, and they did not set out to explore it. In fact, it
was the appearance of life and civilization that incited the
Persians to cross the Zagros Mountains and head down
towards the coast.

The civilizations of that region, born from the waters,
had given water an unequalled importance. Edouard
Dhorme, Professor at the Collège de France, has described this special relationship which existed between the
peoples of the region and water:

---

(1) Sykes, Sir Percy, *A History of Persia*, II, London, 1921, p. 366.

The Sumerians and Akkadians imagined that under our earth at the limits of the median land (Arabistan) there was a great sheet of fresh water which was like the reservoir from which the sources of brooks and rivers burst forth. This water, upon which floated our earth, stretched beyond the horizon and formed a circle analogous to the Okeanos river of the Greeks.... (1).

The most important divinities of the immense pantheon of Sumer, Akkad, Babylonia and Assyria... offered themselves to the adoration of the riverine dwellers of the Euphrates and the Tigris... (2).

Concerning ancient history, this analysis is of interest because of its psychological implications. Further on, it will be seen that the arrival of Persians in Arabistan marked the beginning of a perennial interference in the internal affairs of this region, leading to innumerable conflicts with its inhabitants.

## ARABISTAN AFTER THE ISLAMIC CONQUEST

The presence of the Arabs in this territory is hence multisecular and dates back well before Jesus Christ. After the Bani Tamim, who came to look for water, other tribes settled in Arabistan prior to and following the emergence of Islam (3). Turning to Maxime Rodinson, he has

---

(1) Dhorme, Edouard, *The Religions of Babylonia and Assyria*, P.U.F., 1949, p. 32.

(2) *Ibid.*, p. 138.

(3) The largest tribes that Arabistan welcomed are the following: the Bani al-Am, the Bani al-Hanzala, the Ka'ab tribes, the Bani Rabi'ah, the Bou-Kasseb (including the Bu-Gbis, ad-Dris, al Hanafira, 'an-Nassar, Kàbu ad-Dabis, 'al-Hilàlàt, ad-Dawàlim Bayt Gànim, Kanàn, 'al Bû-màruf, 'al-'Idàn, 'al-Hawàja, 'Ahlul-'Arid, 'al-Baĝaĝira, 'az-Zuwaydàt, Bayt Hàĝ Faysal and 'al-'Atab) and the Bani Tarf. Yet, the greatest branches of the Arabistan tribes up to this day are 'al-Bàwiya, original branch of the Rabi'ah tribe and which is subdivided into ten other branches, such as Bayt-Khazaal, Bani Lam, descending from the Bani Tarf and having five branches: 'al-'Anà-fiĝâ (9 branches), Kutayr (3 branches), 'an-Nassàr (2 branches) and Bani Sàla descending from Bani Tamin (9 branches). Salamàt is one of the branches of 'al-Bàwiya (3 branches), Bayt Sa'd (9 branches), Hamid (7 branches), as-Sarîfâat (2 branches), Bani Tamim (13 branches), 'az-Zarkan (5 branches), 'al-'Akras (3 branches) and over 24 Arab tribes dispersed among the 13 mentioned above.

ascertained the supremacy of the nomadic Arab tribes over this region: "The Arab penetration is ancient. It certainly must have begun before Islam, notably when the Arab tribes were occupying a great part of Mesopotamia... in the 6th century B.C." (1)

The Arab presence took on its present-day political and administrative dimensions "when the Arabs conquered this region in 640 A.D. under the caliphate of Omar Bnul-Khattab". (2) Arabistan from then on remained an Arab province, administratively attached to Bahrain after having been put under the rule of Harqus Ben Zuhair. During certain periods, however, it was attached to Basra. This explains why Arabistan was exposed to numerous crises under the Umayyads and the Abbasids, the most important of which were provoked by the Kharijites, the Qarmatians and the Zanjs. The latter destroyed a great number of cities in Arabistan in 874 A.D.

Historians claim that the revolt of Sahib al-Zanj attained al-Ahwaz. The Orientalist L. Massignon has spoken of the numerous attacks by the Zanjs that the Arabs of this area had to bear: "The country greatly suffered from the Kharijite revolt in the 8th century, the Hindu Jats or Zoot in the 9th and especially from the movement of the Bani Bridi..." (3)

In 935, the governors of the peripheral provinces became more autonomous from the central powers. Under the caliphate of Abul-Abbas al-Muqtadir, the Bani Hamdane took Mosul along with the territories of Bakr,

---

(1) Rodinson, M., *The Arabs*. P.U.F., Paris, 1979, p. 76.

(2) *Dà'irat-al-Ma'àrif al Islàmiyah,* (Islamic Encyclopedia), I. Khuzestan Article, p. 38.

(3) Massignon, *Op. Cit.,* p. 388.

Rabi'ah and Modar. Ibn Wathiq seized Basra and Arabistan was given over to the domination of al-Bridi. The territory of the caliphate was then reduced to Baghdad and its province.

In 936, Mohammed Ibn Wathiq sent an army to combat al-Bridi in order to reconquer Arabistan. However, he sought the protection of the Buwayhids, who, after having helped him, imposed their rule, so that this territory together with Baha 'ud-Dawla became an essential part of their state. This continued until the end of the Buwayhid period in 1055, and then it was the turn of the Saljuqs to occupy the region (1).

To summarize, it can be said that despite the political crises this region experienced, it belonged to an Arab empire that had no boundaries between its provinces. Arabistan was therefore integrated into a larger entity bestowed with political and religious unity under the reign of the Rachidoun Caliphs (2) of the Umayyads and the Abbasids.

Arabistan maintained its Arab character until the fall of the Abbasid caliphate. Later on, in 1258, the Mongols vanquished and destroyed the Abbasid state. Arabistan, like the neighboring territories, then went through a period of decadence even while being coveted by the states of Genghis Khan, Tamerlane and other conquerors.

---

(1) Massignon, *Op. Cit.*, p. 388.
(2) Called the "enlightened Caliphs".

## RETURN TO ARAB POWER

In 1436, the Arab dynasty of the Moucha'chi'iyah regained mastery over Arabistan under its founder Mohammed Al-Moucha'chi'i (1) that Longrigg described as a descendant of the Rabî'ah. He selected the city of Hawizah as capital of his emirate. Following his death in 1458, his son Mohsen took over and constructed a new capital, al-Mohseniyah. He issued money, consolidated relations with Iraq and spread his rule throughout Arabistan.

In 1501, Isma'il as-Safawi founded the Safawid state in Persia, while the Moucha'chi'ins governed Arabistan. Thus, another historical phase commenced such that the Safawids appeared as a new force counterbalancing that of the Ottomans. Between the two empires a ferocious struggle started and Arabistan became one of its battlegrounds. After a Safawid attack, Dezful and Tustar were conquered for a brief period.

Subsequently, Mubârak Ben Abdul-Muttaleb Ben Badrân came to power, and his reign (1588 to 1616) was to be known as a flourishing epoch: he reconquered the cities of Dezful and Tustar and imposed himself throughout the province. The Portugese traveler, Pedro Teiskeira, who visited the region in 1604, wrote:

> The entire province situated to the east of Shatt-al-Arab formed an Arab emirate governed by Mubârak Abdul-Muttaleb, who remained independent from both Persians and Turks, concluding a military agreement with Portugal,

---

(1) Shibr, Jâsem Hassan. *Târîh al-Moucha'chi'in* (History of the Moucha'chi'in) Baghdad, 1954.
Khazaal, Khalaf. *Târîh al-Kuwait as-siyâsî* (Political History of Kuwait) III, Beirut, 1963, p. 90.

the penetration of which into the Arabian Gulf dates from this period (1).

Another voyager, Pietro della Valle, who navigated down the Karun River to where it empties into the Shatt-al-Arab, furnished other details:

> Mansûr..., who governed from 1634 to 1643, dominated Shatt-al-Arab. He permitted no vessel to pass without paying him duties... He was in permanent connection with the Governor of Basra. He obstinately resisted the attempts of Shah 'Abbas to intrude upon the internal affairs of Arabistan. (2)

From the above, it can be concluded that:

1 - Besides its well known fertility, Arabistan was bestowed with an ancient history substantially enriched by the contributions of several civilizations, notably that of the Arabs.

2 - The Persians, as well as other foreign states, were aware of the strategic importance of this Arab region. For that reason they coveted it and wished to subject it to their domination since ancient times. In spite of repeated attempts, provoking hundreds of battles and thousands of victims, the Persians were never able to appropriate this region, which preserved its Arab character.

(1) *The Travels of Pedro Teiskeira: "Kings of Harmuz"* and excerpts from *"Kings of Persia"*. Hakluyt Society, 1902.

(2) *The Travels of Sig. Pietro Della Valle to the East Indies and the Arabian Desert,* Hakluyt Society, 1902.

It still may be asked why conflict between the population of Arabistan and the Persians has persisted from before the 16th century. What had been the economic importance of this region? The Orientalist Louis Massignon analyzed its attraction in the above-cited article:

> The two chief waterways, the Shatt and the Karun, command an entire network of natural routes of economic exchanges the center of which is presently found between Mohammarah in the east and New Basra in the west, as it was ten centuries ago between Old Basra (Zubayr) and Ubullah. These half-water, half-land routes are also used for the export of products harvested and manufactured in the country, like silk cloth from Tustar and, in former times, sugar from Shush. (1)

European vessels had penetrated into the Gulf with the intention of monopolizing the trade as well as the aforementioned products. As G. Curzon has written in his well-known book:

> The Western forces have recourse to methods similar to those which existed in the relations between Arab tribes: maritime alliances, then war; Portugal, Holland, France and England all used these methods. (2)

Thus, the conflict between Arabs and Persians very quickly became international once the Western powers had taken the offensive in the Arabian Gulf region, as we shall now see.

---

(1) Massignon, L. *Op. Cit.*

(2) Curzon, Georges N, *Persia and the Persian Question,* II, London, 1892, p. 323.

# CHAPTER 4

# HISTORICAL CAUSES OF THE CONFLICT : THE MODERN PERIOD

## ENTRY OF THE EUROPEAN POWERS INTO THE GULF

Historically, the European powers intervened very early in the Gulf and did not fail to take advantage of the different contradictions that thrived in this region.

### 1. *Portugese domination*

In the 16th century, the Gulf region underwent the domination of Portugal, the penetration of which was facilitated by an alliance concluded between Lisbon and Persia. The agreement reached during the reign of Shah Ismail as-Safawi allowed both allies to establish a boycott policy towards Arab navigation and trade.

### 2. *Ottoman occupation*

In 1546, the Ottoman expansion attained Basra in order to defeat the Portugese and thwart their alliance with the Persians. Despite Arab support of the Ottomans, Arabistan remained under Portugese domination, whereas Basra was won over by the Ottomans. Portugal's control of Arabistan continued up until 1652, at which time a struggle between English and Dutch influence took over.

### 3. *Rivalry between Holland and Great Britain*

Between 1580 and 1640, when Spain annexed Portugal, England and Holland made their entry into the Gulf; England thus intended to reinforce the security of its communication route towards India. With respect to Holland, its aims were chiefly commercial. "The English made Bandar Abbas the headquarters for their activities. As early as 1635 the English vessels traded with Basra in spite of Dutch competition." (1) This rivalry grew stronger and led to a war between the two countries in 1652. The East Indies Company was about to close its branch offices when Louis XIV, King of France, inflicted such a grave defeat on Holland that it became powerless to protect its interests in the Arab Gulf. (2)

### 4. *Napoleon and the Persians*

Between 1793 and 1809, France negotiated a treaty making Persia its ally in the Gulf. However, the French were not able to implant themselves in that area. The Arab tribes conserved their autonomy in Arabistan and Shatt-al-Arab. Since England feared a French advance towards India, it strengthened its presence in the Gulf and opened consulates in the different countries of that region.

### 5. *Clash between Russians and British*

The English domination did not last long before being shared, for Russia was on the look-out for any weakening of the Persian Empire. Indeed, Peter the Great had declared to his army earlier:

> As soon as you feel the Persian Empire weakening, do not hesitate to invade it through to the Gulf, and from there, if

---

(1) Akkad, Salah : "Colonialism and Oil in the Arab Gulf." *International Political Review*, n° 8, Cairo, April 8, 1967, p. 32 (Arabic).

(2) Curzon, *Op. Cit.*, p. 535.

you are able, continue all the way to the Indies where all the treasures of the world are to be found. (1)

The first Russian interventions in the Gulf date from 1838. Saint Petersburg encouraged the Persian Empire to take hold of the city of Herat which represented an important stronghold for the English on the route to the Indies. (2) Thus, Russia continued to play an active role in the region, interfering in border conflicts between the Ottoman Empire and Persia. The defeat of Russia in 1907 by Japan brought St. Petersburg to conclude a treaty with the English. The Russian influence was confined to the north of Persia. This country thus found itself exposed to two influences : Russian to the north, English to the south. By the terms of the 1907 treaty, Arabistan was to conserve its autonomy. (3)

## 6. *Discovery of Oil*

England was given an exceptional advantage in the region when it obtained, against a moderate sum (some twenty thousand pounds sterling), an authorization from the Shah to undertake research for oil deposits on the Iranian territory. This research was begun as early as 1902 and led to the discovery of the "Bir Soleyman" well in 1908. Naturally, this discovery had the effect of sharpening the imperialist rivalries in that area.

## 7. *German Interference*

At the beginning of the 20th century, Germany was transformed into a power with designs on the Orient. It

---

(1) Sykes, Sir Percy, *Op. Cit.*, p. 254.

(2) Rowlinson H., *England and Russia in the East.* London, 1875, p. 13.

(3) Curzon, *Russia in Central Asia*, p. 378 ; and Najjar M.A., *Political History of Arabistan 1897/1925.* Dar Al-Ma'aref Cairo, 1971, p. 188.

developed commercial relations with Basra, Moham-marah (Khorramshahr) and Ahwaz. The appearance of a third European power in the Gulf jeopardized the existing balance between the Russians and the English. It also pushed these two countries into taking somewhat the same side.

\*
\* \*

Before treating the modern period of Arabistan, the history that has unfolded over four centuries with its suc-cession of events must first be examined. The modern era actually begins with the settlement of the Bani Kaab tribe, which inaugurated an epoch of economic prosperity and political autonomy in Arabistan and the Shatt-al-Arab.

## THE POWER OF THE BANI KAAB :
## FIRST PERIOD

The Bani Kaab make up a tribe of Arab Bedouins having settled in Arabistan. The historian Al-Kalkashandi points out that the Bani Kaab compose one branch of the Amer Bani Sa'sa'a tribe originating from the Arabian Peninsula and having settled in Iraq. (1) All the Bani Kaab, including those established in Arabistan, des-cended from a common ancestor. (2) These men settled on the two banks of Shatt-al-Arab, devoting themselves to farming and livestock. The city of Kabbann, which was formerly a part of the Ottoman Empire, became the

---

(1) Al-Kalkashandi, Abul-Abbas Ahmad, *"Nihayat Al-Arb, Fi Maarifat Ansiba' Al-Arab"* (Knowledge of the Arab Ancestors), Cairo, 1959, p. 329.

(2) Al-Azzawi Abbas, *The History of Iraq between two occupations*, VIII, Baghdad, 1956, p. 38 (Arabic).

capital of their territory (1) as Louis Massignon has ascertained. "The tribe of the Kaab (pronounced "Tcha'b" in Bedouin), traditionally buffalo tenders, solidly established its preeminence over the region and the supremacy of its chiefs, the hereditary sheikhs of the Al-Bou Nasir, over all others." (2)

Lord Curzon drew up a list of the first Kaab chiefs and in it can be found : Nasir-Ibn Mohammed and his brothers Abdallah, Sarhan, Mir Rahman (1690-1722), then Faradj Allah (1722), Tahmaz Ben Khanfar (1732), Bander (1735), Salman (1737-1766), Osman (1737-1764), Ghanim (1766), Barakat (1770), Ghadban (1782), Moubarek (1792), Faris (1794), Alwan (1795), Barakat II (1801), Geith (1812), Mobadir (1828), Abdallah II (1831), Thamr (1837), Faris II (1840), Loutfallah, Mohammed Khan, Rahman and Mir Abdallah Djafar Khan (deposed in 1881 then restored to power in 1889). (3)

The historians who have dealt with the development of the Bani Kaab Emirate point out the rapidity of its territorial expansion. Taking advantage of the conflict between the Persians and the Ottomans over the possession of their territory, the Sheikhs of the Emirate gradually asserted their autonomy and brought law and order to their lands. Persians and Ottomans were finally obliged to accept the situation, and opened relations with the Bani Kaab.

Soon the Emirate procured itself a fleet which by the XVIIIth century became one of the most important in the Gulf. This fleet allowed the Bani Kaab to strengthen their

(1) Lorimers J.G., *Op. Cit.*, I, Calcutta, p. 1627.

(2) Massignon L., *Op. Cit.*

(3) Curzon, *Ibid.*, p. 324.

69

autonomy and extend their influence to the Shatt-al-Arab islands and Basra. (1)

## Louis Massignon has added further detail :

Throughout the eighteenth century their politics [of the Bani Kaab], which remained identical despite a few bloody outbreaks over successions, consisted in conserving the alliance of the Turks, who were ever ready for any retreat on the part of the Persian government. (2)

# THE REIGN
## OF SHEIKH SALMAN BEN SULTAN
## OR THE GOLDEN AGE
## OF ARABISTAN

The Shatt-al-Arab region witnessed remarkable progress under the reign of Sheikh Salman Ben Sultan (1737-1767). The Bani Kaab became the masters of the region : no ship was able to penetrate into the Shatt-al-Arab without having paid them navigation duties. Sheikh Salman so consolidated the fleet of this emirate that it could rival with that of the Ottoman Empire. "It was thus able to extend its power from Abadan Island to the city of Bushire as well as all along the coast of Oman in the Arabian Gulf." (3) The power of Sheikh Salman worried the Persian Empire, which made unsuccessful attempts to defeat it militarily ; similarly, the Ottomans were forced to incline before the power of Salman who not only refused to pay the dues forcibly imposed upon the emirs of this region, but also cut off Iraq's access to Shatt-al-Arab.

---

(1) Mohammed Abdul-Amir, *Maritime forces in the Arabian Gulf during the XVIIIth century*, Baghdad, 1966, p. 41.

(2) Massignon L., *Op. Cit.*

(3) Khazaal, H.K., *Political History of Kuwait*, I, p. 49.

70

The English then attacked the Bani Kaab forces, whose "reputation of bravery had attained Europe by that period". (1) They believed that this Arab force represented "a threat to their commercial interests in the form of the East Indies Company. That was the first military intervention of the English in Shatt-al-Arab and Arabistan. Sheikh Salman succeeded in repelling the fleet sent to attack his forces". (2)

This series of successes of the Bani Kaab consolidated their sovereignty over Arabistan and allowed them to form close relations with the other Arab tribes of the Gulf, particularly those of Qatar, Bahrain, Kuwait and Oman. (3)

At the death of Sheikh Salman in 1767, Karim Khan, Emperor of the Persians, proposed an alliance with the Bani Kaab, which in reality signified recognition of the autonomy acquired by this tribe. (4)

## THE DIVISION OF THE BANI KAAB
## AND THE BIRTH OF MOHAMMARAH

The Bani Kaab split into two clans when Sheikh Mardaw Ben Ali of the Bou-Kasseb tribe gave his authorization for Emir Hajj Youssef Ben Mardaw to settle at the mouth of the Karun River. In 1812 the Emir built the city of Mohammarah (Khorramshahr), provoking a division of the Bani Kaab into two clans : some members of the tribe, the Abou Nasser, remained at Felahiyah

---

(1) Berryne J., *Op. Cit.*, p. 173.

(2) Wilson, *Op. Cit.*, p. 128.

(3) Najjar, Moustapha Abdel, *Op. Cit.*, p. 37.

(4) Wilson, *Op. Cit.*, p. 168.

(Chadkan) and others, under the name of Bou-Kasseb, emigrated to Mohammarah.

Incidents broke out between the two factions of Bani Kaab, to the advantage of the Bou-Kasseb. Hajj Jaber Bou-Kasseb was able, however, to restore the unity of the Bani Kaab under his leadership. Due to him, Mohammarah expanded into the south of Iraq and to the Shatt-al-Arab.

Before going on, the causes of the division of the Bani Kaab should be brought to mind :

*a*) The Persian Monarchs had not forgotten the double defeat of Thi-Qàr (1) and Qadisiyah inflicted on them by the Arabs. For this reason, they were constantly trying to take advantage of any weakness manifested by their neighbors.

*b*) The Bani Kaab tribes had preserved their ties with the Ottoman Empire. They paid exorbitant duties to the Pacha of Baghdad. Furthermore, official documents attest that the territories in which the Bani Kaab were implanted were under Ottoman "suzerainty". (2) Finally, this region had made a pledge of allegiance to the Ottomans at the time of the Iraqi conquest. (3)

*c*) The decline of the Bani Kaab Emirate was precipitated by an internal conflict whose importance was aggravated by the antagonism between Persians and Ottomans.

---

(1) Thi-Qàr is an Iraqi Department, wherein a famous battle between Arabs and Persians once occurred before that of Qadisiyah. This stirring Arab victory was praised by the Prophet Mohammed.

(2) Darwich, Bacha, *Report on the demarcation of Turko-Iranian bounderies*, Baghdad, 1953, pp. 3-5 (Arabic).

(3) Garabiyya, Abdul-Karim, *Introduction to the Modern History of Arabia*, I, Damascus, 1960, p. 106.

The region of Arabistan and Shatt-al-Arab became the object of a ferocious struggle between the two empires, which took turns occupying it. Arabistan and Shatt-al-Arab thus resemble a Middle Eastern Alsace-Lorraine : a land coveted and fiercely disputed by the surrounding countries. This conflict continued through several centuries. Between the 16th and 18th centuries it was punctuated with a series of agreements the most notable of which follow.

## PRINCIPLE AGREEMENTS

● *Omassiyah (1541)*

Between 1508 and 1514 the Persians occupied territories beyond their boundaries, notably, the Shatt-al-Arab. This region was, however, liberated by Sultan Ottoman Selim I. In 1529, profiting from the weakness of Soleiman Al-Kanouni, the Persians took it back until 1542 when, following the signature of the Omassiyah treaty, they were forced to cede it to the Ottomans. (1) Other agreements were to follow :

● *Qasr-e-Shirin (1639)*

In 1623, the Persians took over Shatt-al-Arab, occupying it for fifteen years. In 1639, Sultan Ottoman Mourad IV obliged the Persians to sign the Qasr-e-Shirin treaty by which the Safawid Empire recognized that Iraq and the Shatt-al-Arab belonged to the Ottoman Empire.

---

(1) For more details, cf. Zabet Chaker, *International relations and border agreements between Iraq and Iran,* p. 29 on.

## • *Amir Achraf (1727) and Nader Shah (1747)*

At the beginning of the 18th century, the occupation of the Hawizah area by the Persians triggered new conflicts with the Ottomans, ended in 1727 by the Amir Achraf treaty, article 7 of which stipulates : "because of its contiguity with Basra, the region of Hawizah located within Iraqi territory will be occupied definitively by the Ottoman Empire ; the Persian Empire commits itself not to intervene in the internal affairs of Arabistan". This clause was reiterated in the Nader Shah treaty (1747) which ended further hostilities between the two states.

## • *Ard Roum (Erzeroum) I (1823)*

The border zone remained relatively calm until 1818, during which the Persians again unsuccessfully attacked. After merciless warfare a new protocol was signed, that is, the famous treaty of Ard Roum (1823), reconfirming that the entire Shatt-al-Arab region belonged to the Ottoman Empire.

## • *Ard Roum II (1847)* (1)

The appetite of the Persians, motivated by the strategic interest of this region, was whetted by the attitude of the native tribes. Indeed, the Bani Kaab were desirous of preserving their autonomy, so taking advantage of the rivalry between the Persian and Ottoman Empires, they swung from alliance with one power to alliance with the other. This policy succeeded until the Turks decided to throw all their forces into the balance: a huge army was sent by Istanbul, which occupied not only Arabistan but also pursued the Persian forces to the Zagros Mountains. Only the opening of new negotiations allowed Persia to

---

(1) Cf. Integral text in Appendix V (p. 181).

avoid fighting in order to prevent the fall of Teheran. England and Russia, which then upheld the Persian Empire, imposed their mediation between the two parties. (1) A mixed commission representing the four countries was set up to solve the conflict. This commission met for three years. During their investigations, hostilities again broke out. In 1843, Najib Pacha attacked the Persians. The second treaty of Ard Roum (Erzeroum) was concluded May 31, 1847 between the Ottoman Sultan Abdul-Majid and the Persian Shah Mohammed. For the first time, the Ottoman Empire retreated from Shatt-al-Arab, the western part of which was ceded to Persia. Article 2 of this agreement stipulates that "the Ottoman Empire recognizes the rights of the Persian Empire over the city of Mohammarah (Khorramshahr) and its port, over Khodr Island (Abadan), as well as over the territories found on the east bank of Shatt-al-Arab". The two parties agreed to set their boundaries on the east bank of these straits, placing these waters under the total sovereignty of the Ottoman Empire. The scope of this agreement remained theoretical, however, for several reasons:

*a*) The first is that the native tribes were not consulted beforehand, while their attitude in the past had often provoked or revived the conflict between Persians and Ottomans.

*b*) In both its terms and its effects, the treaty accorded the Persian Empire merely partial annexion of the Shatt-al-Arab. In reality, this region conserved its autonomy with respect to Teheran.

*c*) The Shatt-al-Arab tribes contested the clauses of the May 31, 1847 treaty relative to their territory.

---

(1) Nawar, Abdul Aziz, *Modern History of Iraq*, Cairo, 1968, p. 333 (Arabic).

75

*d*) Finally, the Persian Parliament did not ratify this treaty. Teheran judged its territorial gains as insufficient, demanding the whole region of Shatt-al-Arab, Arabistan and even Iraq. (1)

Despite these difficulties, the commission, composed of Russian, English, Persian and Turkish representatives and charged with bringing the Ard Roum Treaty into effect, proceeded to define the boundaries, especially under British impulsion, for its representatives demonstrated much zeal in accomplishing this task. (2) Finally, the commission met in 1850 and 1851 in Baghdad and in Mohammarah, but it was unable to conclude any protocol due to continuing divergences between the parties. The outbreak of the Anglo-Persian War in 1854 ended its mission. March 26, 1857, the English army led by Sir James Outram launched an attack against Mohammarah and occupied it with the help of Sultan Ottoman. Negotiations were begun with the latter concerning the possible retrocession of Mohammarah to Baghdad. (3) However, before these talks ended, the Paris Treaty (1857) was signed,obliging the British army to retreat from the territories seized from Persia. (4) Discussions over the definition of boundaries in the Shatt-al-Arab and Arabistan, included in the 1847 treaty, were relaunched in 1865. After four years of fruitless negotiations, it was decided that the contested territories would remain under the control of the state occupying them de facto. In fact, this agreement

(1) Husni, Abdl-Razzak, *Modern Political History of Iraq*, III, Sidon, 1957, p. 327 (Arabic).

(2) James (Felix Jones), *Narrative of a journey to the frontier of Turkey and Persia, through a part of Kurdistan*. Submitted to the government on August 16, 1848. Selections from Bombay Government record nº XLIII New Series, pp. 135-213.

(3) Akkad, Salah, p. 161.

(4) Broklman, Karl, *History of the Muslim Peoples*, IV, Beirut, 1955, p. 166 (Arabic translation by Mounir Baalbaki and Nabil Faris).

did not resolve anything. In the next years, Shatt-al-Arab and Arabistan became the theater of new incidents. The region nevertheless remained under Arab control.

● *The Protocol of Constantinople (1913)*

In 1912, the Protocol of Teheran was finally concluded in annex to the Ard Roum Treaty, and was completed by another signed November 17, 1913. (1) The most important clauses of this protocol were the following :

1. Khodr Island, its port and the small islands located near Abadan were taken from the Ottoman Empire, passing over to Persian control.

2. The riverside boundaries of the Shatt-al-Arab were set upon its left bank, from the locality of Nahr Abul-Arabid to the sea.

3. The Persian government abandoned its claims on the city of Sulaymaniyah.

The clauses regarding neighborly relations, navigation, trade and exchange of persons were identical to those of the previous agreements.

The Ard Roum Treaty raises two points :

1. One fraction of the Bani Kaab territory was attached to the Persian Empire, which constituted an undeniable violation of the will of these tribes, above all desiring the preservation of their autonomy. (2)

2. Aside from the constant convetousness of Persia, the Ottoman retreat from this region can be explained by the permanent resistance of the inhabitants to its authority.

---

(1) Cf. Appendix VI (p. 193) for integral text of the 1913 Protocol.
(2) Najjar M., *Ibid.*, pp. 63-64.

Negotiations on the implementing of the 1913 protocol were to be interrupted by the outbreak of the First World War. Iraq was to accede to the statute of independence. The Shatt-al-Arab should incontestably have been consi-dered as an integral part of its territory. The 1913 protocol added nothing to the second Ard Roum Treaty other than a clause conferring to the Sheikh of Mohammarah full rights over the region of Arabistan. This constituted an indirect recognition of the Arab character of that territory by the Persians and the Ottomans. Because of it, the Shatt-al-Arab was to live another period of autonomy starting with Hajj Jaber Mardaw and ending with Sheikh Khazaal.

## THE POWER
## OF THE BANI KAAB:
## SECOND PERIOD

As mentioned above, the Kaab tribes split up into two clans, namely, Al-Boukasseb and Al-Bounasser, at the beginning of the 18th century. The former settled on the Karun River and their first chief, Hajj Youssef Ben Mardaw, founded Mohammarah in 1812.

● *The reign of Jaber ben Mardaw*

In 1837, at the moment he took over, the Sheikh of Sheikhs, Kaab Thamr, attributed the title of governor of Mohammarah to Hajj Jaber Mardaw, the son of Hajj Youssef. In reality, the exercise of that power indispu-tably conferred to Jaber by the Ard Roum Treaty did not prove to be comfortable. Hajj Jaber, whose capital was Mohammarah, while he resided in Basra (1), was troubled

---

(1) An-Nabhani, *Al-Tuhfat Al-Nabhaniyyah*, IX. Cairo. 1342 H., p. 31 (Arabic).

by intertribal wars. He confined himself to an attitude of neutrality while maintaining good relations with both Persians and Ottomans, and notably with the Walis of Baghdad. It was the Persians who first had need of him to quell diverse tribes. Before going into this point, however, it would be useful to recall the words of Louis Massignon explaining the three reasons for the commercial importance of Mohammarah:

> A first reason is that for Mohammarah, merchandise brought by vessels of the high sea by way of the Shatt must be transported by the lighter Karun boats. The second is that the oriental canals bringing merchandise directly from India to Ahwaz by Abadan and Dawraq (Felahiyah) are no longer kept up, so that the only entry route by fluvial navigation is by the Shatt at al-Faw. The third is that Mohammarah is a region less unhealthy and richer in resources than the eastern delta, for it benefits from its proximity to the Shatt and from the loam after flooding. (1)

The tribe which made the most trouble for Hajj Jaber was that of the Rabi'ah, representing a true threat. Hajj Jaber thus turned to an ancient Arab diplomatic practice: he married Noura, the daughter of the chief of the Rabi'ah, Sheikh Talal, in order to appease the opposition of that tribe. One son, Sheikh Khazaal, was born from this union, to become the last emir of autonomous Arabistan. (2)

The permanent conflict opposing Ottomans and Persians, the weakening of these empires, as well as the intelligent diplomacy of Sheikh Jaber would cause Nasser Eddine Chah, ten years after the Ard Roum Treaty, to make of Arabistan an independent emirate governed by

---

(1) Massignon, L., *Op. Cit.*

(2) This contradicts the opinion of Massignon, who described the mother of Khazaal as Persian. Cf. H.K. Khazaal, *Op. cit.*, p. 99.

Hajj Jaber. By the terms of the imperial decree, it was provided that:

> 1 - The Emirate of Mohammarah was to be governed by Hajj Jaber and subsequently by his descendants;
>
> 2 - Customs were to depend upon the Emirate Administration;
>
> 3 - The Shah was to promise not to interfere in the internal affairs of the Emirate. (1)

Once his position was recognized, Hajj Jaber could devote his efforts to the development of the emirate. He followed his traditional policies, such as maintaining good relations with Iraq and expanding navigation in the Shatt-al-Arab. Among his plans for development figured the widening of the Karun River so as to render it fully navigable from its mouth to the port of Tustar in northwest Arabistan. Despite their interest for the emirate's economic development, Hajj Jaber turned down propositions made by England in exchange for the right for its ships to navigate freely upon this river. In this way, Hajj Jaber intended to avoid creating any jealousy likely to invite external intrusions into his territory and thus conserve his autonomy. The politics of Sheikh Jaber were also correctly analyzed by Louis Massignon:

> Hajj Jaber wisely and successfully led the gradual climb of his clan to the rank of tribe and of Mohammarah, his residence as chief of the clan, to the rank of capital of a principality... He succeeded in getting the sanction of the Persian Government for his rupture with Sheikh Al-Mashaïk of Felahiyah by obtaining directly from the court of Teheran his investiture over the city of Mohammarah. (2)

---

(1) Intaki, Abdul-Massih, *The Voyage of King Hussein to the Nile Valley*, Cairo, 1917, p. 207 (Arabic).

(2) Massignon, L., *Op. Cit.*

Massignon continued with this judgment of Miza'al, the son and successor of Hajj Jaber :

> He was to continue his father's policy toward the Persian court, from which he obtained the quite enviable title of "Mo'iyr as Sultanah" in 1889, in exchange for his promise to pay an annual tribute. He had the first palace of Feiliyeh constructed on a lateral canal perpendicular to Shatt-al-Arab.

● *Bloodshed over succession*

It was in this palace that in 1897 tragedy occurred:

> Sheikh Miza'al had three living brothers: Mohammed, his elder, Khazaal and Salman, his younger brothers. Miza'al, by nature rather gentle according to his contemporaries, had since some time become suspicious, no longer holding his two counselors, the Persian Katib Mollah Hassan and the emir of his personal guard, Sheikh Abdallah, in full confidence. It is said that one day he was overtaken by a fear of ambush and had the tallest trees surrounding his palace pruned or cut down. On several occasions he had been warned about the activities of his younger brother Khazaal. The latter was arrested, released, then assigned to residence within the palace. These contradictory measures reflected the hesitations of Miza'al. At the end, the tragedy exploded. That day, while the English steamboat "Malamir" of the Karun River service was just leaving Mohammarah, Khazaal and Sheikh Abdallah slipped into the palace, found Miza'al and assassinated him. In the struggle to master the situation, the conspirators were obliged to kill another fifteen of Miza'al's servants. In the scuffle, the King's belt of gold with a diamond buckle disappeared. It was the symbol of the principality for the people, and Khazaal was so infuriated that he had the head of Miza'al cut off. In the meantime, the wives of the dead man burst into the room. They threw themselves upon the corpse and Khazaal let them take him away to be buried decently. Before nightfall, as news of the murder was spreading, the first of Khazaal's edicts was promulgated in

81

Mohammarah: any funeral ceremony intended for Miza'al was prohibited. (1)

After a moment of emotion, stirred a second time by the unanimous refusal of Miza'al's harem to become that of his murderer, daily life became normal again in Mohammarah. The golden belt "rediscovered" and returned to Khazaal by his brother's wives sealed the reconciliation between them and the new Sheikh. It is hence that Sheikh Khazaal, conferred the official title of "Mo'izz Assaltanah wa Sirdar Arafi" according to protocol, became the absolute master of Mohammarah; (2) Khazaal immediately seized Miza'al's heir, Aboud, who was trying to plot against him, had him blinded with a bayonet, then imprisoned.

## SHEIKH KHAZAAL,
## LAST OF THE BANI KAAB EMIRS

It is certain that the reign of Sheikh Khazaal was capital to the history of Arabistan. After the discovery of oil, the western powers found themselves newly interested in this region and events and conflicts were both amplified. The First World War was to modify the equilibrium of the region: some regimes crumbled as that of Iran, where the Qadjars were supplanted by the Pahlavis, who then attacked the Arab government of Arabistan.

● *Proclamation of Independence of Mohammarah (1902)*

In the manner of Hajj Jaber, Sheikh Khazaal established excellent relations with the neighboring states. He was thereby enabled to lessen Persian pressure on his territory. (3) Taking advantage of the system of alliances

---

(1) Massignon, L., *Op. Cit.*

(2) Az-Zarkali, *al-A'lam* (The Precursors), II, Cairo, 1954, p. 350.

(3) Memoirs of Reza Shah, translated by Ali al-Basri, Baghdad, 1950, p. 28.

and the balance of forces in the region, Sheikh Khazaal was able to lead his emirate to independence. In this undertaking, the assistance of the British proved first to be precious, then destructive. In fact, after having come to his aid, London abandoned Sheikh Khazaal to the hands of his adversaries. At this period, Persia was considerably weakened by the joint attacks of Russia to the north and England to the south. The Anglo-Persian conflict was exploited by Khazaal who created close links with the English in order to ensure the independence of his principality. The creation of an autonomous and powerful emirate facing Persia was in keeping with the strategic views of London, which consequently gave its support to Sheikh Khazaal. Once the oil deposits were discovered, and Russia was engaged to construct a railway line between Teheran and Arabistan, England recognized the independence of Mohammarah (in 1902) and concluded a treaty of military assistance (1905) with Sheikh Khazaal. Moreover, England made sure that neither the Ottoman Empire nor the Arab leaders of the region interfered in the internal affairs of Arabistan. By means of this alliance, Sheikh Khazaal protected himself from both Persia and the Ottoman Empire. In this respect, however, it must be noted that the relations between Arabistan and the government of Baghdad were in general harmonious. Were there not Arab populations to be found on either side of the frontier?

The end of the First World War was marked by the triumph of the Russian Revolution. Moscow temporarily disappeared from the Gulf scene, as did the Ottoman Empire and the other powers. England remained as practically the sole controlling force in this region deliberately described by Western observers as a "British lake". (1)

---

(1) Khazaal H.K., *Op. Cit.*, p. 195.

The development of the international situation led England to conclude a treaty with Wasouk, the Prime Minister of the Persian Empire (August 9, 1919). The aim of this agreement was to secure Teheran against a possible Soviet aggression. Furthermore, England, with the tacit acceptance of the Shah and his government, imposed its supervision over the administrative affairs of Persia. The signing of this document coincided with the dawn of anti-colonial movements in the Middle East, notably that of Reza Khan, who proned Persian nationalism against both the Qadjar dynasty, considered responsible for the collapse of the Empire, and foreign intervention in this country. Reza Khan was assigned the portfolio of defense in the government of Zia-ud-Din, and then was appointed commander-in-chief of the army. He gave the order to arrest all those responsible for the signature of the 1919 treaty with the English. The divergence between the Prime Minister and Reza Khan brought him to leave the country temporarily. (1) The Soviet leaders, having renewed ties with Persia, thought of Reza Khan as a nationalist and revolutionary, and hardly criticized his authoritarian methods of government. Moscow signed a treaty with Persia in 1921 by which Russia renounced all of the privileges formerly accorded it in Persia, and recognized the independence of that state. In return, Russia demanded and gained from Persia the abolition of all privileges held by the other powers. Consequently, Teheran abrogated its 1919 treaty with England. The Soviets opened a consulate in Arabistan. England then reinforced its support of Sheikh Khazaal and advised him to avoid any contact with the Russian Consul. In 1921-1922, Reza Khan attempted to reduce the dissidence having overrun the north of Persia. He then turned against Arabistan.

---

(1) Memoirs of Reza Shah, *Op. cit.,* pp. 41 and 83.

## ● *Persian occupation of Arabistan*

When Sheikh Khazaal became conscious of the danger, he tried to take precautions against the aims of Reza Khan. He tried to break out of the isolation imposed by Great Britain by seeking the support of the Persian tribes implanted on the periphery of the emirate. He came into contact with Youssef Khan, the Bakhtiarian chief (the tribe from which Chapour Bakhtiar, latest Prime Minister of Shah Mohammad Reza Pahlavi, originated), with Golam Reza Khan, Governor of Bachtakwa, as well as with Moujahed Khan Emir of Luristan, and made an alliance with them against Reza Khan. Sheikh Khazaal was appointed head of this coalition (1), the headquarters of which were in Arabistan. The allies of Sheikh Khazaal obtained the support of the Shah exiled in Paris. These events incited Reza Khan to crush this opposition and occupy Arabistan, qualifying it as a "place of turpitude and a threat for the whole Persian Empire". The declarations of Sheikh Khazaal, calling him an "enemy of Islam, usurper of the power in Persia", (2) sharpened his irritation.

Reza Khan and his army started to march on Arabistan via the Isfahan and Shiraz route. England tried in vain to stop him by pretending that Sheikh Khazaal was under its protection. The British Ambassador addressed a letter to Reza Khan enumerating all the interests of Great Britain and justifying its politics in this region. The contents of that letter even today might allow a better understanding of the sensitivity of Europe and the United States regarding the question of oil :

---

(1) Called "Coalition as Sa'adah" (Coalition of Happiness).
(2) Memoirs of Reza Shah, *Op. cit.*, p. 41.

Besides the political and strategic interest of this region, Great Britain holds a particular interest — vital to the English people — in the oil reserves. On the other hand, as you know, the oil pipe-lines extend the length of the Karun River; it is feasible that in case of conflict with the forces of Sheikh Khazaal military operations would cause damage to these pipe-lines. England will consider the Persian State as solely responsible for any damages. In that event, it will be obliged to intervene directly and rapidly so as to defend its interests and those of the petroleum companies. (1)

This warning did not stop Reza Khan in his undertaking. As for Sheikh Khazaal, he had to content himself with the purely diplomatic assistance of England. The latter was careful to preserve its weighty interests in Persia and thus abstained from giving material support to the Emirate of Arabistan. Furthermore, direct English intervention against Persia would have undoubtedly had the effect of throwing that state into the arms of the Soviets. When the Persian army entered Arabistan, Sheikh Khazaal proceeded to make a just evaluation of the forces at play, thereby realizing the imbalance which existed between the military obsolescence of the tribes and the modern army of Persia. Taking care to avoid the destruction of his country (2), he accepted to negotiate with Reza Khan. He did not do this himself, using the pretext of his poor state of health, but charged his son Abdel Karim to discuss the future of the Emirate. (3) Sheikh Khazaal entrusted his son with a letter for Reza Khan in which he explained the reason for his dissidence and pledged submission to the Persian powers. Nevertheless, Reza Khan continued to march. He made his entrance into Mohammarah and occupied Arabistan village by village. He also took over Al-Ahwaz and the

---

(1) Memoirs of Reza Shah, *Op. cit.*, p. 83.

(2) Hachimi, Mohammed, *The Three Heroes*, Baghdad, 1937, p. 81.

(3) *Idem.*

palace of Sheikh Khazaal in which he established his headquarters. When Sheikh Khazaal was able to encounter Reza Khan, the latter appeared cordial and indulgent. He assured him that he would not jeopardize his position.

● *The fall of Sheikh Khazaal*

In Mohammarah, Sheikh Khazaal invited Reza Khan to his Palace in Feiliyeh and accompanied him on a tour through the Emirate. Before leaving Arabistan, Reza Khan set up a military government directed by Fadlallah Khan Zahidi. This officer stayed on good terms with Sheikh Khazaal and tried in vain to convince him to visit Teheran; a trap was then set for him.

While Sheikh Khazaal was in Basra, General Zahidi pretended to have received an order to pull out of the region ; he left Al-Ahwaz and took the direction of Mohammarah. He informed Sheikh Khazaal of this departure. The Sheikh requested confirmation of this news from the British representative in Al-Ahwaz, who reassured him. A reception was planned for the departure of General Zahidi, which was supposed to take place on the private yacht of Sheikh Khazaal anchored in the Shatt-al-Arab facing the Emir's palace. Khazaal sent for his son in Basra so that he could attend the reception. A few hours prior to it, a detachment of the Persian army came on board and proceeded to arrest Sheikh Khazaal and his son, who were deported to Mohammarah, then Al-Ahwaz and finally to Teheran. (1)

April 30, 1925 thus marks the end of the independent Arab government of Arabistan. Jean-Jacques Berreby has commented upon the occupation of Arabistan by the Persians in these terms: "The error of Sheikh Khazaal was

(1) Sheikh Khazaal died in Teheran in 1936.

87

that his emirate was located in a strategic area of the oil world which knows neither laws nor rights." (1)

Shortly afterwards, the Iranian government published a so-called declaration signed by Sheikh Khazaal in which it was indicated that :

1. The Emir of Arabistan, Sheikh Khazaal, abdicated in favor of his son Jasseb.

2. Iran had the right to oversee the internal affairs of Arabistan.

3. Arabistan nullified all of its international agreements, except those reached with Persia.

A lot has been written about the reign of Sheikh Khazaal over the Emirate of Arabistan; the observers' judgments are in great contrast, going from elaborate praise to unconditional condemnation. It is thus that Amin Arrihani, for example, considered him as "the oldest of kings, as having the reputation of most qualified and as the most generous among them". (2) On the contrary, Louis Massignon esteemed that "he took up the life of his predecessors: long days spent napping the day long in his diwan, barely heeding the reports of his secretaries and agents; nights reserved for the harem, a life of indolence interrupted from time to time by hasty skirmishes with rebels, times when he would recover the artfulness and energy of old". (3)

\*
\* \*

---

(1) Berreby J.-J., *The Arabian Gulf*, p. 111.

(2) Ar-Rihani, Amin, *Moulouk Al-Arab* (The Arab Kings). II, Beirut, 1951, p. 186.

(3) Massignon, L., *Op. Cit.*

As for Reza Khan, he became master of the country; the Parliament definitively proclaimed the deposition of Shah Ahmed, who was sojourning in Paris. A new Iranian constitution was drawn up and adopted in December 1925. Reza Pahlavi became Shah in April 1926, thus inaugurating a new period in Iranian history.

# CHAPTER 5

# RESISTANCE OF ARABISTAN TO THE PERSIAN OCCUPATION

## THE COLONIZATION OF ARABISTAN

After occupying Arabistan, Iran modified the name of this territory in calling it Khuzestan, in an attempt to deprive it of everything that made it Arab. Moreover, the Iranian authorities prevented the Arab language from being taught there. However, "events have shown that most of the tribes living in these regions refused to collaborate with the Persian authorities". (1)

The measures taken by the Persian authorities against the rights of the Arab people of Arabistan can be resumed as follows :

1) Arabistan was considered as the 10th province of Iran. A military governor was appointed to head the administration of this region ; meanwhile, the existing Arab institutions (political, administrative and judiciary) were suppressed.

2) Several military bases and barracks were put up in the region of Arabistan. This "militarization" of the administration proves that the Persian presence was foreign in the eyes of the native population. It is for this reason that the Arab people of Arabistan never stopped claiming its right to liberty and independence.

---

(1) al-Akkad, Salah, *Op. Cit.,* p. 234.

3) An area of 9,800 sq. miles of Arabistan was definitively joined to Persia. Arab tribes were forcibly transferred to northern Iran and replaced by a population of Persian origin. This policy is identical to that practiced by "The Union and Progress Commitee" (U.P.C.), in power just before the collapse of the Ottoman Empire, the aim of which was to forcefully render Turkish the Arab population then under its domination. This policy was and still is racist and anti-Arab.

4) The localities, cities, rivers and mountains of Arabistan changed designations under the Persian occupation. Persian names were attributed to them.

5) The Iranian government forbade the use of Arabic in the local courts, thus largely blocking the access of Arab citizens to jurisprudence. Later, the Shah gave the order to purge the Persian language of its Arab terms. Despite these maneuvers, Arabic has remained the first language used by the inhabitants of Arabistan. Furthermore, among other decisions concerning the region, the Iranian Cabinet suppressed the teaching of Arabic, ordered the closing of private schools which teach this language and prohibited its use in official acts. Orders were given that passports were no longer to be issued to Arab citizens wishing to continue their studies in the Arab countries. One exception was made for Saudi Arabia for the duration of the annual pilgrimage to Mecca. Passports were delivered only for that country and for one month, and the trip had to be made by plane.

6) The Persians represent only a tiny minority within the overall population of Arabistan. However, they have monopolized the administrative jobs as well as those of the diverse productive sectors and services. The Cabinet blocked access to the civil service, the army and the security forces to all Arabs. There was no other choice remaining for the region's inhabitants than to work in farming or fishing or as dockers at the ports of Arabistan.

7) The Iranian government promulgated a law by which the Arab tribes were dispossessed of their properties which were then placed under the authority of the regime's military governor. An agrarian reform was passed somewhat later, "legalizing" the expropriation of the Arab farmers, whose lands were distributed to Persian peasants. No Arab was allowed to acquire farmland without previous authorization accorded by the Iranian Cabinet.

8) Even the most elementary sanitary infrastructure is lacking in this region ; the hospitals are insufficient in number and poor in equipment.

9) The Persian government authorized all members of the police and the army to arbitrarily arrest any Arab citizen, thus creating a climate of terror and oppression in Arabistan.

10) Arab books found in either bookshops or individual homes were confiscated.

11) In the region of Al-Hawizah and those regions adjacent to the Iraqi province of Missan, the water irrigating the lands of the Arab tribes was cut off and diverted toward lands occupied by the Persian population. These practices caused a massive exodus of the Arab population towards the cities for their lands no longer sufficed for their needs.

12) The Iranian government taxed the earnings of the Arab peasants very heavily. The workers, in great majority Arab, were also highly charged.

*
* *

By these practices, the Persian leaders intended to abolish even the designation of this region, having become "Khuzestan", from the collective memory. Some apparently misinformed observers of today's war between Iraq and Iran have been taken in by this contrivance, such as Eric Rouleau, who has not hesitated to write that "the Iranian Khuzestan has been rebaptized 'Arabistan' by the Ba'athist regime". (1) In fact, as proved by the map reproduced here from an article published in 1908 by Louis Massignon, the most famous French Orientalist, the region is historically known under the name of Arabistan.

---

(1) *Le Monde*, January 6, 1981.

## ARAB RESISTANCE BEFORE
## THE FALL OF THE PAHLAVI MONARCHY

Despite all of these discriminatory measures, as well as the terror and torture practiced by the Iranian authorities, they were unable to completely subjugate the Arab population. The insurrections and revolts practically never stopped, for the Arabs pursued their struggle for independence and liberty. The most important Arab revolts having broken out over the last fifty years are the following :

1) The revolt of Sheikh Khazaal's soldiers on July 22, 1925, that is, three months after the occupation of the region by Persia. This revolt was led by Shalash and Sultan who proclaimed the independence of al-Mohammarah. Yet, the Iranian artillery savagely bombed the city overrun by the rebels, and a great number of them were imprisoned, then executed.

2) The same year of 1925 saw Sheikh Abdel Mohsen al-Khaqani take the lead of an Arab revolt in al-Mohammarah. This uprising seriously worried the Iranian authorities. The rebels sent two memoranda to Baghdad demanding the independence of Arabistan and the return of Sheikh Khazaal to the control of his kingdom.

3) In 1928, an insurrection broke out in the region of Al-Hawizah, led by the martyr Mohieddine Az-Ze'baq, Chief of the Shurfa tribes. He was able to form a government which resisted the Persians for six months. The women of Arabistan participated in this revolt.

4) A movement of support of the struggle in Arabistan existed from 1929 to 1939 in Iraq. Directed by Sheikh Hàdi Kàshef al-Ghata', this association sent a memorandum to the League of Nations. This document

requested that a referendum on the autodetermination of Arabistan be organized.

5) In 1940, the Kaab tribe directed by Sheikh Haidar al-Kaabi staged a revolt in the al-Dabis River region, pushing the Persian forces out of the area. The Iranian authorities were unable to crush the uprising until they captured and executed Sheikh al-Kaabi.

6) The al-Ghajriyyah rebellion in 1943, under the direction of Sheikh Jasseb, son of Sheikh Khazaal, was upheld by different tribes. The Persian army suffered heavy losses before regaining control of the resistance.

7) In 1944, Sheikh Abdallah, son of Sheikh Khazaal, presently living in Kuwait, vainly attempted to incite the Arab tribes to revolt, for several tribal chiefs had refused to participate in the insurrection.

8) The Bani Tarf rose against the Persians in 1945. Reza Shah seized the occasion to deploy an unprecedented repression against the Arab tribes. He gave the order for sixteen of their chiefs to be buried alive to set an example so as to dissuade the population from other revolts. The members of the Bani Tarf tribe were deported to the north of Iran.

9) In the same year, the revolt of Sheikh Mazkhour al-Kaabi broke out in the region of Abadan ; the Iranian military barracks were attacked in that city. That revolt was severely repressed.

10) When the Arab League was created, the Arabistan problem brought up considerable discussion within the new organization. On February 7, 1946, the tribes of Arabistan submitted a memorandum requesting that the situation in Arabistan be included in the agenda of debates

in the Arab League Council. (1) This request was met with fierce opposition on the part of the Egyptian delegate, who justified his position by insisting on family connections between the Iranian and Egyptian dynasties (the Shah had married Fawziyah, the sister of King Faruq). Moreover, also using this tactic the Iraqi representative emphasized the ties of friendship that existed between Abdul-Ilah, regent of the Iraqi Kingdom, with Mohammed Reza Pahlavi. In reality, the question was never dealt with. Nevertheless, the Arabistan tribes addressed another complaint to the Arab League against Iran's methods, expressing their desire to see the Persian occupation ended (August 22, 1946).

11) In 1946, the youths of the region created an association for the defense of Arabistan, whose goal was to draw international attention to the problem. The same year, the As-Sa'adah (happiness) party was created with an identical aim. (2)

12) In 1956, the rise of Arab unionist and nationalist currents in Syria and Egypt restored hope to Arabistan's inhabitants. At that moment, the first political organization of contemporary Arabistan was created, namely, the Arabistan Liberation Front. From the start, it organized a mass demonstration to support the Egyptian people against the English-French-Israeli attack of 1956.

13) The People's Liberation Front of Al-Ahwaz was launched in 1958, advocating armed resistance as the strategy to liberate Arabistan. The Front accounted for over a hundred military operations against the Persian occupant. During the struggle against the Iranian authorities, the Front lost 27 of its militants.

---

(1) Cf. Integral text in Appendix VII (p. 207).

(2) According to certain historians, ''As-Sa'adah'' may get its name from the ''Coalition of Sa'adah'' (Coalition of Happiness) created by Sheikh Khazaal with neighboring tribes in order to resist Reza Khan.

14) In 1959, the political organizations of Arabistan held a congress known as the National Congress of Arabistan. It led to the creation of the High National Committee of Arabistan, the objective of which was to continue the struggle against the Persian power. The Iraqi Revolution of 1958 brought support to the militants of Arabistan whose intention was to bring about a general revolt in order to obtain the independence of their province.

15) In 1963, the question was once again submitted to the Arab League Council, but without success. The Arab countries divided themselves into allies and enemies of the Shah's regime. Iraq thus showed itself to be one of the Arab countries that was most attentive to the cause of Arabistan, due to its geographical and historical ties with this region.

16) The Arabistan Liberation Front recommenced its activities after the wave of repression it had undergone in 1964. This decision was taken at a meeting held in Kuwait, after which the party became the National Liberation Front of Arabistan.

17) 1968 saw the creation of the Arab Revolution Movement for the Liberation of Arabistan, but it was dissolved in 1969 upon the initiative of its founders.

## ARAB RESISTANCE AFTER
## THE FALL OF THE SHAH

The Arab struggle grew considerably more intense towards the end of the Shah's reign. Arabistan took an active part in the revolt against the imperial power and contributed to its downfall. They had hoped that by supporting Khomeiny and by getting rid of the Shah they would be able to recover their right to freedom and to self-determination. However, when Sheikh Mohammed Al-Khaqani, the representative of Arabistan, came in April 1979 to submit his people's demands to Ayatollah Khomeiny in person, the latter refused to receive him. (1)

● *What were these demands ?*

1) Recognition of the Arab identity in Iran and its inclusion in the Iranian Constitution (the new Iranian Constitution does not mention this point). (2)

2) Creation of a regional council in Arabistan, an initiative destined to materialize the granting of some autonomy. The council would promulgate all laws necessary to the internal administration of the region.

3) Creation of Arab courts whose jurisdiction would handle all disputes between Arab citizens.

4) Recognition of Arabic as the second official language of Arabistan (after the Persian language).

5) Teaching of Arabic in every primary school.

6) Opening of an Arab university in the autonomous zone, responding to the needs of the Arab population.

7) Creation of a sufficient amount of jobs for the Arab population.

8) Recognition of the freedom of information and press in Arabic.

9) Allotment of a part of the earnings derived from Arabistan's oil toward the improvement of this area.

---

(1) Afterwards, it was Dr. Hanzal Khazaal who came to visit him to reiterate these demands. Khomeiny refused to hold the interview in Arabic. Abul-Hassan Bani Sadr acted as interpreter.

(2) The texts of the new constitution of the Islamic Republic were published in the *Kayhan Journal,* April 28, 1979.

10) Possibility for Arab citizens to sign up in the local army and police without discrimination.

11) Revision of laws concerning the distribution of land.

● *What was the result of these demands ?*

1) The regime of Khomeiny replied to these demands by repression. Even when the population persisted, his answer was a categorical refusal. Arbitrary arrest and execution went on. The religious leader of the Arabistan population, Sheikh Mohammed al-Khaqani, was arrested and confined in Qom, in a place located near the residence of Ayatollah Khomeiny.

2) General Madani, Commander of Naval Forces, undertook the disarmament of the Arabistan Arabs and ordered arrests, thus provoking incidents that left 500 dead, 320 wounded and led to the arrest of 700 militants.

3) Iran decided to put pressure on the surrounding countries to prevent them from sending aid to the inhabitants of Arabistan. Ayatollah Khalkhali, President of the Revolutionary Courts, paid a visit to Bahrain, where he was to accuse Iraq, along with other Gulf countries, of sending weapons to Arabistan and to Mohammarah. Furthermore, he demanded that certain persons having "collaborated" with the Shah's regime and who were supposedly taking refuge in the Gulf area, be turned over to him. He also solicited that the opening of delegations of both the revolutionary authorities and the Iranian party "Fidaiyou Khalq" be authorized in the Gulf countries.

4) The month of April 1980 constituted an important turning point in the struggle of Arabistan. A fresh outbreak of acts of resistance was once again directed against a regime that had not freed itself of the Shah's politics.

Military operations were aimed at official buildings and oil complexes the chief labor force of which comes from Arabistan. By April the incidents were daily. Three revolutionary organizations — "Movement of the Mujahidin of the Arab Muslim People", "Popular Movement of Arabistan" and "The Political Organization of the Arab People of Arabistan" — led this resistance.

On April 30, 1980, a revolutionary group from the province of Arabistan occupied the Iranian Embassy in London and took its diplomatic corps as hostages. The principal demand of these revolutionaries was recognition by the government in Teheran of Arabistan's autonomy along with the liberation of several hundred prisoners. During his trip to the Gulf, Sadegh Ghotbzadeh spoke with the commando over the telephone and afterwards announced that those with whom he had spoken expressed themselves fluently in Persian and that he had told them of his government's wish to execute the prisoners from Arabistan at the same time as refusing their conditions. This operation was ended six days later when the British security forces attacked the Embassy, killing the revolutionaries and two hostages.

5) Ghotbzadeh declared that the Iranian government would take national differences into account, but that it would never tolerate demands for autonomy of any community whatsoever. He made still another somber proclamation by which the 1975 Algiers agreement was abrogated. (1)

---

(1) *Al-Mostaqbal Review,* n° 123, June 30, 1980.

## THE OCCUPATION OF ARABISTAN
## AND NAVIGATION
## IN THE SHATT-AL-ARAB

In spite of these revolts and unceasing protests, the occupation of Arabistan since 1925 was a step allowing Iran to take control of a part of the Shatt-al-Arab waters.

> The Iranian authorities did everything possible to make the Shatt-al-Arab the common property of Iran and Iraq. It is for this reason that in November 1934, Iraq raised the question, asking that the conflict between the two countries be settled by means of negotiation. But Iran took advantage of the weakness of Iraq's political leadership following the coup of Bakr Sidqî, to reiterate its claims to Shatt-al-Arab, obliging Iraq, despite itself, to give its authorization for Iran to share navigation in the Shatt-al-Arab. This rendered the Iraq-Iran boundaries very delicate. (1)

> Prior to the Second World War, more precisely in July 1937, a border agreement (2) was reached under the patronage of Great Britain that brought the boundary back to the Iranian bank of the Shatt-al-Arab, the waterway being wholly attributed to Iraq. (3)

The founding of the Iraqi Republic in 1958 caused a deterioration in relations between the two countries. The all-powerful Shah officially denounced the treaty of 1937, reaffirming Iran's rights over half the Shatt-al-Arab's waters. Despite diverse tentatives of mediation, frontier incidents multiplied. To weaken Baghdad, the Shah supported the Kurds under General Barazani, fighting against

---

(1) Berreby, Jean-Jacques, *Op. cit.*, p. 109.

(2) Cf. Integral text of this agreement in Appendix VIII (p. 211).

(3) *Le Monde*, September 29, 1980.

the central power in Iraq. (1) After the construction of refineries in Abadan, close to the east coast of the Shatt-al-Arab, Iran extended its claims to the islands in the Gulf, immediately after Great Britain's declaration regarding its retreat from the zone eastward of the Suez Canal. As already mentioned, "in 1971, the Shah occupied the three islands in the Strait of Hormuz, belonging to the Gulf Emirates, believing that he was to become the policeman of the Gulf". (2) "Baghdad was the only capital to protest against this annexion. This objection was not followed up." (3)

The tension in the relations between the two countries continued until a climax was reached towards the beginning of 1975, after which both sides were brought to the table of negotiation upon the initiative of late Algerian President Houari Boumediene, which led to the Declaration of Algiers on March 6, 1971 and the conclusion of a new treaty. Two important factors in the internal situation of Iraq encouraged its leaders to make certain concessions to Iran.

When the October War exploded in 1973,

> Iraqi forces were at the time deployed along the eastern front in full readiness for any Iranian aggression on national soil. In order to provide proper conditions for moving the Iraqi forces to the battle with the Zionist enemy, the Revolution Command Council issued a statement on October 7, 1973 in which it reaffirmed Iraq's readiness to settle the problems with Iran peacefully. So, Iraq sent its striking forces to Syria where they had the honor of taking an effective role in protecting Damascus from falling and checking the Zionist advance within Syrian land.

---

(1) Cf. *Le Point,* n° 419, September 29, 1980.
(2) *Idem.*
(3) *Le Monde,* September 29, 1980.

From the realistic point of view, issuing that statement implied Iraq's readiness to consider the claims of Iran in Shatt-al-Arab. (1)

## Furthermore, it is incontestable that

Our people offered all sacrifices needed in the battle which lasted twelve months, that is, from March 1974 to March 1975. The casualties of the Iraqi Army in that battle exceeded 16 thousand martyrs and wounded soldiers, while the total figure of the casualties of the people in general was more than 60 thousand killed and wounded.

Despite the valiant performance of our Army in fighting the puppets and those who have been backed up by the American-Zionist and Iranian forces, and despite the high morale of our men, it was impossible to ignore the material and objective requirements of the battle. Those requirements are sometimes of supreme significance in determining a lot of political and military outcomes.

The question reached a very crucial point when our supplies and essential ammunition began to run out and three heavy shells were all that remained for the Air Force. (2)

Nevertheless, the Algiers agreement was not to be respected by the Iranian side any more than the preceding ones.

---

(1) Taken from the Iraqi President's speech on September 17, 1980. (Cf. Integral text in Appendix XI, p. 223).

(2) *Idem.*

# CHAPTER 6

# THE COURSE OF THE WAR : THE FIRST PHASE

It is incontestable that relations between Iraq and Iran had deteriorated since the return of Khomeiny to Teheran and even before, as a study of each country's declarations will confirm. A reliable review such as "Géopolitique du Pétrole" had pointed out the possibility of war between Iraq and Iran and continued its analysis in exposing that which it called "the military imbalance" between the two countries.

> From the standpoint of land forces, the disproportion between the army bequeathed to the Republic of Khomeiny by the Shah and that of the Iraqi regime is no less considerable: approximately 400,000 soldiers serving Iran and a little over 200,000 for Iraq... Iran theoretically disposes of a more modern and complete armament than does Iraq, but the corps of Iranian officers is still under the effects of the purges, trials and executions of its most prestigious generals... (1)

For the Arab countries it was clear that since the return of Khomeiny to Iran, neighborly relations with that state had started to deteriorate, which would lead the two countries towards war in early September 1980. It could have been expected that the Iranian Revolution, which had upheld that of the Palestinians, would proclaim that the Shah had illegally conquered Arab lands in the Gulf. It

---

(1) *Géopolitique du Pétrole*, December 31, 1979.

ought to have decided to restore these lands to their Arab and Muslim inhabitants, since it had announced its revolutionary nature to all Muslims. It was also expected that Iran would apply the agreements signed with Iraq by which it promised to maintain courteous relations and not to threaten the security of neighboring countries. These hopes proved to be in vain.

In fact, as previously seen, the new Iranian leaders have taken it upon themselves to undermine the security of the other Arab and Muslim countries. They have declared that the territories forcibly annexed by the Shah would remain Iranian. They even went as far as to claim Iraq and the other Gulf countries as Persian territories. Furthermore, they have adhered to a policy of interference in the internal affairs of the Arab regimes, especially that of Iraq. The authorities in Iran have maneuvered in various ways to create difficulties for the Iraqi government and have unceasingly invoked its downfall.

● *Military provocations*

The hostility expressed by the Iranian demonstrators and leaders against Iraq was accompanied by aggressions and military provocations that have led to a state of war. Before this degradation of the situation, the Iranian forces had committed 244 border violations or acts of aggression against Iraq by air, sea and land in the period from February 23, 1979 to July 26, 1980. (1) Among these acts should be included bombings of Iraqi border posts, the capture of soldiers belonging to border units, the interception of civil planes and aggressions against Iraqi and foreign ships in the Shatt-al-Arab. The Iraqi forces answered these aggressions in trying to limit them. During

---

(1) Official Memorandum about the Iraq-Iran border conflict, Foreign Affairs Ministry of Iraq. November 1980.

this period, Iraq sent 240 official notes to the Embassy of the Iranian Republic in Baghdad (1), giving an account of the aggressions, their date, form and consequences. Moreover, Iraq sent official notes to most of the regional and international organizations (2) : the League of Arab States, the U.N., the Nonaligned Movement, the Organization for African Unity, the Conference of Islamic Nations, etc. Even though these organizations were informed of the events having taken place on the Iraq-Iran border, Teheran did not take the notes of protest into consideration, thus violating international laws and rules as well as the conventions concluded between the two countries.

● *Military concentrations and the triggering of clashes*

At the end of July 1980, movements and concentrations of Iranian troops were observed near the border with Iraq. The Iranian artillery started violently bombarding the Iraqi border posts. It is thus that July 28th the post of al-Chîb was attacked and seriously damaged. These skirmishes soon took the appearance of a real war. Teheran did not hesitate to boast : "When the Iranian army marches toward Baghdad, no one will be able to hold it back. By means of a mere communiqué we shall be able to decree the fall of the Iraqi regime."

By August, the amplitude and violence of the clashes became unbearable for the Iraqi authorities. On the 6th, for example, Iran tried to compromise the Soviet Union by demanding that it halt its deliveries of weapons to Iraq. August 27th, Teheran announced that combats had grown in importance in the Qasr-e-Shirin sector and had

---

(1) Cf. Appendix IX (p. 217).
(2) Cf. Appendix X (p. 219).

extended to all frontier posts in the region. The Iranian army used "ground-to-ground" missiles for the first time. (1)

## THE WAR

On the morning of Thursday, September 4th, violent air and naval fighting burst out after the shelling of several Iraqi villages, namely, Khanaqîn, Muzayriah, Zurbatiyah, Qata'Mandali and Mustapha Lwand, and the oil installations of Naft Khâneh by Iranian forces. According to the military communiqués of both countries, these battles caused a great number of victims, dead or wounded. Two of Iran's Phantom bombers were shot down. Equally violent combats continued on September 5th and 6th. These brought about the destruction of the oil plants in that region as well as of numerous military posts. The Iraqi forces went into action by shelling the villages of Qasr-e-Shirin and Mehran.

● *The liberation of two regions : Zein al-Qaws and Saif Saad*

The Iraqi government was surprised by the intensity of these combats and attempted to put an end to the hostilities by diplomatic means. It sent an official note to the Iranian Embassy in Baghdad in which they were informed of the damage caused in Iraq by Iranian artillery. The Iranian forces nevertheless pursued their operations; thereafter, the Iranian aviation attacked the posts of al-Hussein, Kouteiba, Houk and Ghazâli, as well as the village of Khanaqîn.

---

(1) *Le Monde,* August 29 and September 29, 1980.

September 9th, the Iraqi army was moved to the border and following a violent struggle, forced the Iranians to retreat from the region of Zein al-Qaws. Afterwards, Iraq demanded by way of an official note that Iran return the Iraqi territories it was occupying in violation of the agreements concluded between the two countries, in particular, the 1975 Algiers treaty. That note was left unanswered. On the contrary, Iran multiplied its acts of aggression. Fighting recommenced at Diyala and Wasit. On September 10th, the Iraqi forces liberated the region of Saif Saad, subsequent to clashes during which the head of Iranian military operations, General Chabni, was killed (the helicopter in which he was accompanied by numerous Iranian officers was shot down). In addition, two Phantoms and several tanks were destroyed. Naval combats resulted in the sinking of two Iranian patrol boats. By September 16th, the Iraqi forces had already liberated 125 sq. miles of the territory attributed to Iraq by the Algiers agreement.

The pursuit of hostilities from then on remained uninterrupted. Iran decided to close its airspace. Bombings in the region of Shatt-al-Arab were intensified and several ships were hit. All around the world, attention was drawn to this region, especially after Teheran's threat to prohibit navigation in the Strait of Hormuz and the Shatt-al-Arab zone.

## ABROGATION OF THE 1975
## ALGIERS AGREEMENT

In the evening of September 17, 1980, the members of the Iraqi National Assembly were convoked to an emergency session. Upon entering the auditorium, the representatives looked solemn ; they knew that crucial decisions were to be taken. Some were seeking information about the outcome of the fighting. When the deputies had taken their seats, President Saddam Hussein took his place on the platform and pronounced a speech that was to become historic: (1)

> Following the signing of the Accord, negotiation and contacts were held in view of enforcing its clauses, especially those concerning demarcation, fixing border pillars and other technicalities. Three basic protocols were signed on the basis of the Accord, namely, the protocol of delineation of river borders, the protocol of redemarcation of land borders and the protocol on border security.

> The Iranian side benefitted at an early stage from the protocol of delineation of the river borders in Shatt-al-Arab, whereas additional time was normally required for the implementation of the protocol of land borders. The measures of returning these territories to Iraq were delayed owing to the conditions of the former Iranian regime in 1979 and 1980. The new regime assumed office while our territories were still under the other party's control. We then understood the new regime's need for some time to honor its commitments under the Accord. But since the first day of the assumption of power by this ruling group in Iran, we noticed an aggressive stand on their part, and a breach of neighborly relations... They, therefore, fully bear the legal and de facto responsibility of rendering this accord null and void...

> Since the rulers of Iran have violated this accord from the very beginning of their assumption of power through unmasked and deliberate interference in the domestic affairs of Iraq and... by refusing to return the Iraqi territories that we were obliged to liberate by force, for these reasons, I hereby announce before you that the Accord of March 6, 1975 is terminated on our part too. (The Revolution Command Council issued a decree to this effect.)

> Therefore, the legal relationship in Shatt-al-Arab must return to what it was prior to March 6, 1975. This river must recover its Iraqi Arab identity as it had been throughout history in name and in reality, with all the disposal rights emanating from full sovereignty over the river.

---

(1) Cf. Integral text of the speech in Appendix XI (p. 223).

During the night, Mr. Tareq Hamad-al-Abdallah, Secretary General of the R.C.C., was seen on television, informing the Iraqi people of the decisions taken by that Council and unanimously adopted by the National Assembly. The Algiers agreements and their annexes were thus abrogated.

● *The provisions of the Algiers agreement can be summarized in three points* (1) :

1) The two contracting parties recognize that the Shatt-al-Arab is principally an international route of navigation. Consequently, they engage themselves to abstain from any exploitation likely to disturb navigation within the Shatt-al-Arab, in the territorial waters of these two countries and in all parts of the navigable channels in territorial water leading to the mouth of the Shatt-al-Arab.

2) Both parties will once again be able to restore security and mutual confidence along their common boundaries. The two parties promise to bring into effect a very strict and efficient control on the borders they share so as to put an end to all subversive infiltrations, whatever their origin.

3) Measures will be taken to carry out the demarcation of land boundaries between the two countries.

It should be noted that no mention is made in these dispositions of Iraq's renunciation to its demand of evacuation of the three islands in the Strait of Hormuz that were occupied in 1971 by the Imperial navy.

● *Significance of the abrogation of the Algiers agreement*

The decision to annul the agreement took on a further

---

(1) Cf. Appendices XII (p. 227) and XIII (p. 241) for integral text of the agreement and annexes.

dimension when the Iraqi authorities put the following measures into effect as a result :

1 - All vessels wishing to use the Shatt-al-Arab were obliged to fly the Iraqi flag and to conform to the orders of the Iraqi authorities. For example, "for the first time since 1975 a Japanese ship has undertaken the crossing of the Shatt-al-Arab with an Iraqi pilot and with the Iraqi flag raised high on the mast". (1)

2 - The Shatt-al-Arab was reinstated as an Iraqi national waterway under the full sovereignty of Baghdad, as it already had been in the past (see above).

3 - The decision of Iraq gave it total sovereignty over its sea and air, in addition to the right to define the rules of navigation in the Shatt-al-Arab.

4 - The absolute sovereignty of Iraq over the Shatt-al-Arab conferred it the legal right to determine all penal and civil questions concerning this region. The duty to oversee all expenses and repairs due to navigation was additionally attributed to Iraq.

5 - The port authorities both inside and outside Iraq were informed that they were to refer to the orders of the Port of Basra and to the navigation rules effective in the Shatt-al-Arab before the agreement of 1975. These rules were related to the control of river traffic, to navigation licenses and to port duties.

6 - The owners of ships using the Shatt-al-Arab were warned of the necessity to abide by these instructions and to remain in contact exclusively with the Iraqi patrolers in charge of meeting them at the entrance to or exit from the Shatt-al-Arab.

In fact, Iraq and Iran had both recognized on several

---

(1) *Le Monde*, September 21-22, 1980.

occasions that the Algiers agreement had not been respected. "The Iranian Head of State, Abul Hassan Bani Sadr has admitted that Iran had not applied the Algiers agreement, forseeing the restitution to Iraq of certain territories administered by Iran, but he assigned the responsibility for this shortcoming to the Shah's regime." (1)

The Iraqi Minister of Foreign Affairs, Saddoun Hammadi, has in turn indicated that "the Algiers agreement includes a passage stipulating that if any article is violated, the whole protocol becomes null and void... At least two articles have failed to be respected : that involving the restoration of the Zein al-Qaws and Saif Saad sectors, and another, the question of security... Teheran allowed one of General Barazani's sons to enter Iran so as to use him for reviving agitation in Iraqi Kurdistan". (2)

## LIBERATION
## OF THE SHATT-AL-ARAB

On September 17th, Iranian bombings of the Shatt-al-Arab were intensified. Fierce combats took place in the port of Mohammarah and at the Abadan airport. The headquarters of the Iranian armed forces announced in a communiqué that the area of fighting henceforth included the entire region of the Shatt-al-Arab. The same message indicated that the Iraqi side of the Shatt was being shelled by Iranian missiles and heavy artillery. The Iranian army made it known that an Iraqi border post and ammunition depot had been obliterated. After that, five Iranian warships were destroyed at the Khosrowabad base, to the south of the port of Abadan, as well as this base's installations.

---

(1) *Le Monde,* September 19, 1980.
(2) *Le Monde,* October 7, 1980.

Baghdad announced that the Iraqi forces had attacked Iranian warships which had intercepted and machine-gunned the English ship "Orient Star" on its way to the port of Basra. Navigation was practically cut off in the Shatt-al-Arab. Moreover, Iranian patrolers intercepted a Kuwaiti vessel which was directed toward the port of Basra bearing the Iraqi flag. Another ship, the "Lucile", registered in Singapore, was caught under Iranian fire in the port of Mohammarah ; it, too, was flying the Iraqi flag.

By September 21st, the Iraqi forces had finished liberating all territories attributed to Iraq according to the Algiers agreement. Baghdad then proposed an opening of negotiations with Teheran in order to find a just solution to the conflict, that is, one that would take the interests of both countries into account while respecting the agreements concluded between them. Iran rejected this offer and intensified its military operations in the afternoon of September 21st. The Iranian forces set about the systematic bombing of Iraqi cities, factories, schools and hospitals, and shelled the boats anchored in the Shatt-al-Arab. In the evening of that day, 125,000 Iranian reservists came to reinforce the "Guardians of the Revolution" and the Iranian army, in conformity with a decision of the authorities of Teheran obliging these reservists to get to the eastern front by October 3rd.

Until that date, the news agencies had met with difficulties in trying to obtain information from the Iranian side due to the breakdown in communications between Teheran and the outside world. The Iranian radio picked up in Paris and in London constituted the major source for Iranian news and communiqués.

According to "Le Monde", the Iranians bombarded military objectives in Iraq, causing damage to six airports ; 47 persons were killed and 100 wounded. Iran also

114

gave orders for merchant vessels found in the Shatt-al-Arab to leave the area as fast as possible.

## THE IRAQI COUNTER-ATTACK
## ON SEPTEMBER 22nd

After weighing the gradual transformation of the clashes into an open war, and in retaliation to Teheran's attempts to paralyze navigation in the Shatt-al-Arab, the Iraqi Revolution Command Council was resolved to strike hard once and for all.

On September 22nd, the Iraqi air forces raided ten army and air force bases located inside Iranian territory. These raids caused heavy damage and even destroyed such airports as Kermanshah, Sanandaj and Al-Ahwaz, in addition to the army bases of Hamadan, Teheran, Isfahan, Dezful, Shiraz and Tabriz. In return, Iranian planes carried out raids on Basra and Wasit in Iraq. Teheran warned the Gulf countries against any attempt to attack Iran by air, sea or land from their territories.

● *Intensification of military operations and the Strait of Hormuz threatened with closure*

On September 23rd, the military situation was aggravated when Iranian aviation bombed six Iraqi airports and launched raids against Baghdad, Nineveh and Basra, causing the destruction of this city's petro-chemical plant. It was then that the Iraqi forces penetrated by about fifteen kilometers into Iranian territory and laid seige to the villages of Sumar, Qasr-e-Shirin, Zahab and Charmel. Furthermore, they tightened their control of the city of Mohammarah, and destroyed part of the Abadan refineries.

115

It was only at this time, when fighting gained in intensity and spread to the region of the Shatt-al-Arab, that the conflict took on an international dimension. Highly industrialized states started to fear that their economy, progress and prosperity were in danger, especially after the repeated threats of Iran to close the Strait of Hormuz. Taking note of these threats, President Saddam Hussein declared that

> ...the Iranian attempts to take control of the navigation in the Strait of Hormuz represent a step towards an all-out war and create the circumstances for foreign intervention in the affairs of the region. Iraq will not remain passive in front of this new situation, but will take all necessary measures to bring the Iranians to respect the rights of others as well as international law. (1)

We shall not linger any longer on the military details and the destruction caused by this war. The military messages emanating from both countries are extremely contradictory ; it is therefore difficult to have an exact idea of the extent of the damages and to evaluate the losses in lives and equipment.

## FIRST REACTIONS
## FROM THE INTERNATIONAL COMMUNITY

### a) Waldheim's appeal

International circles attentively observed the evolution of the war and its effects upon the world situation. On September 22nd, the Secretary General of the United Nations, Kurt Waldheim, sent out an appeal to both countries, inviting them to cease fire and to open negotiations. This request was transmitted to the representatives of the two countries in the United Nations. (2) Iraq

---

(1) *Le Monde,* September 23, 1980.

(2) *An-Nahar,* September 23, 1980.

responded favorably to this invitation, but put three conditions upon the stopping of combats :

1 - Respect of Iraqi sovereignty over the frontier zone separating it from Iran.

2 - Respect and recognition of Iraqi sovereignty over the Shatt-al-Arab.

3 - Iran's retreat from the islands of Abu Musa and the two Tumbs.

With regard to the Iranians, they altogether failed to reply to Kurt Waldheim.


*b) An appeal from Europe*

Due to the efforts of Jean François-Poncet, French Minister of Foreign Affairs, the European Community indicated its interest in these "naval and air battles over such a powder keg". In view of Iranian threats relative to the Strait of Hormuz, the Committee of Nine published the following declaration on September 23rd :

1. The nine states of the European Community express their strong concern over the military confrontation between Iraq and Iran.

2. Noting the bilateral nature of the current conflict, they underline the need to avoid anything that could extend it. In this regard, they rely upon the continuing restraint of all other states, notably that of the Great Powers.

3. They approve of the appeal communicated by the Secretary General of the Conference of Islamic Nations in favor of an immediate cease-fire and, referring themselves to the discussions already underway thanks to Mr. K. Waldheim, Secretary General of the U.N.O., they declare their readiness to support any international initiative apt to favor a political solution to the argument.

4. They recall the extreme importance that the freedom of

navigation in the Gulf represents for the entire international community, and the necessity of not infringing upon it.

5. They decide to continue following the developments of the situation with the utmost attention and remain prepared to contribute their help in seeking a solution. (1)

## c) *Appeal from the Security Council*

The Security Council met in the late afternoon of September 23rd, and after several hours of discussion, its President, the Tunisian Taeib Slim, made its appeal to the belligerents known :

> The members of the Council are extremely preoccupied by the idea that this conflict is destined to grow more and more serious and that it may represent a severe threat to international peace and security. They heartily welcome and fully support the appeal that the Secretary General addressed to both parties September 22, 1980, along with his offer of mediation to resolve the present conflict. The Council members have asked me to represent them in appealing to the governments of Iraq and Iran to take the first step in view of a solution to their dispute by abstaining from all armed activity and all acts likely to aggravate the dangerous situation which presently exists, and by settling their argument by pacific means.

The Iraqi delegate, Salah Omar al-Ali, participated in the meeting, but his Iranian colleague was absent. (2)

## d) *The Soviet-American talks* (3)

The United States Secretary of State, Edmund Muskie, met his Soviet colleague, Andrêi Gromyko, at the

---

(1) *Le Monde*, September 25, 1980.

(2) *Le Monde*, September 24, 1980.

(3) Cf. *Herald Tribune* and *Le Matin*, September 26, 1980.

headquarters of the Soviet delegation to the United Nations in New York. Their conversations chiefly dealt with the Iraq-Iran conflict. This was the first demonstration of the misgivings of the two powers.

Observers noted that the position of both Moscow and Washington was characterized by a hesitant, prudent neutrality. This impression was confirmed afterwards. The Soviet-American talks did not lead to any concrete proposition which would have permitted the Security Council to find a solution to the conflict.

### e) France's worry

France, which offered the most active diplomacy among the Western countries, once again expressed its apprehension in view of the increasing deterioration of the situation in the Gulf. The French Cabinet published a communiqué on September 24th, in which it expressed its disapproval of any military action that would result in the halting of navigation in the Gulf :

> The French government expresses its serious preoccupation about the consequences of the military confrontation opposing Iraq and Iran. France observes that the dispute having brought about these clashes is strictly bilateral and considers that it must become the object of a political settlement.
>
> It relies on the other states, notably the Great Powers, to demonstrate the greatest reserve so as to favor this objective. France emphasizes the importance of maintaining the freedom of navigation in the Gulf for the entire world community as well as the necessity of not endangering it. (1)

---

(1) *Le Monde,* September 25, 1980.

● *Contacts between Moscow and Paris*

While the French Cabinet was meeting to discuss the consequences of the war, a special envoy of the Iraqi President, Mr. Tareq Aziz, arrived in Paris with a note for President Valéry Giscard d'Estaing informing him of the latest developments. This visit to Paris of the Iraqi Deputy Premier was the follow-up to a three-day official stay in the Soviet Union, which was in the scope of normal Soviet-Iraqi consultations.

Following his interview with the French President, Mr. Tareq Aziz gave a press conference at the Iraqi Cultural Center in Paris on the afternoon of September 23, 1980, addressing himself to over 150 newspapermen from the French and foreign media. To a question about the possibility for negotiation, the Iraqi Deputy Premier was to reply:

> We have no other aim or objective than to see our rights put into effect. If the opposing party wishes to speak with us, we are disposed to listen and to discuss with them. We do not reject any initiative that would favor a settlement of the conflict on a peaceful basis. This initiative could come from any country in the world, except Israel, which we do not recognize, or the United States.
>
> Iraq does not wish to prolong the conflict. If the Iranian leaders announce today that they accept the moderate conditions of Iraq, the Iraqi authorities will immediately react in a positive manner...

He went on to explain these conditions :

> 1) Recognition by Iran of the sovereignty and rights of Iraq over its national territory.
>
> 2) Establishment of neighborly relations with Iraq and the Arab nation.
>
> 3) End to all interference in the internal affairs of bordering countries.
>
> 4) Stopping of every kind of act of aggression.

120

Mr. Tareq Aziz concluded by explaining that Iraq did not wish to prolong the struggle and then asserted:

> If we say that, it is not because we are weak but because our position is strong. (1)

## IRAQ REPLIES AFFIRMATIVELY TO THE APPEAL OF THE SECURITY COUNCIL

On September 24th, Dr. Saddoun Hammadi, Iraqi Minister of Foreign Affairs, dispatched a letter to the President of the Security Council and to the Secretary General of the United Nations, in which he transmitted the Iraqi answer to the request sent the day before by the Security Council. This letter asserted :

> Iraq considers that since the Algiers agreement dated March 6, 1975 has not been respected by the Iranian side, it is abrogated in virtue of the provisions of Article 4 of this agreement. Iraq has taken this decision after having exhausted all peaceful means over the past three years in trying to urge Iran to abide by this protocol. Iraq has firmly declared that it had no designs upon Iranian territory and that it had not wished to declare war with Iran nor to enlarge the combat zone. But Iran has on its own initiative undertaken to extend the conflict, bringing Iraq to retaliate by attacking objectives located inside Iranian territory. Our goal is to preserve the interests of Iraq, of the Gulf region and of the international community. (2)

● *Iran admits the superiority of Iraq*

On September 24th, Iranian President Bani Sadr recognized Iraqi military superiority. In the meantime, Khomeiny entreated the Iraqi army and people to "rise up against the Ba'athist regime". (3)

---

(1) Notes taken by a delegate of E.M.A.

(2) *An-Nahar*, September 26, 1980.

(3) *An-Nahar*, September 25, 1980.

In the field of operations, the war was then becoming characterized by the intensive use of aviation against the petroleum complexes. Naval combats were intensified in the Shatt-al-Arab. Iraqi military communiqués reported raids by Iranian aviation against the refinery in Naft Chaabiyah and the oil terminal of Basra. These attacks also hit economic centers and the civilian population.

Regarding the Iraqi air forces, they shelled Iranian positions, for instance, the base at Tabriz as well as the airport and the Ahwaz installations. Iran announced an Iraqi raid on the islet of Kharg where the main outlet of Iranian oil is to be found ; two oil reservoirs caught fire. Moreover, Iraqi forces took over full control of the region of Qasr-e-Shirin and Mehran.

On September 25th, the Iraqi army arrived at the entrance to the city of Mohammarah. Before furthering its advance, the first accomplishment was to destroy the wall of sand erected by the Iranians all along the Shatt-al-Arab facing Basra. In little time, Mohammarah was to find itself under the threat of the Iraqis, who meanwhile were continuing to progress within Iranian territory. The Iraqi flag was raised over the prefecture of Mehran. The Iraqi army also invested the oil plant of Chah Abad. Iran announced that its aviation had carried out three raids over the city of Kirkuk, damaging its airport and petroleum installations. Other Iranian attacks struck the towns of Arbil, Mosul, al-Kut and Basra.

## IRAQ RECOVERS
## ALL CONFISCATED TERRITORIES

The Iraqi Defense Minister, General Adnan Khairallah, announced during a press conference held on September 24th that Iraqi forces had regained all stolen Iraqi territories. He declared:

The penetration of our forces inside Iranian territory, beyond the international borderline, is a reaction against Iran's closing of the Shatt-al-Arab and its threat to close the Strait of Hormuz, which is a strategic passageway not only for Iraq but for all countries in the region. This threat involves the interests of the Third World countries, all the more so since we know that Europe and Japan along with a great number of countries worldwide, fulfill their energy needs in this region.

## The Iraqi Defense Minister was to add :

The war can be stopped if Iran recognizes our rights, otherwise it will continue and we will be forced to strike vital points in Iran till the day they recognize our legitimate rights... We have demanded total sovereignty over the Shatt-al-Arab, but we have no territorial ambitions. In particular, we do not have the intention of seizing the oil reserves of Arabistan because we have enough oil.

## General Khairallah concluded his press conference in the following terms:

We befriend and respect the peoples and armed forces of Iran. The latter have been forced into fighting to satisfy the designs of the Iranian leaders. (1)

---

(1) *Le Monde*, September 26, 1980.

123

# Chapter 7

# THE COURSE OF THE WAR :
# THE SECOND PHASE

## NEW INITIATIVES FOR PEACE

Three international initiatives have thus far become the basis for diplomatic efforts aimed at finding a solution to the Iraq-Iran conflict. The first is that of the Security Council which adopted a resolution demanding a cease-fire by both of the belligerents. The second emanates from the Islamic countries that decided to send a delegation assigned to a "goodwill mission" between the two capitals, Baghdad and Teheran. This delegation was headed by Pakistani President Zia-ul-Haq, in his capacity as President of the Conference of Islamic Nations (C.I.N.), who was accompanied by Mr. Habib Chatti, Secretary General of the C.I.N. The third initiative was that of Fidel Castro, President of the Movement of Nonaligned Countries, whose Minister of Foreign Affairs, Isidoro Malmairca, was in charge of transmitting messages to the Presidents of Iraq and Iran and was to discuss with them the means of putting an end to the hostilities.

● *Iraq's Acceptance vs. Iran's Refusal*

Dr. Saddoun Hammadi, Iraqi Minister of Foreign Affairs, declared that his country would favorably accept any proposal for mediation, along with any international initiative "regarding the problems that are at the origin of the present conflict, whether it be at the level of international or regional organizations, so as to identify our rights

and guarantee them as well as our national interests".
Dr. Hammadi was to add:

> Iraq, aware of its responsibilities and basing itself on the
> principle of nonalignment and on the United Nations
> Charter, has defined its policy after having proved that it
> has the possibility to defend its sovereignty and its rights
> by military means, once political means have been
> exhausted. In accordance with its principles, Iraq
> announces that it wishes to preserve world peace. By the
> same token, it appreciates the concern of many countries
> anxious to maintain security in this region. Iraq under-
> stands and shares the preoccupation of these countries and
> would like it to be known that Iraq realizes its responsibil-
> ities toward the vital economic interests of the world,
> especially with regard to petroleum.

The Iranian Prime Minister, Mohammed Ali Radjai,
on the contrary, has clearly rejected these diverse initiatives. In an interview given prior to the arrival of the
Pakistani President and Mr. Habib Chatti, Mr. Radjai
made the announcement that "My country is ready to
welcome all personalities, but we shall never accept to
receive a mission of good will. Furthermore, we shall
never declare that Iran is prepared to negotiate".

● *Iraq announces the stopping of fighting before the
decision of the Security Council*

While tentatives at mediation in the Iraq-Iran conflict
were at a standstill and the United Nations was inviting
the belligerents "to abstain from any new recourse to
force", Iraq proclaimed that it was ready to accept an
immediate cease-fire. On the morning of September 28th
(9: 55, local time), President Saddam Hussein asserted in
a radio-broadcast speech: (1)

> We proclaim to the entire world that Iraq is prepared to
> stop fighting if the other side accepts this earnest plea.

---

(1) *Le Monde*, September 30, 1980.

## The President then added that :

Iraq is disposed to negotiating directly with the Iranian party, or through a third party or any international organization, in order to reach a just and honorable solution guaranteeing our rights. Our forces are now holding the positions assigned them at Qasr-e-Shirin, Mehran, Sarbil Zahab, Ahwaz and Mohammarah, the pearl of the Shatt-al-Arab, the city that got rid of its mourning clothes today and put on an Arab dress, that of victory.

We are not taking advantage of our military victory to formulate demands to which we have no right... We are asking the Iranian government to legally and virtually recognize our legitimate rights, namely, Iraqi sovereignty over its national territory as well as its river and sea waters. We also want Iran to desist from its illegal occupation of the three islands, Greater and Lesser Tumbs and Abu Musa, and to cease its interference in our internal affairs and in those of the other countries of the region. This battle is not ours alone, but rather that of all Arabs so as to maintain the Arab character of the Gulf, to push aside the danger of Persian expansionism and to avoid the intervention of external powers.

On the evening of the same day (6: 30 p.m. local time), the United Nations Security Council unanimously adopted a resolution presented by Mexico and Norway, which states :

> 1 - The Council demands that Iraq and Iran immediately abstain from any further recourse to force and that they settle their argument by pacific means and in conformity with the principles of justice and international law;

> 2 - It invites them to accept all appropriate offers of mediation and conciliation;

> 3 - It requests that other states demonstrate great moderation and that they abstain from any act likely to cause an escalation or extension of the conflict;

> 4 - It expresses its support of the Secretary General's efforts and his offer of good offices;

> 5 - It recommends that the Secretary General prepare a report for the Security Council within forty-eight hours. (1)

● *The efforts of the Islamic Conference*

At the same time as the Iraqi Head of State was making his speech, the Pakistani President Zia-ul-Haq and Mr. Habib Chatti were stopping over in Amman on their way to Baghdad. The Pakistani President and Mr. Chatti had already met President Abul Hassan Bani Sadr in Teheran, but Khomeiny had refused to receive them. President Zia-ul-Haq commented the earlier interview in these terms: "Iran is still in a phase where mediations lead to nothing." One of the collaborators of Bani Sadr declared that "the Pakistani President did not obtain any result... We shall continue fighting until the last Iraqi soldier has evacuated Iranian territory". (2)

---

(1) *Le Monde*, September 30, 1980.

(2) *An-Nahar*, September 29, 1980.

The Iraqi Head of State, Saddam Hussein, had reacted positively during a telephone conversation to the proposition of Mr. Zia-ul-Haq to come to Iraq to carry out a mission of mediation. President Hussein told him the following:

> Even though it finds itself in a position of force, Iraq favorably accepts the Islamic initiative and encourages any initiative of peace undertaken by the international organizations in which Iraq is a member or by regional organizations and friendly countries. (1)

While in Baghdad, the Pakistani President had a series of official talks with the Iraqi Head of State in the presence of Emir Hassan ben Talal, Prince and heir of the Jordanian Kingdom. During these interviews, Iraq confirmed its readiness to both facilitate and contribute to the success of the mission of the C.I.N. president.

President Zia-ul-Haq then went to New York after passing through Paris, where he spoke with Valéry Giscard d'Estaing. When he was leaving the Élysée, he affirmed that "the talks that he had had in Baghdad had given him real hope of finding a solution to the Iraq-Iran conflict". (2)

● *The initiative of the nonaligned countries*

The initiative of the nonaligned countries was no more successful than the two preceding ones. Following the visit of the Cuban Foreign Affairs Minister to Iraq on September 26th, an official spokesman announced: "Iraq has accepted Cuba's 'goodwill mission', the aim of which is to put an end to this conflict." (3) "On the other hand, by way of Prime Minister Mohammed Ali Radjai, Iran

---

(1) *An-Nahar,* September 28, 1980.

(2) *An-Nahar,* October 1, 1980.

(3) *An-Nahar,* September 28, 1980.

renewed its refusal to accept any mediation as long as the Iraqi forces were in Iran." (1) The visit of the Cuban Minister of Foreign Affairs to Iran thus ended in failure. Mr. Radjai explained: "Castro has misunderstood the revolution of our people if he is asking us to sit at the negotiation table with Iraq..." (2)

● *The declarations of the Iranian ambassador in Moscow*

The Iranian rejection of any attempt to settle the conflict was clearly evidenced by the declaration of Mohammed Mokri, Ambassador of Iran in Moscow who, during a press conference held September 29th (3), indicated that Iran did not assign any great importance to the 1921 treaty with Russia, and specifically articles 5 and 6 which were denounced by the Islamic Republic (4). Mr. Mokri added that the opening of negotiations with Iraq depended on several conditions :

— The downfall of the regime of Saddam Hussein and his replacement by the true representatives of the Iraqi people.

— Iranian occupation of the Iraqi city of Basra as a guarantee for payment of war indemnities. After paying these reparations, the population of this city would be

---

(1) *As-Safir,* September 28, 1980.

(2) *An-Nahar,* October 3, 1980.

(3) *Le Monde,* October 1, 1980.

(4) Article 6 of that treaty stipulates that:

"In the case in which a third power would try to pursue a policy of usurpation by armed intervention in Persia, or would like to use the Persian territory as a base for operations against Russia, and in the case where a foreigner would threaten the boundaries of Russia or its allies, a threat that the Persian government would not be able to stave off after a preliminary warning by Russia, the latter would have the right to advance its troops into the country in view of military operations necessary for its defense. However, Russia promises to withdraw its troops from Persian territory as soon as the peril is averted."

asked to pronounce itself by vote upon its connection to Iraq or to Iran.

— The organization of a vote in Iraqi Kurdistan for autonomy or for its attachment to Iran.

● *Opposite reactions of Iran and Iraq to the Security Council resolution*

After having approved of the opening of negotiations, the President of the Iraqi Republic dispatched a letter that was received by the Secretary General of the United Nations on September 29th. (1) In it, he stated that Iraq accepted the terms of the resolution adopted by the Security Council and promised to cease fire on condition that this would be reciprocated. The next step, according to the Iraqi Head of State, should have been the opening of "negotiations, directly, by mediation, or by the representatives of an international organization or any body that we respect and in which we trust, in view of finding an equitable and honorable solution which would guarantee our rights and our sovereignty".

> On the other hand, the Islamic Republic refuses any direct or indirect dialogue with Iraq, as long as the Iraqi troops have not withdrawn... The propositions included in your letter and in the resolution of the Security Council cannot be taken into consideration by our government. (2)

This excerpt from the reply to Mr. Waldheim's letter signed by Bani Sadr and dated September 22nd as well as to the resolution adopted on September 28th by the Security Council, accurately reflects Iran's categorical rejection of all demands to end the fighting.

---

(1) *Le Monde*, October 1 and 3, 1980.  Cf. text of this letter in Appendix XIV (p. 265).

(2) *Le Monde*, October 30, 1980.

# RECRUDESCENCE
# OF MILITARY OPERATIONS

While these diplomatic efforts were being made, air raids were striking the cities plus the oil and industrial complexes of both countries, notably Teheran, Mosul and Kirkuk. It was during this period that the exports in Iraqi oil feeding the pipelines that cross Turkey and Syria were interrupted. The intensification of military operations culminated on September 27th, a key date in the course of the war. Combats were then flaring on the outskirts of Al-Ahwaz, the capital of Arabistan, and in some parts of Mohammarah. The same day, the Iraqi forces published communiqué nº 41, addressed to the army and people of Iraq as well as to all Arab countries, the terms of which were as follows:

> Your glorious army has arrived in Al-Ahwaz ! ! ! Right now it is with your Arab brothers who belong to the tribes of the Bani Ka'ab, Bani Tarf, Kinana, Bani Lâm, Tamim, Malek, Sawari, Salamât al-Muhaysin, Sakhr and Mawsa-wiyah... All of them are under the protection of your army which has glorified the soil of Arabistan and has in turn been glorified by this soil, its history and its martyrs. Thus, our glorious army has attained its strategic ends as defined by its leaders. Its duty is now to consolidate this victory. (1)

Simultaneously, the Iranian radio was broadcasting a speech by Khomeiny instructing the religious leaders to prepare the people for war. The Imam announced that his country would carry on the struggle to its last soldier. Observers noted that this was the first call to arms from the "Guide of the Revolution". They also noticed that this appeal represented an implicit confession of the Iraqi forces' progression inside Iranian territory.

---

(1) *Ath-Thawra* (Baghdad), September 28, 1980.

● *Bombing of the Iraqi nuclear research center*

On September 30th, thick black smoke was seen rising from Baghdad : Iranian aviation had just hit the thermal power plant in Dawra. During that raid, which caused the death of fifteen persons, oil supplies belonging to the plant were set on fire. In the meantime, Phantom F4's were attacking concrete buildings in the region of Ashtar to the east of Baghdad, at the entrance of which a sign announced "Electronic Industries". What was really involved was the Franco-Iraqi nuclear research center housing the Isis and Osirak reactors (which the Iraqis call Tamuz 1 and 2).

The identity of the attacking planes has not been formally established. Radio-Teheran denied Iran's responsibility for this raid. According to diverse sources (1), it could have been Israeli fighters that had organized the attack. The statements of certain top Israeli leaders tend to corroborate this thesis. Forty-eight hours before the attack, General Yehoshua Seguy, Chief of the Israeli military intelligence services, declared his surprise that "Iran had not yet attempted to bombard the Iraqi nuclear reactor in construction near Baghdad". The Israeli newspapers dwelt on the details of this raid before a sudden blackout on the affair. (2)

In an interview by the Kuwaiti newspaper "Al-Anba' ", President Saddam Hussein evoked this affair for the first time:

> We have in our possession several elements which cannot be divulged at the present time. However, I am able to affirm that Iran bombed these nuclear plants with the

(1) Cf. For example, *L'Express* and *Le Monde*, October 4, 1980.

(2) Annexed to the present work (Appendix XV), an excerpt can be found from an article by Israeli Political Science professor, Shlomo Aronson, on "The nuclear factor in the Middle East". This article reveals the confusion which surrounds the raid on the Iraqi nuclear generators.

assistance of a foreign power which owns the same type of plane (Phantom), that is to say, Israel. We struck down some of the planes that bombed the plants, and the Iranian pilots thus captured confessed that Iran participated in this operation. On the other hand, we were unable to find the rest of the aviators whose planes were shot down because the safety button that was supposed to eject the pilot in case of emergency was removed, inevitably bringing about their death. The reason for doing this was to dissimulate the identity of these pilots. (1)

For years the French-Iraqi nuclear cooperation has provoked strong reactions in Israel, despite repeated claims from Baghdad and Paris that the Isis and Osirak reactors were destined solely for civil use. Unlike Israel, Iraq adheres to the nuclear nonproliferation treaty and has consented that its nuclear complexes be inspected by the International Atomic Energy Commission (I.A.E.C.). Baghdad therefore has no intention of using the 93 % enriched uranium fuel delivered by Paris for military objectives. On September 24th, Jean François-Poncet, French Foreign Affairs Minister, on a visit to New York, emphasized the purely peaceful nature of Franco-Iraqi nuclear cooperation "despite all the news published here and there". Finally, the French Government explained that:

> The delivery to Iraq of highly enriched uranium is not exceptional since the great majority of research reactors functioning throughout the world, and in particular those delivered by the United States, use this kind of combustible. It corresponds only to the requirements of the research reactor supplied, is programed in consequence and is subject to all necessary safety measures. (2)

---

(1) *Al-Anba'*, January 19, 1981.

(2) Cf. *Official Journal of the French Republic*, September 24, 1980 and *Le Monde*, September 26, 1980.

● *Iraq vainly calls for a cease-fire*

October 1st, Iraq invited Iran to cease fire from October 5th through 8th. This entreaty followed Baghdad's acceptance of the mission of mediation offered by Mr. Zia-ul-Haq and Mr. Chatti. Iraq laid down the following conditions before the cease-fire could take effect:

— An end to the Iranian attacks against Iraqi forces.

— An end to the concentrations and movements of troups.

— No more reconnaissance flights or propaganda campaigns against Iraq.

On October 2nd, the Iraqi military command announced that military operations would from then on be restricted to the defense of the strategic areas already held. At this same moment, Teheran was proclaiming a general counter-offensive. Fierce combats took place in Arabistan, especially in the regions of Mohammarah, Dezful, al-Ahwaz and Abadan. The Iranian Chargé d'Affaires at the United Nations, Mr. Jamal Shemirani, had rejected the Iraqi proposal for a cease-fire, explaining that Teheran would persist in its refusal as long as the Iraqi army had not regained the positions it occupied prior to the war. The Iranian attitude caused Iraq to intensify its attacks so as to oblige its adversaries to sit down at the table of negotiation. Starting on October 3rd, the Iraqi forces applied themselves to the cutting off of all supply routes to Iranian towns.

The cease-fire proposed by Iraq was to go into effect on October 5th, but instead, four Iranian planes carried out a raid over the suburbs of Baghdad, hitting economic and civil targets. It was after this attack that Iraq made known its will to go on fighting against Iran whatever the period of time and the sacrifices required. Iraq had weighed the Iranian acts of refusal of all international resolutions, mediations and appeals to lay down its arms.

The war then entered a new operational stage. The intransigence of Iran progressively discouraged those who had exerted themselves in trying to find a solution to the conflict. The Iraqi Revolution Command Council observed this situation in a long communiqué:

> Despite the contempt shown by the Iranian authorities for these good intentions, praised by the Islamic states as well as by international circles known to be friendly; despite the publication of a communiqué signed by Khomeiny rejecting the proposal for a cease-fire, the Iraqi government has fully kept its engagements towards the Islamic states and the entire world. In this way, the President of the Republic, Commander-in-Chief of the Iraqi Armed Forces, has given the order to stop all military operations, the cease-fire going into effect October 5th, 1980 at dawn. And, indeed, the Iraqi Armed Forces have scrupulously respected these instructions. However, the government of Teheran has rebuffed this initiative by continuing to this very day its acts of aggression against our armed forces and against Iraqi territory. It is thus that their ground forces triggered aggressions against our armed forces while Iranian aviation and the navy were simultaneously raiding civil sites inside Iraqi territory.

> By proclaiming before the entire world that it has faithfully filled its engagements, the Iraqi government demonstrates by words and by acts its good intentions, its solid commitment to principles, its sincere desire to put an end to hostilities in such a way that a just solution can be found, based on the speech pronounced by the President of the Republic, Commander-in-Chief of the Armed Forces, on September 28, 1980.

> Let it once again be recalled that in this speech, the President of the Republic had announced Iraq's will to decree the stopping of fighting if the other side engaged itself to respect this earnest plea. Moreover, our country is ready to negotiate with the Iranian party in view of finding an honorable and just solution which guarantees our rights

136

and respects our principles. What we demand, the President said, is that the Iranian government recognize outright, both legally and in practice, the legitimate historical rights of Iraq over its territories and its waters; that it commit itself to a true policy of good neighborliness; and that it abandon its racist, aggressive and expansionist tendencies as well as its spiteful attempts to interfere in the internal affairs of the countries in the region.

Lastly, the Iranian Government must restore all lands spoiled from our native land and present a clear idea of its claims and of its viewpoint as to the rights of Iraq and the Arab Nation. Yet, the behavior of the Iranian authorities confirms what we have always said about the expansionist aims of a regime whose irresponsibility towards its peoples is equalled only by its contempt for the rest of the world. We are convinced that the only effective means to bring these authorities to reason is to strike them painful blows so as to oblige them to recognize law and reality.

Conscious of its responsibility with regard to the region and the world, and respecting the parties having generated these good initiatives, Iraq is firmly decided to pursue its just and honorable struggle for its legitimate historical rights.

### • *Iran's isolation and the Iraqi diplomatic campaign*

President Bani Sadr complained about the isolation of Iran from the rest of the international community: "We should not ignore what is said of us throughout the world. We are isolated because international public opinion has judged our actions as unrightful." This declaration translates the internal dissension, the divergences of viewpoints and the contradictions between what the Iranian leaders say and what they do.

Considering the absence of any cohesion within the Iranian political leadership, the Iraqi authorities launched an enormous diplomatic campaign, the echo of which was amplified by the internal unity reigning in Iraq. President

Saddam Hussein had messages transmitted to twenty-seven states, defining the position of Baghdad and recalling its proposal for a peaceful settlement to the conflict. Mr. Naïm Haddad, President of the National Assembly and member of the R.C.C., undertook a tour of the Eastern European countries (Bulgaria, Czechoslovakia, Rumania, Poland, East Germany and Hungary). Mr. Abdel Fattah Mohammed Amin, member of the R.C.C. and Minister of the Regional Administration, also went on a tour of several countries in Western Europe (Italy, Austria, West Germany, Spain and Sweden). Mr. Kassem Mohammed Khalaf, Minister of Higher Education and Scientific Research, visited India, Indonesia, Sri-Lanka, Bangladesh, China and Japan. Mr. Hachem Hassan Aqrawi, State Minister, went to Nigeria, Senegal, Mali, Madagascar, Mozambique, Tanzania, Zambia and Kenya. Mr. Karim Mahmoud Hussein, Youth Minister, met with the Turkish and Greek authorities. Mr. Hikmat Ibrahim, member of the Revolutionary Council, left for Belgrade just a few days later, while Mr. Abdel Wahab Mahmoud, Minister of Agriculture, departed for South America.

● *Crossing the Karun*

At the same time as the Iraqi special forces were just finishing beseiging Mohammarah, on the night of October 10th, a detachment from the Iraqi army was continuing its advance over the Al-Ahwaz route, before heading toward the south along a line parallel to the Shatt-al-Arab. This maneuver was the prelude to the most noteworthy military operation of the war.

Iraqi tanks succeeded in forging their way through the 9 m. separating the al-Mohammarah-al-Ahwaz route from the banks of the Karun. This river crosses the southern part of Mohammarah before emptying into the Shatt-al-Arab, and therefore constitutes the northern extremity of the Island of Abadan. During the night the Iraqi tanks moved ahead until they finally reached the Karun. Crossing it a 310 yard long floating bridge was set up in order to permit the tanks to take up positions on the opposite bank before sunrise. Both the observers and the military correspondents estimated that this could be thought of as one of the most skillful maneuvers of modern warfare. In the morning, the Iraqi forces surprise attacked the Iranian units to be found on the al-Ahwaz-Abadan route. They took numerous prisoners and seized a considerable amount of weapons and heavy material, namely, British-made Chieftain tanks, American M-60's and 175 mm., recoilless guns from the same origin (these guns achieved notoriety when Israel used them against Egypt under President Nasser during the 1968-1969 war of attrition). This material was in perfect condition and was carried by the Iranian prisoners themselves towards Basra behind the Iraqi lines, once again making use of the floating bridge to cross back over the Karun.

The Iraqis were trained on this material and then made rapid use of it against the Iranian forces, as mentioned by the Iraqi military communiqués published in December, 1980. Part of the Iranian armament was exhibited in Zawra' Park in Baghdad. Furthermore, 50 tanks were given to Jordan.

Crossing the Karun allowed the Iraqis to completely surround Abadan Island to the east, north and west, and to take control of all roadways connecting the Abadan refineries to the rest of Iran. During this operation, a great number of Iranians were taken prisoner, and among them, Mr. Mohammed Jawad Tandkuyan, Petroleum Minister, captured on October 31st. In addition, the Iraqi forces destroyed the oil pipelines between the refinery of Abadan and al-Ahwaz. They also blew up the strategic pipelines buried 3.3 yds. underground.

### • *The fall of al-Mohammarah*

The communiqués emitted by both sides give dates for the fall of Mohammarah that contradict those of the press releases. These divergences may be explained by the complex topography of this city, which extends around 3 3/4 m. in length and 2 1/2 m. in width. The city is divided into five large sections : A huge, modern port upon the Shatt-al-Arab, bordered by the old city to the north and the new city to the east. The Island of Abadan makes up the southern section, that is, the opposite bank of the Karun. To the northeast, a group of military buildings and barracks form the fifth section.

This structure explains why the takeover of Mohammarah was achieved in several stages. The first phase ended in the occupation of the port by Iraqi forces. The final "mopping-up" went on during and after the crossing of the Karun, and the most ferocious fighting occurred at this time, in each and every street. The Iraqi special forces demonstrated their ability to engage in street combat.

In the speech that he addressed to the Iraqi soldiers on October 18, 1980, on the eve of the feast of Al-Adha, President Saddam Hussein cited these battles as an example :

> You, my brothers who are fighting and wrenching the land of al-Mohammarah free from the enemy, you are paying with your blood each inch won over from the enemy. By your combat, you are writing a page of history as you edify the past, present and future of your nation. You are struggling for the reawakening of the Arabs.

On November 8, 1980, the Iraqi newspapers devoted their headlines to what they called "the final touch". By this, they were referring to the Iraqi actions in the city of

Mohammarah. That very day, the popular army (1) had finished clearing the barricades, tanks and burning tires left by the Iranians in the main streets of the city. In the meantime, civil technicians were laying telephone lines and assuring the postal and telegraphic services in the city.

The battle for the control of the port made international news due to the considerable number of foreign ships found there, waiting to unload the merchandise imported by Iran. These boats had been stuck for quite a while and ultimately were hit by Iranian fire. The latter forces were trying to put pressure on the Iraqis and get them to stop their advance.

The commander of the Iranian navy announced that his country was going to mine the Strait of Hormuz to prevent any international humanitarian attempts to rescue the crews on the stranded boats. Furthermore, on October 14th, the Iraqi President made it known to Kurt Waldheim that his country had started to evacuate the vessels blocked inside the port of Mohammarah and that Iraq would inform the United Nations of the completion of this operation. Additionally, a director of the Iraqi General Company of Ports indicated that the states to which these ships belonged had been informed of the steps taken by Baghdad. He added that four boats belonging to Greece, Yugoslavia, Italy and South Korea had been directed to the port of Basra. (2)

---

(1) The popular army is a paramilitary formation composed of civilians. It groups together very well trained youths, workers and peasants. Their mission in wartime is to defend strategic institutions and, if necessary, to participate in the fighting. 35,000 members of this army took part in the war against Iran. Mr. Taha Yassin Ramadan, member of the R.C.C. and First Deputy Premier, is the commander of the popular army.

(2) *An-Nahar,* October 15, 1980.

The "mopping-up" of Mohammarah and the crossing of the Karun completed the Iraqi victory that had by then become undeniable. Eye witnesses visited this region during the first two weeks of November. They travelled all along the front from Qasr-e-Shirin in the north to Abadan in the south, passing by the regions of Bostan (Bsaytin) and Khafajiyah. Their testimonies confirmed that the Iraqi army controlled an entire region "stretching 13-17 miles inside Iran along a 350 mile front." (1)

While the Iraqi army was pursuing its advance on all fronts, the popular army was assuring the defense of those cities and complexes liberated, for example, Moham-marah, Qasr-e-Shirin, as well as the villages of the Bostan region. The civilian groups for popular action undertook the marking out of roads and the construction of dams. The above-mentioned witnesses described Iraqi society at war as a machine whose parts are well lubricated : each individual has an assigned task that he fulfills with total abnegation.

## THE SECRET
## OF THE IRAQI SUCCESSES

In his press conference held in Baghdad on November 10, 1980, the Iraqi president emphasized the high level of consciousness attained by the Iraqi people during the war.

● *We consider the wars of 1956, 1967 and 1973 as our own experiences.*

The experience of the Arabs in the war involving Syria, Jordan and Egypt in 1967 is our own, and that of October

---

(1) Press conference of President Saddam Hussein on November 10, 1980.

1973 led by Syria and Egypt on the front lines, with all of their military potential against the Zionist entity, is again our experience as Arabs.

All these wars are full of lessons rich in both positive and negative aspects. The element of surprise by our enemy does not allow us to justify the possibility of losing the battle, nor does the fact that their mobilization within five days instead of over a week had temporarily thrown us off. It would in no way excuse us not to have minutely calculated everything, just as we cannot use the excuse that our stocks were sufficient for two months, whereas the war may be prolonged to over four months.

## • The longest contemporary war

That is why we may declare in all frankness and sincerity that we are satisfied with our calculations in front of our new enemy who imposed this war upon us and that we have accepted. Our calculations are still right, and what is more, the positive elements which have arisen in our favor at the Arab, international and Iraqi levels, as well as the technical aspects, among others, have revealed themselves even more auspicious than those considered when we took the decision for confrontation.

You may say that this is the vague language already heard from other people. But I ask you this: What duration are you speaking about? The war has lasted over two months. This is the longest armed conflict between two countries in the history of modern wars, with the exception of wars of independence which have a different nature and meaning. We have already been fighting two months. Notwithstanding the ultra-sophisticated arsenal that the United States of America and other countries have stored in Iran, the military plans in its possession today, as well as the experience acquired by that country prior to the fall of the Shah thanks to the CENTO pact, we have succeeded in fighting them for two months, improving our military positions and progressing.

## ● *An Iraqi Arab strategy*

It has been said that this progression is slow. In the beginning you called it rapid, at least some of you during the first week. It has been said that the Iraqis had thrown themselves into a war without having taken any precautions with regard to their means of communication, and without having sufficiently weighed the defensive measures that the enemy would take. Then you, or some of you at least, started to criticize us for our slowness, declaring that either our tactics were inspired by those of the Soviet Union or that they were of Western or Oriental inspiration. As for myself, I would say that their inspiration is solely due to the Iraqi Arab strategy. They derive from the lessons we have learned, lessons that are common to all Arabs, even to those who today manifest their ill-will. The latter have obliged us to calculate precisely by accounting for their possible dealings. Thus, we were not surprised by them ; what did surprise us, however, was the support of so many well-intentioned people at the international and Arab levels, who demonstrated more support than could have been hoped for. When it must confront a situation, the calculations of our country with regard to its men, its institutions, its people and its leaders, or other aspects, take the worst eventualities into consideration. The same information media had predicted our failure at the time the March 1970 Manifesto was proclaimed. But we did not fail. They believed that Iraq had launched itself into a tremendous adventure and that it was taking the risk of division. But on the contrary, the unity of Iraq was reinforced. These same circles had also forecast our failure at the time of nationalization, saying that we had gotten ourselves involved in a foolish adventure. But we have succeeded. Not content with that, they dreamed of the appearance of a conflict between civilians and military, but its dream was not to come true. The same milieux predicted we would fail in the war against the rebel factions in 1974, a war that lasted 12 months. We have won a victory and their forecast proved false.

It is again those sources which, not having received central instructions from Zionist circles, remained silent during the first week of the war. As we ourselves had foreseen,

144

they were taken by surprise. As soon as they had received instructions from the Zionists, in particular, and others who wish neither the victory of Iraq nor the development of the Arab Nation, they went on the offensive. That is exactly what happened.

I am not speaking of those among you who are asking questions. On the contrary, we have always said that we were grateful to those who question us because discussion and concerted action are the indispensible ways and means for reaching the truth. But we resent those who know this truth and elude it by avoiding to speak of the matter.

## • Mobilization of the Iraqi people

So try to pass through the Abadan-al-Mohammarah, al-Mohammarah-al-Ahwaz or al-Mohammarah-Dezful sectors, you will see dozens of miles of paved roads. This work was carried out not by Iraqi soldiers, but by Iraq. It is the Iraqi civilian organizations that did this on the army's back lines, since everyone fights in their own way in Iraq. The engineer, the officer, the soldier, the popular army, the drivers of bulldozers and tractors, the peasant, the artist, the writer, the man of letters and the journalist, each one in his own area. The Iraqi children that you can see accomplishing their duty in the field of civil defense also had the honor of participating in the battle. You will see dozens of miles of road laid out behind the army, conceived in accounting for winter and possible upheavals due to the will of man or to natural elements that could happen to the Dez Dam or to the al-Karkheh River after the winter rains.

The war started on September 4th. The Iranian enemy launched it against our people and against our country. In the month of September, it was not yet winter. One week to ten days after September 22nd, as soon as our ground forces entered Iranian territory and the fighting took on a new and larger dimension, we began laying out roads in order to link the paved ones to the centers of command of the Iraqi army fighting at Dezful, al-Ahwaz, al-Mohammarah, Abadan, Qasr-e-Shirin, Mehran and other zones. Perhaps you would say: Look at these people from the Third World countries... They are never capable of calculating as do the great powers, nor as those who know

145

science and how to manipulate it. Perhaps you would say: Oh! The Arabs! Surely the Zionist entity and its sympathizers say: Look at the Arabs! They have not thought of the winter... They have not taken the dam on the Dez into account nor the other Iranian rivers that may possibly undergo violent changes due to nature or to the Iranians.

Perhaps you will say, now that we have told you how we improved the roads: the Iraqis therefore want to settle in rather than to leave these territories. But we shall answer by stating that our behavior is constantly inspired by this noble saying: 'For your life on earth act as if you were going to live forever, and for life-after-death, act as if you were going to die tomorrow'. Our mothers and children would never pardon us for neglecting to take the steps necessary to face winter and its rigors.

## IRAN AT THE U.N.:
## RADJAI'S SPEECH

The Iranian Prime Minister's visit to New York on October 17th astonished diplomatic circles. Mr. Radjai was going to the United Nations to expose the Iranian point of view. His trip was aimed at breaking out of Teheran's isolation.

The same day that Mr. Radjai arrived in New York, the Iraqi president was meeting with Mr. Habib Chatti, Secretary General of the Conference of Islamic Nations, and reconfirmed to him that Iraq was ready to accept an immediate cease-fire and to open negotiations based on the respect of Iraqi rights and notably upon the sovereignty of Baghdad over its lands and its territorial waters. The visit of the Iranian Prime Minister only served to reflect the "embarrassment" of Teheran over a war that was still going on with Iraq. (1)

---

(1) *Le Monde,* October 17, 1980.

Prior to the meeting between Radjai and Waldheim, the latter had received a message from General Zia-ul-Haq, President of the Conference of Islamic Nations, which contained a proposal for a three-day cease-fire to take effect Saturday, in the evening of October 18th, for the feast of Al-Adha. Iraq accepted this proposal but Mr. Radjai turned it down during a press conference held in New York on October 18, 1980.

On October 17th, the Iranian Prime Minister gave an hour-and-a-half speech in front of the Security Council. He explained Iran's position at the same time as he attacked Arab nationalism: "The Super Powers want to create a new Israel in the Middle East, under the colors of Arab nationalism". He also criticized the use of Soviet arms by the Iraqis, recalling "the Soviet aggression against Afghanistan" before evoking "the Soviet arms arriving to Akaba on their way to Iraq". The remainder of the Iranian Prime Minister's intervention was limited to insults against Iraq and its leaders, before concluding somewhat paradoxically: "We are not here to ask for anything whatsoever from the Security Council." (1)

## THE IRAQI THESIS

During the October 15th session devoted to the Iraq-Iran conflict, Dr. Saddoun Hammadi was the first to speak before the Security Council. After having laid out the Iraqi point of view in detail and after presenting a

---

(1) Cf. U.N.O., S/PV 2251, p. 21.

Note : In a statement to the Lebanese weekly *Al-Hawadess* N° 1271 of March 13, 1981, published in London, the Iraqi Minister of Defense Adnan Khairallah declared that "Honestly speaking, we have not received a single bullet from the Soviet Union since the beginning of the war until now."

record of the relations between the two countries since the return of Khomeiny to Teheran, he concluded:

> Iraq does not stand for war, nor does it believe in the use of force in international relations. Iraq, as its record proves, and particularly so in its frontier relations with Iran, has always adhered strictly and honorably to the letter and spirit of its international commitments. But at the same time, Iraq does not accept any form of threat or aggression against its sovereignty and dignity, and we are ready to make all the sacrifices necessary for the preservation of our legitimate rights and vital interests.

> Concern has been expressed regarding the repercussions of the recent events on the world economic interests which might be adversely affected. Let me point out at once that Iraq is keen to protect within its ability the economic interests of other nations. So any attempt to widen the character and scope of our problem with Iran would endanger the situation. Such an attitude would invite further foreign intervention in our part of the world which we earnestly want to keep outside the sphere of influence and rivalry of the Big Powers, in the interest of international peace and security, and world economic prosperity.

> It is well known to the Council and the international community as a whole, that Iraq has responded favorably and positively to the various calls addressed to it and the efforts made to stop the fighting and move towards a peaceful settlement of the present conflict. We have cooperated with the Security Council from the outset and have participated in its deliberations. Our response to this Council's resolution no. 479 of September 28, 1980 was prompt and positive; our President informed the Secretary-General (document S/14203 of September 20, 1980) that... 'we naturally accept the above-mentioned resolution... and declare our readiness to abide by it if the Iranian side does likewise', and that 'we hope that the Security Council will take the necessary measures to urge the Iranian side to abide by that resolution'. (1)

> Iran, Mr. President, officially rejected the call of the Council. Moreover, in response to the goodwill mission

---

(1) Cf. United Nations, S/14203, p. 2.

undertaken by the President of Pakistan and the Secretary-General of the Islamic Conference we offered a unilateral cease-fire from October 5-8, which actually went into effect at dawn on October 5th. Iran's response was a large-scale attack on land, sea and in the air.

I should finally like to reaffirm before the Council that Iraq does not stand for the use of force in international relations. We firmly believe in the peaceful settlement of disputes. We fully realize that, as a developing country, we need to utilize all our energies and resources for social and economic development. But at the same time we cannot stand idle against any encroachment upon our legitimate sovereign rights in our total territories, security, peace and well-being. (1)

● *Where are Iran's boundaries?*

When the members of the Security Council evoked the possibility of an Iraqi retreat and especially the American declarations, Dr. Saadoun Hammadi addressed messages to the Foreign Affairs Ministers of its member states. These notes reflected Iraq's genuine desire to find a final solution to the conflict. Iraq was reaffirming that it had no designs on Iranian territories, but that it would not give up its legitimate rights over its own territory as well as absolute sovereignty over the Shatt-al-Arab.

According to Dr. Hammadi, to propose an eventual Iraqi retreat is not realistic for three reasons:

1 - The unique borderline agreement between Iraq and Iran is that of 1913. The 1975 agreement was implicitly abrogated by Iran, after which Iraq did the same. The agreement of 1937 had been unilaterally nullified by the Shah.

So what must be the extent of an eventual Iraqi retreat? On this point, the content of Dr. Hammadi's mes-

---

(1) Cf. Integral text of the speech in Appendix XVI (p. 271).

sages was explained by President Saddam Hussein during his November 10, 1980 press conference :

> Our rights are clear, our territory is clearly defined, as well as our sovereignty over the usurped Arab territories. The Iranian territory is equally well defined. What we demand is that Khomeiny tells us precisely which are the geographic boundaries of Iran, an initiative which up to now he has not wanted to take. Ask him this question and you'll see that he won't tell you where those boundaries are to be found. Then you will understand how much of an expansionist Khomeiny is.

> Ask the Iranian leaders where exactly their land and sea borders with Iraq and the Arab countries of the Gulf are located. You will see how they evade the question, for they want to expand to the detriment of the Arabs.

2 - After all this has happened, how can anyone imagine a retreat of the Iraqi armed forces ? How can one guarantee that Iran will not then undertake a war against Iraq and occupy its territories ? If we want to be realistic in speaking of a retreat, that is, an outcome representing a definitive solution to the conflict, the legitimate claims of Iraq must be considered, as well as giving guarantees that would avoid a new outbreak of fighting.

3 - Iraq seeks peace with Iran along with that between Iran and the other Arab countries. "We want final and precise boundaries and we intend to obtain respect of the principle of non-interference of a country in the internal affairs of any other", concluded Mr. Hammadi.

● *Project for a conclusive peace*

It was in this setting and in response to questions raised by journalists during the press conference referred to above that President Saddam Hussein explained his concept of a conclusive peace and the normalization of Iraqi-Iranian relations:

> We have spoken more than once of the criteria that we

think would guarantee good relations or normal relations between Iran and us, as Iraqis and as Arabs.

Indeed, I can briefly recall the essential elements:

— that they respect our rights and that we respect theirs;

— that illegitimate rights not be imposed on us by force;

— that we respect their security and that they respect ours;

— that we respect their sovereignty and that they respect ours;

— and that we respect the path that they have chosen and that they respect the one adopted by us.

As to whether we prefer bilateral or territorial guarantees under the auspices of the Islamic Conference or other international instances, well, the only guarantee is that we agree among ourselves and that there be mutual respect for our rights, besides the fact that Iran must respect Arab rights, and the Arabs those of Iran. If we learn that this is not possible, we will envisage other, broader guarantees.


## WHAT IS ARABISTAN'S FUTURE?


On the occasion of the 11th Arab Summit in Amman, President Saddam Hussein elucidated the Iraqi viewpoint concerning the future of Arabistan during a press conference held on November 27, 1980 in the presence of Emir Hassan, Crown Prince of Jordan :

It is up to the people of Arabistan, as with the other peoples of Iran, to decide upon their own fate. From then on, speaking of this question without accounting for the will of the peoples in the region would constitute an encroachment upon this will.

151

In a previously cited interview with President Saddam Hussein published in the Kuwaiti newspaper "Al Anba" (1), the following dialogue was reported to have taken place:

Q — Are you going to demand the creation of an autonomous government for the Arab citizens of the region of Arabistan as one of the conditions for a cease-fire?

> THE PRESIDENT — Regarding this problem, our position is in fact identical whatever country is involved. The Kurdish minority in Iraq has actually obtained an autonomous government, which is understandable. In Iran, five different ethnic groups coexist. If circumstances permit the Iranian minorities to govern themselves in one way or another, we agree. We are prepared to offer our support in such a case, which is in full concordance with our convictions and our policies. However, it is not right that we Iraqis make such proposals in place of the Iranian ethnic communities.

Q — Why don't you make this gesture anyway, for the people of Arabistan and you are both Arab ?

> THE PRESIDENT — Up till now we have not regarded the situation created by the state of war, but we have adopted a general position on this issue instead. It is natural that we offer our assistance to the Arab brothers living there, especially against an enemy state with which we are still in war. We uphold any people who is seeking to obtain its rights as well as to decide upon its own future.

Q — Why hasn't Iraq conquered Abadan when it is militarily capable of doing so ?

> THE PRESIDENT — In the conflict with Iran, our principle has been to avoid carrying on a war of conquest. If we have extended the fighting into Iranian territory, it is to protect our own cities from danger and to keep our people

(1) January 19, 1981.

safe from the Iranian bombs, raids and terrorism that they have already exposed us to. We also want to regain our rights usurped by Iran. If we know that a given military operation, for instance, the takeover of a city, would lead us closer to this objective, then we would go ahead with it. On the contrary, if we can practically attain the same objective without necessarily proceeding to an operation of conquest, then we shall not do it. I do not exclude the possibility of conquest nor of military occupation, but I contend that the general situation is defined by factors which are not wholly military in nature.

In a series of articles published in Paris in the "Al-Watan al Arabi" review under the title "The Iraqo-Iranian Conflict", Iraqi Deputy Premier, Tareq Aziz writes:

> With respect to Arabistan, it is not logical nor appropriate to raise the question while the Arab situation is not yet ready for it, and neither are the Arabs of Arabistan sufficiently prepared for it themselves, even though it is they who are primarily concerned by the problem. In any case, Iraq is the firmest advocate of their cause. (1)

Speaking on March 14, 1981 before a fresh batch of Iraqi Popular Army fighters on their way to the battle front, President Saddam Hussein declared what observers considered to be a step ahead regarding the question of Arabistan :

> *Our people in Arabistan should prepare themselves to exercise legitimate national rights over their territories and to play their role as a people having possessed its own characteristics throughout history and at present having all the prerequisites to establish themselves nationally. (2)*

---

(1) *Al-Watan al Arabi,* January 22, 1981.

(2) *Baghdad Observer,* March 15, 1981.

## WHERE ARE WE GOING?

The war is now entering into a new phase. The counter-offensive launched under the direction of Iranian President Abul Hassan Bani Sadr in early 1981 has ended up in the destruction of the Iranian tank forces. Observers have described this event as one of the biggest tank battles in modern warfare. In Iran, internal struggles were never more fierce, as shown by the scathing accusations exchanged by the President of the Republic and the Prime Minister, the latter blaming Bani Sadr for the total failure of the counteroffensive. The religious leaders themselves have become aware of the defeat that Iran has suffered. Iraq, in the meanwhile, has gradually been improving and consolidating its military positions, as it extended its territorial control along the front.

At the same time, United Nations delegate Olaf Palme was carrying out his second visit to Baghdad and Teheran. He returned to New York more optimistic than after his first visit in mid-November 1980. At the end of January 1981, the Islamic Summit was held in Taif (Saudi Arabia). But in spite of the numerous appeals made by the Muslim heads of state, Iran refused to take part in it.

At the Summit of Taif a cease-fire between Iraq and Iran was requested in addition to a nine-state committee being created under the name of the "Reconciliation Committee", designed to seek a solution to the conflict. In his speech (1) before the C.I.N., which groups 42 states, President Saddam Hussein affirmed that the chances of restoring peace were still alive, "if we trust in law and reason, without hate or fanaticism". (2)

---

(1) Summary of a speech given by President Saddam Hussein at the Islamic Conference in Taif on January 28, 1981 (cf. Appendix XVII, p. 289).

(2) *Al-Anwar,* January 29, 1981.

Further attempts were made to convince Iran to negotiate by the Foreign Affairs Ministers during the Conference of Nonaligned Countries, meeting in New Delhi from
February 9-13, 1981, but these too proved to be unsuccessful due to the unacceptable conditions set by
Teheran for the opening of such talks. This attitude
sharply contrasts with that of the Iraqi leaders who during
this same conference declared that they would listen to
any proposal for a peaceful settlement of the conflict.

On the last day of February 1981, the Islamic Goodwill
Mission arrived in Teheran headed by Ahmed Sekou
Touré, President of the Republic of Guinea, and having as
members President Zia-ul-Haq, of Pakistan, President
Zia-ur-Rahman of Bangladesh, President Dawoodo
Gawara of Gambia, the Turkish Prime Minister,
Mr. Yasser Arafat, Chairman of the Palestine Liberation
Organization, the Foreign Ministers of Malaysia and
Senegal, as well as Mr. Habib Chatti, Secretary General
of the Islamic Conference. The Mission was received at
the airport by Bani Sadr himself, and then by Khomeiny,
who received them at his home in Teheran and who
reprimanded the Taif conference for having listened to
President Saddam Hussein's 80-minute exposé of the
Iraqi point of view. In a 5-hour meeting with the Mission,
attended by members of the Iranian Defense Council,
President Bani Sadr reviewed "the conditions Iran considered necessary for peace". All observers agreed that
the declarations of the Iranian officials on the task of the
Mission were "mostly intended for internal consumption,
rather than to solve the conflict" (1).

The Islamic Goodwill Mission arrived in Baghdad in
the evening of March 4th, and was accorded an official
welcome headed by President Saddam Hussein. Talks

---

(1) *An-Nahar*, March 2, 1981.

between the Iraqi side and the Mission started less than an hour later. Heading the Iraqi party, President Hussein affirmed that "any solution which does not take the reasons behind the war into consideration, including Iraq's full sovereignty over Shatt-al-Arab and its lands, cannot be a just and logical one. Any withdrawal before Iran's recognition of these rights, as well as their providing practical and legal guarantees to Iraq, cannot be materialized. The President also stressed that Iraq fully adheres to what it has announced and to the Islamic Conference's resolutions, namely, stopping the fighting and conducting negotiations to reach an agreement ensuring the legitimate rights of both parties under the auspices of the Goodwill Mission". (1)

The Goodwill Mission paid a second visit to both capitals and made some proposals for a peaceful solution. Iran hastily turned them down before any Iraqi commentary could be made.

The Nonaligned countries also made a new initiative and named a special committee with the same aim. After meeting in Geneva, this committee left for Beirut, where they consulted with Yasser Arafat. After these consultations the committee did not pay visits to either Baghdad or Teheran, perhaps due to a belief that circumstances were not yet ripe for this mediation, or to their desire to give the Islamic Goodwill Mission a chance to follow up on its initiative.

* *
*

(1) *Baghdad Observer,* March 15, 1981.

Hence, the Iranian position is clear: Khomeiny rejects negotiation and conciliation of any kind at a moment when Iran is facing interior dissension and a ferocious power struggle between its various political factions, in addition to the growing clamor of its ethnic and national groups for autonomy. This situation has obliged Khomeiny to name a permanent committee to conciliate these different groups, including a representative of both the President of the Republic and the Prime Minister. The question that arises is the following: how can a leader who is unable to reconcile his own contradictions be expected to find reconciliation with others? On the other hand, the Iraqi position firmly adheres to the defense of its sovereignty and national rights, and the more bloodshed there will be, the more extensive its demands.

While evoking Iran's disintegration during the precited speech to Iraqi Popular Army soldiers on March 14th, President Saddam Hussein committed himself to helping the different peoples of that country: "Bani Sadr is surprised and so is his master Khomeiny, how Iraq is fighting with such determination for the seventh month running, while the population of Iran is three times that of Iraq. The longer the fighting goes on the greater our determination, and the more rights merited". The President added that Iraq is ready to offer all moral and material assistance to the Iranian peoples of Kurdistan, Baluchistan, Azerbaidjan, as well as to all honorable citizens to live in honor and peace, so as to establish neighborly relations with Iraq. He then said that "Iranian rulers are disintegrating while we in Iraq are intensifying our unity, they are standing on the brink of collapse while we are firm in our positions. The Iranian peoples are living in despair, poverty and humiliation, while our people are living in prosperity and stability... We never wished to see Iran dismembered. We wanted Iran to be a neighborly country, capable of resolving all its problems and maintaining its integrity, but from now on, we shall not anticipate this wish because a country harboring enmity to the Arab nation and to Iraq ought to deteriorate and disintegrate. This is our strategy, which we have disclosed since a long time''. (1)

In the future, will the various attempts to put an end to the war triumph, or shall we be spectators to a fresh outburst of fighting ? In the latter case, will it be an all-out war or will it be on a more limited scale, taking the form of a war of attrition ? Finally, will the internal troubles known to exist in Iran be resolved so as to permit a responsible leadership to take over and to head Iran toward dialogue and toward a just and lasting peace ?

---

(1) *Baghdad Observer,* March 15, 1981.

# CONCLUSION

As this study comes to an end, it would appear that the Arab-Persian conflict finds its roots in history, even from the pre-Islamic period. Whatever form it has tended to take, the nature of the antagonism between Arabs and Persians has a perennial aspect. Bearing in mind the historical context, the following remarks can be made:

1) The region of Shatt-al-Arab, including Arabistan and the other lands in question, is Arab due to its geographical and historical background, its economy, its nationality and its culture. The Arab character of this area has been legally recognized by international treaties concluded throughout its history.

2) The dominion of the Arabs over these territories is intimately linked to their history and to their extremely close relations with Iraq. Western travelers have testified to the fact: "This region is as different from Iran as Germany is from Spain." (1) It is for that reason that "even if Iraq and this region have known different destinies imposed by the course of history at certain times and over very brief periods, their peoples share the same national identity; one part of this area was always incorporated in Iraq and was in permanent contact with its inhabitants. It underwent all the external influences that Iraq was subjected to." (2)

---

(1) Wilson, *Op. Cit.*, p. 93.
(2) Longrigg, H.S., *Four Centuries of Modern Iraq*, Oxford, 1925, p. 5.

159

3) An economic unity undeniably exists between the two banks of the Shatt-al-Arab, which belong to the same agricultural and climatic family: "It was discovered that both banks were rich in 'black gold' at a period when the Iranian substratum was believed to be diminishing. This pushed the Europeans into occupying Arabistan in addition to Iraq, considering this region to be extremely advantageous for commercial and industrial exploitation". (1)

4) A cultural whole is represented in the fields of language, customs, traditions, sciences, art and literature. Hence, the population of this region is different from the Persians on the cultural plane. Ethnically, it is composed of "immigrant Arabs, part of the Arabs of Iraq and the Arabian Peninsula, all descendants or natives of these countries. They speak the same language as the Arabs and possess the same customs. Their love of freedom is as vivid as that of their brothers in the desert... They were convinced of the impossibility for the Persians to settle on the coast, thus exposing themselves to the invasions of the Arabs, who spent their lives on the seas". (2)

5) Throughout their history, the Persians have demonstrated racist tendencies: "They have since long ago tried in vain to destroy the Arab entity and its power in Arabistan, due to their extreme hatred for the Arabs and their historical tendency to aggress all people who are not Persian". (3)

These quotations are evidence that this region has always been a political and cultural battleground between the Arabs and the Persians.

---

(1) Bereby, J.J., *Op. cit.*, p. 111.
(2) Berryne J., *Op. cit.*, pp. 166-170.
(3) Wilson, *Ibid.*, p. 136.

Despite its origins in the historical conflict opposing these two countries, the Iraq-Iran war has its own particular dynamics. In this respect, the following elements can be discerned:

1) The war broke out following an Iranian attack against Iraq and due to the declared intentions of Khomeiny to provoke internal problems and civil war in Iraq. In retaliating, Iraq thus purely and simply practiced its right to self-defense.

2) We must constantly keep in mind one basic truth, that is, the masses were mobilized in Iran so as to put an end to the Shah's power. This goal was reached and represents a tremendous success for the Iranian people. However, this war against Iraq and Teheran's campaign of hatred against the Iraqi leaders can hardly stir the enthusiasm of the Iranians. The latter are chiefly interested in the reconstruction of the country and by the solutions that must be sought for the many problems poisoning their daily lives. The anti-Iraq hostility would seem to emanate from Khomeiny's state of mind; it is for this reason that it cannot be eternal.

3) The Iranians counted on a split in the internal forces of Iraq, but they lost their bet: this country has confronted the war behind a solid interior front and a unified political leadership.

4) This war is different from all classic warfare between two neighboring countries because its consequences concern the entire Arab world. Even if the conflict is resolved in the near future, it will continue to show an aftermath in different fields in more than one Arab country for years to come.

5) The war has thrust the Middle East into a new phase of its history. It is not easy for the observer to outline all of

its consequences. Without any doubt, this war marks a decisive turning point in the history of the region. Just as the times prior to the war displayed specific features, the post-war period will witness the revision of numerous values. This new factor will produce its effects in both inter-Arab relations and the relations between the Arabs and the rest of the world.

The case of Iran is similar: the ordeal it is undergoing as well as the crisis it is living through will bring about a reaction from the population such that the country will extricate itself from the difficulties it knows today. The interest of the Iranian people, after having suffered through long years of oppression and injustice, is hardly to pursue with arms and an identical frame of mind the external politics of the Shah, characterized by aggression, expansionism and domination over the Arab neighbors.

This war will help the Iranian people to discover the sharp reality and true meaning of events. These new truths issued from the war will be forcibly imposed upon Iran, especially among the alive and active forces of that society, hoping to create a solid basis for the revolutionary changes and desiring the edification of a modern, democratic society in which all Iranians would live in an atmosphere of liberty, fraternity and justice, without internal discrimination and without unjustified external conflicts, notably with its Arab neighbors.

*Until when?*

However true it may be to speak of a historical antagonism between Arabs and Persians, this absolutely does not mean that it must persist in the present and in the future. If we have dwelled upon this aspect, it is in order to explain to those who are foreign to the Middle East the course of events leading up to the war.

The experiences of a great number of peoples prove that peaceful and just solutions based upon mutual understanding constitute the best way to put an end to conflict. On the contrary, experience also proves that partial solutions do not lead to peace, but quite often become the detonator or catalyzer of future confrontations. Such precedents as Alsace-Lorraine, well known to all, need not be recalled here in order to demonstrate the correctness of our conclusions, reached after thorough research. The Iraq-Iran war is in itself an exemplary case.

# APPENDIX

# APPENDIX
# I

## NATIONAL DECLARATION
## OF PRESIDENT SADDAM HUSSEIN
## (FEBRUARY 8, 1980)

In view of the present international situation and its possible future developments, and in light of the serious possibilities threatening the Arab sovereignty and national security, on the one hand, and world peace and security, on the other, and in response to the calls of national responsibility towards the Arab nation's land, culture and heritage, and in accordance with the principles of the Nonaligned Movement,

Iraq finds it proper to take an initiative by issuing the following declaration which it intends to be taken, first, as a charter regulating the national relations among Arab countries, and secondly, as a pledge from the Arab nation to the states neighboring the Arab homeland, which declares its respect and commitment to it.

The following are the tenets of the Declaration :

1. The rejection of the presence of foreign armies and military forces or any foreign forces and military bases or any facilities in any form, or under any pretext or cover or for any reason whatsoever in the Arab homeland. Any Arab regime that fails to abide by this tenet should be isolated and boycotted politically and economically. Its policies should be resisted by all means available.

2. Prohibiting the use of armed forces by any Arab country against any other Arab country. All disputes that may arise among Arab countries should be settled by peaceful means and in accordance with the principles of joint national action and the supreme Arab interests.

3. The tenet mentioned in Article 2 applies to the relations of the Arab nation and its countries with the neighboring nations and states — no armed forces should be used to resolve disputes with these states except in defending sovereignty or in self-defense and in cases where the security and fundamental interests of the Arab countries are threatened.

4. Solidarity of all Arab countries in the face of any foreign aggression or violation committed by any foreign power against the territorial integrity and sovereignty of any Arab country, and in the event of any foreign power declaring war on any Arab country, all Arab countries should jointly resist that aggression or violation and use all means available including military action to thwart it, while a total political and economic embargo should be imposed upon the aggressor. The embargo can be extended to cover all other fields, should that be necessary and in the interst of the nation.

5. Affirming the commitments of Arab countries to the international laws and conventions regarding the use of water, air and land by any country that is not at war with any Arab country.

6. Keeping away from the arenas of international conflicts and wars, and adopting a neutral and nonaligned stand towards any party of the conflict or war except when the Arab territorial integrity and sovereignty and the rights of Arab countries which international laws and conventions guarantee are violated by any side in the

168

conflict; prohibiting the participation of Arab military forces — whether in full or in part — in wars and military disputes inside and outside the area on behalf of any foreign country or foreign party.

7. Commitment of Arab countries to establish advanced and constructive inter-Arab relations so as to prepare a solid ground for an advanced joint Arab economic structure and Arab unity. Arab countries should be keen not to commit any act that may harm these relations or preclude their continuity and development, regardless of the differences in the Arab regimes and the inconsequential political disputes which may arise among them, so long as they remain committed to the tenets of this Declaration.

Arab countries abide by the complementary national economic principle while Arab countries of competent economies pledge to offer all kinds of economic aid to the Arab countries so as to prevent them from depending on foreign powers — a dependence that may affect their autonomy and national will.

8. While laying down the tenets of this Declaration, Iraq affirms its readiness to abide by it in respect of every Arab country and every party that is committed to it. Iraq is also ready to discuss it with the Arab brothers and to listen to their comments about it so as to enhance the effectiveness of its tenets and improve upon its contents.

Iraq also affirms that this Declaration is by no means intended to be a substitute for the existing Arab League Charter and the Joint Arab Defense and Economic Co-operation Treaty. Rather, Iraq deems it a reinforcement of the Charter and Treaty and an attempt to develop them in such a manner as to help them match the newly created conditions and dangers threatening the Arab nation, and a fulfillment of the national responsibilities to face the present and future circumstances.

Great people of Iraq!

Masses of the glorious Arab nation!

In making this Declaration, Iraq is prompted by its sense of national responsibility, which surpasses any subjective or regional interest. While offering this Declaration to the Arab governments which will be responsible for ratifying and abiding by it, we strongly uphold the view that the tenets of this National Declaration can be implemented so as to make it a Charter of Arab relations only through the struggle of the Arab masses and with their support and backing, as it guarantees their national aspirations of freedom and independence and paves the way for Arab unity.

SADDAM HUSSEIN

Chairman of
The Revolution Command Council
President of the Republic of Iraq

Baghdad, February 8, 1980

# APPENDIX
## II

## MESSAGE FROM THE IRAQI GOVERNMENT TO THE GOVERNMENT OF Mr. MEHDI BAZARGAN, HEAD OF THE PROVISIONAL GOVERNMENT OF IRAN
### (FEBRUARY 13, 1979)

The Iraqi Government presents its compliments to Mr. Mehdi Bazargan, President of the Provisional Government in Iran, and would like to define its stand on events in neighboring Iran as follows:

1. The firm policy of the Republic of Iraq of patronage of the July Seventeenth Revolution under the leadership of the Arab Ba'ath Socialist Party, is to establish strong brotherly relations and relations of fruitful cooperation with peoples and countries neighboring Iraq, on the basis of respect of sovereignty, non-intervention in the internal affairs of others and respect of the peoples' legitimate aspirations in accordance with the principles they choose by their own free will. The Iraqi Government has always been keen on precisely and faithfully applying this policy whenever the governments of the neighboring countries adhered to it themselves.

2. Iraq, in addition to the aforementioned general principles, has a special outlook on the relations with the

171

two neighboring peoples of Iran and Turkey. These two peoples are not merely neighboring, but they are brotherly ones, linked with the Arab people in general and the Iraqi people in particular, by deep-rooted Islamic ties and common historical relations over the centuries. We believe that the nature of these religious and historical relations should be a strengthening factor of the positive relations in recent times between Iran and Iraq and other Arab countries.

3. The peoples of Iraq, who struggled for tens of years against colonial domination, a decomposing royal regime and against all forms of tyranny and exploitation, and whose struggle was crowned by the July Seventeenth 1968 Revolution led by the Arab Ba'ath Socialist Party, ensuring freedom, justice, and progress to them, views with sympathy and support the struggle waged by the neighboring and friendly people of Iran for freedom, justice and progress; it also feels proud of this victory scored by the Iranian people and happy for them.

4. The Iraqi Government views with much satisfaction the statements of Ayatollah Al-Khomeiny, the famous religious leader, and the leading personalities in the Iranian Popular Movement about the relations with Arabs, and the attitude toward the Zionist usurper. It considers these statements as expressing the conscience of the free Iranian people, who should stand at the side of the brotherly Arab people in its just struggle against oppressive Zionism, and the imperialism which supports it. This is a basic feature of a free people, and it is one of the basic factors of the Islamic link between the Arab and Iranian peoples which we hope will be supported by its practical application in the present and the future. We also view with much satisfaction your statements and stands assuring the existence of an independent side in the tendencies of the Iranian Popular Movement, since this is

the firm, principal and practical stand of the Arab Ba'ath Socialist Party and Iraqi Government. For its protection we paid much, especially at those times when most parties in the region were following policies of subordination to foreign and colonial powers. Iran's joining us in this way is considered, in our view, to be an important positive change in the region which will help to support its independence and development.

5. We wish the welfare of the neighboring and friendly Iranian people and look forward to establishing stable relations with the new Iran, relations of fruitful cooperation to reinforce the common ties and to serve the mutual interests of the two countries, as well as to consolidate freedom, peace and stability in this region.

# APPENDIX
# III

## MESSAGE FROM DR. SAADOUN HAMMADI, FOREIGN MINISTER OF THE REPUBLIC OF IRAQ, TO DR. FIDEL CASTRO, CHAIRMAN OF THE SIXTH NONALIGNED SUMMIT (APRIL 2, 1980)

Excellency,

You are doubtless aware of the role played by the delegation of the Republic of Iraq in supporting the admission of Iran as a member of the Nonalignment Movement during the Sixth Summit Conference of the Movement convened in Havana (September 1979) after the recent change that took place in Iran. Iraq's support emanated from its belief that Iran, following the changes taking place in it, would liquidate the vestiges of the expansionist and racist policies pursued by the Shahinshah regime, contribute to the strengthening of the Nonalignment Movement, enhance its unity and active role in international relations, and promote the spirit of cooperation among the member states of the Movement, in consensus with the principles, objectives and resolutions of that Movement. The actions and practices of the Iranian Government, and the statements made by Iranian officials at the highest level, however, proved otherwise. Iran is still acting in the same manner as it did ·

175

under the previous regime. It is still pursuing the same expansionist and racist policies, the seizure of lands by force and the issuing of threats. It perpetuates its illegitimate occupation of the three Arab islands in the Arab Gulf (Greater Tumb, Lesser Tumb and Abu Musa), interferes in the internal affairs of other states, and threatens the use of force against member states of the Movement. This runs counter to the principles and objectives of the Nonalignment Movement.

It may be appropriate to refer in this connection to the statement made by Abul Hassan Bani Sadr, the President of the Republic of Iran, in the periodical called "an-Nahar al-Arabi wa al-Dawli" published in its number 151 dated March 24, 1980, to the effect that Iran would not forego its claims on the three Arab islands and that the Arab countries of Abu Dhabi, Qatar, Oman, Dubai, Kuwait and Saudi Arabia are not independent states as far as Iran is concerned.

Mr. President,

I feel confident that you will agree with me that the above statement constitutes a direct threat against and a flagrant interference in the internal affairs of a group of member states of the Movement. This undoubtedly creates an atmosphere of tension among the member states of the Movement, leads to a disturbance of the security and peace in the area, stirs up conflicts among the member states of the Movement, and consequently satisfies the objectives of the enemies of the Movement who aim to weaken its unity.

This indicates that Iran has begun to lose the conditions of membership of the Nonalignment Movement, in view of its failure to abide by its principles which call for non-interference in the internal affairs of others, refrainment from the threat of the use of force, and respect for the sovereignty and independence of other states.

The Government of the Republic of Iraq would like its non-recognition of the illegitimate occupation by Iran of the three Arab islands (Greater Tumb, Lesser Tumb and Abu Musa) and all the results that may ensue from such an occupation to be put on the record, and demands the immediate withdrawal of Iran from these islands.

I shall be grateful, Excellency, if you will kindly circulate this letter to the member states of the Nonalignment Movement as an official document of the Movement.

Please accept, Excellency, the assurances of my highest consideration, along with my heartfelt greetings.

Dr. Saadoun Hammadi,
Minister of Foreign Affairs
of the Republic of Iraq.

His Excellency, Dr. Fidel Castro Ruz,
President of the Sixth Conference of the
Nonaligned Heads of State and Governments, Havana.

APPENDIX
IV

MESSAGE FROM DR. SAADOUN HAMMADI,
IRAQI MINISTER OF FOREIGN AFFAIRS,
TO DR. KURT WALDHEIM,
SECRETARY GENERAL OF THE U.N.
(APRIL 2, 1980)

H.E. Dr. Kurt Waldheim
Secretary General of The United Nations.

I would like to refer to the statements of Abul Hassan Bani Sadr, the President of the Republic of Iran, to the Arab and International "An-Nahar" Journal published in its issue No. 151 dated March 24, 1980, which states that Iran will neither evacuate nor restore the three Arab islands and that the Arab countries (Abu Dhabi, Qatar, Oman, Dubai, Kuwait, Saudi Arabia) are not independent as far as Iran is concerned.

The above-mentioned statements confirm the policy of Iran which aims at the perpetuation of the illegitimate occupation of the three Arab islands (The Greater Tumb, the Lesser Tumb and Abu Musa). The statements also constitute a direct threat and a flagrant interference in the internal affairs of a group of member states of the United Nations Organization as well as ignoring the independence of these countries. This creates an atmosphere of tension and leads to provoking conflicts and disturbing world peace and security in the area. It runs counter to the objectives of the United Nations Charter which are aimed at preserving world peace and security.

The Government of the Republic of Iraq would like to stress its non-recognition of the illegitimate occupation by Iran of the three Arab islands (The Greater Tumb, the Lesser Tumb and Abu Musa) and all the consequences related to this illegitimate occupation. It also requests that Iran withdraw from the three islands immediately and desist from pursuing an aggressive and expansionist policy, issuing threats and interfering in the internal affairs of the Arab Gulf countries. It further requests that Iran respect the independence and sovereignty of those countries in conformity with the Charter and aims of the United Nations and in the interest of maintaining peace and security in the area.

I shall be grateful if you will kindly circulate this letter to the member states of the Security Council and the General Assembly as an official document.

With best compliments.

Dr. Saadoun Hammadi
Minister of Foreign Affairs
of the Republic of Iraq.

Baghdad, April 2, 1980

# APPENDIX
## V

## TREATY OF ERZEROUM
### (MAY 31, 1847)

### ARTICLE ONE

The two Mussulman Powers waive the totality of their existing pecuniary claims on one another, provided that nothing in this arrangement shall affect the provisions made for the settlement of claims to which Article 4 relates.

### ART. 2

The Persian Government undertakes to cede to the Ottoman Government all the lowlands — that is to say, the land in the western part of the province of Zohab; and the Ottoman Government undertakes to cede to the Persian Government the eastern — that is to say, all the mountainous — part of the said province, including the Kirind Valley.

The Persian Government abandons all claim to the city and province of Suleimania, and formally undertakes not to interfere with or infringe upon the sovereign rights of the Ottoman Government over the said province.

The Ottoman Government formally recognizes the unrestricted sovereignty of the Persian Government over the city and port of Mohammarah, the island of Khirz, the anchorage, and the land on the eastern bank — that is to say, the left bank — of the Shatt-al-Arab, which are in the possession of tribes recognized as belonging to Persia. Further, Persian vessels shall have the right to navigate freely without let or hindrance on the Shatt-al-Arab from the mouth of the same to the point of contact of the frontiers of the two Parties.

## ART. 3

The two Contracting Parties, having by the present Treaty waived their other territorial claims, undertake forthwith to appoint commissioners and engineers as their respective representatives for the purpose of determining the frontiers between the two States in conformity with the preceding article.

## ART. 4

Both Parties are agreed as to the appointment forthwith, by both Parties, of commissioners for the purpose of adjudicating and making a fair settlement in all cases of damage suffered by either Party since the acceptance of the friendly proposals drawn up and communicated by the two Mediating Great Powers in the month of Jemaziyyu-'l-evvel, 1261, together with all questions of pasturage dues since the year in which the arrears in the payments of the latter began.

## ART. 5

The Ottoman Government undertakes that the fugitive Persian Princes shall reside at Brussa, and shall not be permitted to leave that place or maintain secret relations with Persia. The two High Contracting Powers further undertake that all the other refugees shall be handed over in conformity with the earlier Treaty of Erzeroum.

## ART. 6

Persian merchants shall pay the Customs dues on their goods, in kind or in cash, according to the current present value of such goods, in the manner specified in the article relating to trade in the Treaty of Erzeroum concluded in 1238 (1). No additional charge whatsoever shall be levied over and above the amounts fixed in the said Treaty.

## ART. 7

The Ottoman Government undertakes to accord the requisite privileges to enable Persian pilgrims, in accordance with former treaties, to visit the Holy Places in the Ottoman dominions in complete safety and without vexatious treatment of any kind. Further, the Ottoman Government, being desirous of strengthening and consolidating the bonds of friendship and concord which should subsist between the two Mussulman Powers and between their respective subjects, undertakes to adopt such measures as may be most appropriate to ensure the participation, not only of Persian pilgrims, but of all other Persian subjects, in all the said privileges in the Ottoman dominions, in such manner as to protect them from any sort of injustice, molestation, or incivility, whether in respect of their commercial activities or in any other respect.

Furthermore, the Ottoman Government undertakes to recognize Consuls to be appointed by the Persian Government in places in the Ottoman dominions where their presence may be required on account of commercial interests, or for the protection of Persian merchants and other Persian subjects, save only in Mecca the Revered and Medina the Resplendent, and to respect in the case of the said Consuls all the privileges due in virtue of their official character and accorded to Consuls of other friendly Powers.

(1) A.H. 1238 — A.D. 1823.

The Persian Government, for its part, undertakes to accord reciprocity of treatment in every respect to Consuls to be appointed by the Ottoman Government in places in Persia in which the latter may consider the appointment of Consuls to be necessary, as also to Ottoman merchants and other Ottoman subjects visiting Persia.

## ART. 8

The two High Contracting Mussulman Powers undertake to adopt and enforce the measures necessary to prevent and punish thefts and brigandage on the part of the tribes and peoples settled on the frontier, to which end they will quarter troops in suitable localities. They further undertake to do their duty in respect of all forms of aggressive acts, such as pillage, robbery, or murder, which may occur in their respective territories.

Contested tribes the suzerainty over which is not known shall be left free by the two High Contracting Powers to choose once and for all and to specify the localities which they will henceforward always inhabit. Tribes the suzerainty over which is known shall be compelled to come within the territory of the State to which they belong.

## ART. 9

All points of articles of previous treaties, and especially of the Treaty concluded at Erzeroum in 1238 (1), which are not specifically amended or annulled by the present Treaty, are hereby reaffirmed in respect of any and all of their provisions, as if they were reproduced in their entirety in the present Treaty.

---

(1) A.H. 1238 — A.D. 1823

The two High Contracting Powers agree that, when the texts of this Treaty have been exchanged, they will accept and sign the same, and that the ratifications thereof shall be exchanged within the space of two months, or earlier.

*EXPLANATORY NOTE RELATIVE TO CERTAIN STIPULATIONS IN THE PROPOSED TREATY OF ERZEROUM, ADDRESSED BY THE BRITISH AND RUSSIAN AMBASSADORS AT CONSTANTINOPLE TO THE OTTOMAN GOVERNMENT ON APRIL 26, 1847, AND THE PORTE'S REPLY*

The undersigned, representing the Mediating Courts of Great Britain and Russia, have had the honor to receive the identic note, with annex, which His Excellency Ali Effendi, Minister of Foreign Affairs, was pleased to address to them on the 11th instant, relating to the Turco-Persian negotiations.

The undersigned are highly gratified to note from the communication in question His Excellency's statement, on behalf of the Sublime Porte, of the decision to issue instructions forthwith to the Ottoman Plenipotentiary at Erzeroum to sign the articles of the Treaty with the Court of Persia unamended, according to the text drawn up by the Commissioners of the two Mediating Courts, as submitted for the acceptance of the Governments concerned by their plenipotentiaries at Erzeroum, subject to explanations by the representatives of the said Courts at Constantinople to the Sublime Porte on certain points which the latter does not consider sufficiently clear.

The points on which the Sublime Porte requires explanations are as follows:

1. The Sublime Porte presumes that the clause of Article 2 of the draft Treaty ceding the city, port, and anchorage of Mohammarah, and the island of Khizr, to Persia, cannot include either the territory of the Sublime Porte comprised (1) outside the city or the other ports of the Sublime Porte situate in these parts.

The Sublime Porte is also concerned to know whether, under the terms of another part of the same article relating to tribes which, while actually belonging to Persia, may happen to be divided, one half being settled in Ottoman territory and the other half in Persian territory, it follows that those parts of the tribes which are in Turkey will also become subject to Persia, and the territory in their possession will accordingly also be ceded to Persia; and whether Persia will be entitled at some future date to dispute with the Porte the right to the possession of such territory.

2. The Sublime Porte is concerned to know whether, under the existing terms of Articles 1 and 4, the Persian Government is entitled to include the pecuniary compensations as between the two Governments which it had entirely renounced, in the category of individual claims. The Porte understands these claims to apply solely to certain pasturage dues and to losses incurred by the respective subjects of the two Governments as a result of the activities of brigands and the like.

The Sublime Porte further asks whether the Persian Government's assent will be obtained on the question of fortifications added to Article 2, as also in respect of the

---

(1) The word "situate" is used instead of "comprised" in the extract communicated to the Persian Envoy in January 1848.

passages regarding reciprocity which were omitted in Article 7 of the Commissioners' draft.

The undersigned Representatives, being anxious and bound to dispel the uncertainties of the Sublime Porte on all the above questions, hereby declare as follows:

*Ad. 1.* The anchorage of Mohammarah is the part situate opposite the city of Mohammarah in the Haffar Canal, and this definition is not susceptible of any other interpretation.

The undersigned Representatives are further in agreement with the Ottoman Minister in the view that, in ceding to Persia in the region in question the city, port, anchorage of Mohammarah and the island of Khizr, the Sublime Porte is not ceding any other territory or any other ports there may be in this region.

The undersigned Representatives further declare that Persia will not be entitled on any pretext whatsoever to put forward claims in regard to the regions situate on the right bank of the Shatt-al-Arab, or to the territory on the left bank belonging to Turkey, even where Persian tribes or parts of such tribes are established on the said bank or in the said territory.

*Ad. 2.* As regards the Sublime Porte's apprehension that Articles 1 and 4 of the draft Treaty may be irregularly interpreted in such a way as to give rise to the revival by the Persian Government of the pecuniary claims as between the two Governments, the undersigned Representatives hereby declare that, inasmuch as it is explicitly stipulated in Articles 1 and 4 of the draft Treaty that all claims of this kind from whatever source are, and are to continue to be, waived, there can be no resumption of the discussions on the matter in any case, and that only the claims of individuals will be entitled to satisfaction by the two Parties respectively; and, further, that the examination and validity of such individual claims will be subject, as agreed, to a special commission to be appointed ad hoc and that the decision as to what claims are to be regarded as individual claims will also have to be referred to this commission.

In reply to the two subsidiary questions raised at the conclusion of His Excellency 'Ali Effendi's note, the undersigned Representatives believe that they are justified in stating that the Persian Government will readily agree to the insertion in Article 7 of the clauses with regard to reciprocity of treatment to be observed by both Governments in the mutual interest of their respective subjects, pilgrims and Consular Agents. As regards the question of fortifications, they can only express their personal opinion that a reciprocal undertaking on the part of the two Mussulman Governments not to fortify the banks of the Shatt-al-Arab would constitute one more guarantee of the maintenance of peaceful relations between the two countries, well calculated to powerfully cement the bonds of goodwill which is the object of the Treaty in question.

The undersigned Representatives are accordingly entirely prepared to support the fulfillment of the wishes of the Sublime Porte on this point through the intermediary of their colleagues in Teheran; and they have reason to hope that their representations in this connection will not be without effect.

At the same time, the undersigned Representatives are of the opinion that the signature of the Treaty might without inconvenience take place without waiting for the issue of the negotiations on the special point in question, as to which there would be no difficulty in subsequently appending an additional clause to the Treaty.

The undersigned, etc.

OUSTINOF,
H. WELLESLEY.

Pera, April 14 (26), 1847.


## REPLY OF THE OTTOMAN GOVERNMENT TO THE BRITISH AND RUSSIAN AMBASSADORS AT CONSTANTINOPLE


I am in receipt of Your Excellencies' collective official note of April 14th (26th) last in reply to my official note to Your Excellencies asking for certain explanations on the subject of the Persian Treaty.

Your Excellencies' note states in regard to the territories and tribes to which Article 2 of the draft Treaty relates that, although the Sublime Porte agrees in this article to the retention by Persia of the city and port of Mohammarah, the anchorage opposite the city in the Haffar Canal and the island of Khizr, the Sublime Porte does not thereby cede any other port or territory in this region; and, further, that the Persian Government will not be entitled to put forward any claim to proprietary rights either in respect to the regions situate on the right bank of the Shatt-al-Arab or in respect to the regions belonging to the Sublime Porte on the left bank, even where a Persian tribe or part of such tribe is established in such regions;

189

further, that the claims as between the two Governments which are waived in their totality by both Governments under Article 1 will not be included in the category of individual claims to which Article 4 relates; and, further, that you have good grounds for hoping that the Court of Persia will readily agree to the insertion of the clause embodying the principle of reciprocity which was omitted in Article 7.

The Sublime Porte is satisfied with the above official explanations and assurances; and His Majesty the Sultan, having complete confidence in the two Mediating Courts and their Representatives, has ordered in the exercise of His Sovereign Will that instructions should be issued to His Excellency Enver Effendi, Plenipotentiary of the Sublime Porte at Erzeroum, to sign the draft Treaty submitted by the Commissioners of the two Mediating Courts without amendment, on the understanding that the Court of Persia will accept the assurances which have been given by the Representatives of the two Mediating Courts to the effect that it will raise no claim going counter to those assurances, and on the further understanding that, in the event of any such claim being raised, the Treaty will be deemed to be null and void.

It is for the purpose of bringing all the above considerations to Your Excellencies' notice that this official note has been drawn up and is communicated to you.

(L.S.) Es-Said Mehmed Emin 'Ali.

Jemaziyyu-'l-evvel 29, 1263.

*REPLY OF THE PERSIAN ENVOY ACCEPTING THE EXPLANATIONS GIVEN BY THE MEDIATING REPRESENTATIVES AT CONSTANTINOPLE TO THE OTTOMAN GOVERNMENT ON APRIL 26, 1847.*

I hereby declare to Your Excellency that, in virtue of the mission with which I am entrusted by my Government for the exchange of ratifications of the Treaty of Erzeroum, I concur entirely with the explanations given to the Porte by the Representatives of the Mediating Powers with reference to the three first points of Your Excellency's communication. I further declare with reference to the fourth point of the same communication that I have no objection to the insertion in Article 7 of the passages in regard to reciprocity of treatment to be observed by the two Governments in relation to their respective subjects, pilgrims and Consular Agents, and further that, in the matter of fortifications, His Majesty the Shah agrees that so long as Turkey refrains from the construction of fortifications on the right bank of the Shatt-al-Arab opposite Persian territory, Persia will for her part refrain from such constructions on the left bank, possession of which is assured to her under the provisions of the Treaty.

In faith whereof I have signed these present and sealed them with my seal.

(Signed) MOHAMMED 'ALI.

Pera, Sefer 23, 1264, corresponding to January 19 (31), 1848.

To His Excellency Lord Cowley,
His Britannic Majesty's Envoy Extraordinary and
Minister Plenipotentiary, etc.

191

# APPENDIX
# VI

## PROTOCOL RELATING TO THE DELIMITATION OF THE TURCO-PERSIAN BOUNDARY, SIGNED AT CONSTANTINOPLE ON NOVEMBER 4 (17), 1913

The undersigned: His Excellency Sir Louis Mallet, Ambassador Extraordinary and Plenipotentiary of His Britannic Majesty to His Majesty the Sultan; His Excellency Mirza Mahmud Khan Kajar 'Ahd-i-Shamus Saltaneh, Ambassador Extraordinary and Plenipotentiary of His Majesty the Shah of Persia to His Majesty the Sultan; His Excellency M. Michel de Giers, Ambassador Extraordinary and Plenipotentiary of His Majesty the Emperor of Russia to His Majesty the Sultan; His Highness Prince Said Halim Pasha, Grand Vizier and Minister of Foreign Affairs of the Ottoman Empire; have met for the purpose of recording in the present Protocol the Agreement concluded between their respective Governments with regard to the Turco-Persian boundary.

They began by recapitulating the progress, up to date, of the negotiations recently instituted among them.

The Joint Commission provided for in Article 1 of the Protocol signed at Teheran between the Imperial Ottoman Embassy and the Persian Minister of Foreign Affairs in view of determining the bases for negotiations relating to the delimitation of the Turco-Persian boundary held eighteen meetings, the first on March 12 (25) and the last on August 9 (22), 1912.

On August 9 (22), 1912, the Imperial Russian Embassy at Constantinople addressed to the Sublime Porte a note, under No. 264, stating that "the Imperial Government considers that too much emphasis cannot be laid on the necessity of putting into effect without delay the explicit stipulations of the Treaty of Erzeroum, which are tantamount to the restoration of the status quo of 1848".

The Imperial Embassy at the same time forwarded to the Imperial Ottoman Government a memorandum showing the frontier-line in detail in conformity with the stipulations of the treaties in force.

The Imperial Ottoman Government replied to this communication by a note dated March 18 (31), 1913, No. 30469/47. It stated that "the Sublime Porte, being anxious to comply with the desire expressed by the Imperial Russian Government by eliminating any cause of difference in its cordial relations with the latter, and wishing, further, to demonstrate to the Persian Government its entire good faith in regard to the dispute existing on the subject between the two countries, has decided to accept the line mentioned in the aforesaid note and memorandum of the Ambassador of His Majesty the Emperor of Russia for the delimitation of the northern part of the Turco-Persian frontier from Serdar Bulak to Bane — that is to say, down to the 36th parallel of latitude."

Nevertheless, the Imperial Ottoman Government suggested a number of modifications in the line proposed in the memorandum annexed to the note of the Imperial Russian Embassy dated August 9 (22), 1912, No. 264.

The Imperial Ottoman Government also appended to

its note "an explanatory note on the situation of the Zohab boundary and the arrangement that it would be able to accept in order to reach a final and equitable understanding with the Persian Government on that part of the frontier."

The Imperial Russian Embassy replied by a note dated March 28 (April 10), 1913, No. 78. It noted the statement "by which the Imperial Ottoman Government recognizes as a principle for the delimitation of the Ararat-Bane section the exact sense of Article 3 of the Treaty of 1848, known as the Treaty of Erzeroum, as set forth in the note of August 9 (22), 1912, No. 264". As regards the modifications proposed by the Sublime Porte, the Imperial Embassy stated (with a reservation on the question of Egri-chai) that it could not sufficiently emphasize the necessity of making no change in the line established in its note of August 9 (22), 1912.

As regards the question of Zohab, the Imperial Russian Embassy, while reserving the right to submit its detailed observations concerning that frontier, expressed "its opinion on the whole of the Ottoman draft, which does not seem to it to guarantee sufficiently, for the future, the maintenance of order and peace on the frontiers."

On April 20 (May 3), 1913, the Russian and British Embassies addressed an identic note to His Highness Prince Said Halim Pasha, accompanied by a memorandum summarizing their point of view regarding the delimitation of Zohab and the regions situate south of that district.

This exchange of notes was followed by conversations between Their Excellencies M. de Giers and Sir Gerard Lowther, of the one part, and His Late Highness Mahmud Shefket Pasha, of the other part. The result of these conversations was recorded in an aide-mémoire presented by His Excellency the Russian Ambassador to His Highness the Grand Vizier on June 6, 1913, and in the note from the Sublime Porte addressed on June 26 (July 9), 1913, No. 34553/95, to the Russian Embassy, and on July 12, 1913, to the British Embassy.

On July 29, 1913, a "declaration" was signed in London by Sir Edward Grey and His Highness Ibrahim Hakky Pasha concerning the demarcation of the southern boundary between Persia and Turkey.

The Imperial Russian Embassy then proceeded to recapitulate the principles of delimitation established in the correspondence concerning the Turco-Persian boundary. It addressed to the Sublime Porte a note dated August 5 (18), 1913, No. 166. An identic note was addressed to the Sublime Porte by the British Embassy on the same date.

The Sublime Porte replied to these communications by identic notes dated September 23, 1913, No. 37063/113.

As a result of subsequent negotiations, the four plenipotentiaries of Great Britain, Persia, Russia, and Turkey, agreed on the following provisions:

## I

It is agreed that the boundary between Persia and Turkey shall be defined as follows:

The boundary in the north shall start from boundary-mark No. XXXVII on the Turco-Russian frontier, situate close to Serdar Bulak, on the crest between Little and Great Ararat. It shall then drop southwards by way of the ridges, leaving on the Persian side the valley of Dambat, Sarnvtch, and the water system of Yarym-Kaya, which rises to the south of Mount Ayubeg. The boundary shall then leave Bulak-bashi, in Persia, and shall continue to follow the highest ridge, the southern extremity of which is situate at about 44°22' longitude and 39°28' latitude. Then skirting the west side of the marsh which extends to the west of Yarym-Kaya, the boundary shall cross the Sary-Su stream, pass between the villages of Girde-baran (Turkish) and Bazyrgan (Persian), and, ascending to the ridge to the west of Bazyrgan, follow the watershed formed by the Saranli, Zenduli, Gir-Kelime, Kanly-baba, Geduki-Khasined, and Deveji ridges.

After Deveji, the line shall cross the valley of Egri-chai at the place to be designated by the Delimitation Commission in conformity with the status quo, leaving the villages of Nado and Nifto in Persia.

The ownership of the village of Kyzyl-Kaya (Bellasor) shall be established after an examination of the geographical situation of the village, the western side of the watershed in that region being allocated to Turkey, and the eastern side to Persia.

Should the final boundary line leave outside Ottoman territory a section of the road which passes close to Kyzyl-Kaya and connects the district of Bayazid with the province of Van, it is understood that the Persian Government shall give free passage over this section of the road to the Imperial Ottoman Posts and to travellers and goods, other than military troops and convoys.

The frontier shall then ascend to ridges forming the watershed: Kyzyl-Ziaret, Sarychimene, Dumanlu, Karaburga, the hill between the reservoirs of Ayry-chai (Persian) and of Jelli-gol (Turkish), Avdal-dashi, Reshkan, the hill between Akhurek and Tavra Bevra-begzadan, Gevri-Mahine, Khydyr-baba, Avristan.

As regards Kotur, the Protocol of July 15 (28), 1880, known as the Protocol of Sary-Kamiche, shall be applied in such a way that the village of Kevlik shall remain in Turkey, and the villages of Bilejik, Razi, Gharatil (Haratil), the two Jelliks, and Panamerik, shall remain in Persia.

The frontier following the Mir-Omar ridge shall ascend the mountain of Surava, and, leaving Khanyga on the Turkish side, shall pass by way of the watershed formed by the pass of Borush-Khuran, the mountain of Haravil, Beleko, Shinetal, Sardul, Gulambi, Kepper, Bergabend, Peri-Khan, Iskander, Avene, and Kotul. The valley of Bajirga shall remain in Turkey, and the villages of Sartyk and Sero in Persia, and the frontier shall pass from the southern extremity of Kotur over the ridge rising to the west of the Persian village of Behik, and, following the peaks of Seri-Baydost, shall join the crest of Mount Zont.

From Mount Zont the frontier shall continuously follow the watershed between the Persian districts of Ter-gever, Desht and Mergever, and the Turkish sanjak of Hakkiari — that is to say, the crests of Shiveh-Shishali, Chil-Chovri, Chel-Berdir, Kuna-Koter, Kazi-beg, Avukh, Mai-Helaneh, the mountains to the west of Binar and Delamper; then, leaving on the Persian side the basin emptying by way of Ushnu into the lake of Urumiya, including the sources of the Gadyr river known as Abi-servi-gadyr (the valley of which is situate to the south of Delamper and to the east of Mount Girdeh), it shall reach the pass of Keleh-Shin.

To the south of Keleh-Shin the frontier shall leave on the Persian side the reservoir of Lavene, including the valley of Chumi-Geli (situate to the east of Zerdegel and to the southwest of Spi-rez), and on the Turkish side the waters of Revanduz, and shall pass by the following peaks

198

and passes: Siah-Kuh, Zerdeh-Gel, Boz, Barzin, Ser-shiva, Kervi-Khoja-Ibrahim. Thence the frontier shall continue to follow towards the south the main chain of Kandil, leaving on the Persian side the basins of the affluents of Kialu on the right side: the Purdanan Khydy-rava and Talkhatan streams.

It is understood that the Turkish tribes which are in the habit of spending the summer in the said valleys at the Gadyr and Lavene springs shall still have the use of their pastures under the same conditions as in the past.

Having reached the summit of Seri-Kele-Kelin, the line shall pass over Zinvi-Jasusan and the pass of Bamin, and shall cross the Vezne river near the Purde-Berdan bridge. The Delimitation Commission will have to decide as to the future of the village of Shenieh, on the basis of the general principle of the status quo.

After Purde-Berdan, the frontier shall ascend over the chains of Foka-baba-kyr, Berne-spian, Berne-Adul-Fath and the pass of Kaniresh. It shall then follow the water-shed formed by Lagav-Ghird, Donleri, the pass of Khan-Ahmed, and the southern extremity of Tepe-Salos. The frontier will thus pass between the villages of Kandol (Turkish) and Kesh-keshiva and Mazynava (Persian), and reach the course of the Kialu River (the Little Zab).

After joining the source of the Kialu River, the frontier shall follow it upstream, leaving on the Persian side the right bank (the Alani-ajem) and on the Turkish side the left bank of that river. On reaching the mouth of the Khileh-resh River (an affluent of the Kialu on the left side), the frontier shall follow the course of that river upstream, leaving on the Persian side the villages of Alot, Kivero, etc., and on the Turkish side the district of Alani-Mavont. At the southwestern extremity of Mount Balu, the frontier shall leave the course of the Khileh-resh

River, and, ascending over the northwest extremity of the Surkew chain, extending to the south of the Khileh-resh River, shall pass over the Surkew ridge, leaving the districts of Siwel and Shive-Kel on the Turkish side.

On reaching the astronomical point of Surkew almost at latitude 35°49', the frontier shall pass in the direction of the village of Champar-aw, the future of which shall be decided by the Delimitation Commission on the basis of the accepted principle of the status quo. The line shall then ascend over the chain of mountains which form the frontier between the Persian district of Baneh and the Turkish district of Kyzyieja; Galash, Berdi-Kechel, Pusht-Hangajal, Du-bera, Parajal, and Spi-Kana, after which it shall reach the pass of Now-Khuvan. Thence, still following the watershed, the frontier shall turn southwards and then westwards, passing by way of the summits of Vul-Guza, Pushti-Shehidan, Hazar-Mal, Bali-Keder, Keler-Melaik, and Kuhi-Koce-resha, separating the Turkish district of Teretul from the Persian district of Merivan.

From there, the frontier shall follow the course of the Khalil-Abad brook downstream as far as its confluence with the Chami-Kyzylja, and then this last-named river upstream as far as the mouth of its left affluent flowing from the village of Bnava-Suta; it shall follow this Bnava-Suta brook upstream and, by way of the passes of Keli-Naveh-Sar and Keli-Piran, shall reach the pass of Surene, known, it appears, by the name of Chigan (or Chawkan).

The main chain of Avroman, extending in the direction northwest-southeast, shall then form the frontier between Persia and the Ottoman district of Shehrisor. On reaching the peak of Kemadjar (southeast of Kala-Selm and northwest of Sheri-Avroman), the frontier shall continue to follow the main ridge as far as its ramification on the western side, rising to the north of the valley of Dere-Vuli, leaving the villages of Khan-Germela and Nowsud on the Persian side. For the remainder of the frontier as far as Sirvan, the Commission shall — by way of exception — delimit the ground, taking into consideration such changes as may have occurred there between the year 1848 and the year 1905.

South of Sirvan, the frontier shall begin close to the mouth of the Chami-Zimkan, shall pass by way of Beyzel (Bezel) Mountain, and shall descend to the Chemi-Zerishk watercourse. Next, following the watershed between this last-named watercourse and the river which, rising in the Bend-Bemo, bears, according to the identic map, the name of Pushti-Gherav (Arkhevendu), it shall ascend to the summit of Bend-Bemo.

After following the ridge of Bamu (Bemo), the frontier, on reaching the defile of Derbendi-Dehul (Derbendi-Hur), shall follow the course of the Zengeneh (Abbasan) River as far as the point nearest to the summit of Shevaldir (astronomical point) and situate below the village of Mamyshan. It shall ascend this summit and shall next pass by way of the crest of the hills forming a watershed between the plains of Tileku and Serkaleh, then by way of the chains of Khuli-Baghan, Jebel-Ali-Beg, Bender-Chok-Chermik, Sengler, and Asengueran, as far as the point in the Tengi-Hamman defile situate opposite the northern extremity of the Karawiz Mountains.

Thence the frontier shall follow the course of the River Kuretu as far as the village of that name. The future of the village of Kuretu shall be decided by the Delimitation Commission on the basis of the nationality of its inhabitants. Thence the frontier shall pass by way of the road between the villages of Kuretu and Kush-Kurrek, then along the crests of Mounts Kishka and Ak-Dag, and then, leaving Kala-Sebzi in Persia, it shall turn southwards as far as the Ottoman post of Kanibez. Thence it shall follow the course of the Elvend river upstream as far as the point a quarter of an hour's distance downstream from its confluence with the Gilan watercourse; from that point it shall continue as far as the Naft-Su, skirting the Ab-Bakhshan in accordance with the line agreed upon with the late Mahmud Shefket Pasha and shown roughly on the map annexed to the note of the Imperial Russian Embassy dated August 5 (18), 1913, and leaving Naft-Mukataasy to Turkey. Thence, the frontier-line, following the Naft-Deressi, on reaching the point where the Qasr-e-Shirin road cuts that waterway, shall continue along the mountains of Varbulend, Konerigh-Keleshuvan, and Jebel-Gerebi (the extension of the Jebeli-Hamrina-chin).

The Delimitation Commission shall draw up a special agreement for the distribution of the Gengir (Sumar) waters between the parties concerned.

The part of the frontier between Mandali and the northern point of the line indicated in the declaration made in London on July 29th (Shuaib) between Hakky Pasha and Sir E. Grey not having yet been discussed in detail, the undersigned leave the establishment of that part of the frontier to the Delimitation Commission.

As regards delimitation from the region of Hawizah as far as the sea, the frontier-line shall start from the place called Umm-Shir, where the Khor-el-Duvel divides from the Khor-el-Muhaisin with the Khor-el-Azem, nine miles northwest of Bsaytin, a place situate at latitude 31°43'29''. From Umm-Shir, the line shall turn southwestwards as far as longitude 45° (1), at the southern extremity of a small lake known also by the name of Azem and situate in

---

(1) This should read 47°45'.

the Khor-el-Azem some distance northwest of Shuaib. From this point the line shall continue to the south along the marsh as far as latitude 31°, which it shall follow directly eastwards as far as a point northeast of Kushk-i-Basra, so as to leave this place in Ottoman territory. From this point the line shall go southwards as far as the Kaiian canal at a point between the Nahr-Diaiji and the Nahr-Abu'l-Arabid; it shall follow the medium filum aquae of the Khaiyin Canal as far as the point where the latter joins the Shatt-al-Arab, at the mouth of the Nahr-Nazaileh. From this point the frontier shall follow the course of the Shatt-al-Arab as far as the sea, leaving under Ottoman sovereignty the river and all the islands therein, subject to the following conditions and exceptions:

(a) The following shall belong to Persia: 1. the island of Muhalla and the two islands situate between the latter and the left bank of the Shatt-al-Arab (Persian bank of Abadan); 2. the four islands between Shetait and Maawiyeh and the two islands opposite Mankuhi which are both dependencies of the island of Abadan; 3. any small islands now existing or that may be formed which are connected at low water with the island of Abadan or with Persian terra firma below Nahr-Nazaileh.

(b) The modern port and anchorage of Mohammarah, above and below the junction of the river Karun with the Shatt-al-Arab, shall remain within Persian jurisdiction in conformity with the Treaty of Erzeroum; the Ottoman right of usage of this part of the river shall not, however, be affected thereby, nor shall Persian jurisdiction extend to the parts of the river outside the anchorage.

(c) No change shall be made in the existing rights, usages and customs as regards fishing on the Persian bank of the Shatt-al-Arab, the word "bank" including also the lands connected with the coast at low water.

203

*(d)* Ottoman jurisdiction shall not extend over the parts of the Persian coast that may be temporarily covered by water at high tide or by other accidental causes. Persian jurisdiction, on its side, shall not be exercised over lands that may be temporarily or accidentally uncovered when the water is below the normal low-water level.

*(e)* The Sheikh of Mohammarah shall continue to enjoy in conformity with the Ottoman laws his rights of ownership in Ottoman territory.

The parts of the frontier not detailed in the abovementioned frontier-line shall be established on the basis of the principle of the status quo, in conformity with the stipulations of Article 3 of the Treaty of Erzeroum.

## II

The frontier-line shall be delimited on the spot by a Delimitation Commission, consisting of commissioners of the four Governments.

Each Government shall be represented on this Commission by a commissioner and a deputy commissioner. The latter shall take the commissioner's place on the Commission in case of need.

## III

The Delimitation Commission, in the performance of the tasks devolving upon it, shall comply:

1. With the provisions of the present Protocol;

2. With the Rules of Procedure of the Delimitation Commission annexed (Annex (a)) to the present Protocol.

## IV

In the event of a divergence of opinion in the Commission as to the boundary of any part of the frontier, the Ottoman and Persian commissioners shall submit a written statement of their respective points of view within forty-eight hours to the Russian and British Commissioners, who shall hold a private meeting and shall give a decision on the questions in dispute and communicate their decision to their Ottoman and Persian colleagues. This decision shall be inserted in the minutes of the plenary meeting and shall be recognized as binding for all four Governments.

## V

As soon as part of the frontier has been delimited, such part shall be regarded as finally fixed and shall not be liable to subsequent examination or revision.

## VI

As the work of delimitation proceeds, the Ottoman and Persian Governments shall have the right to establish posts on the frontier.

## VII

It is understood that the concession granted by the Convention of May 28, 1901 (9 Sefer, 1319, of the Hegira), by the Government of His Imperial Majesty the Shah of Persia to William Knox D'Arcy and now being worked, in conformity with the provisions of Article 9 of the said Convention, by the Anglo-Persian Oil Company (Limited), having its registered office at Winchester House, London (the said Convention being referred to hereunder as "the Convention" in Annex (B) of the present Protocol), shall remain in full and unrestricted force throughout the territories transferred by Persia to Turkey in virtue of the provisions of the present Protocol and of Annex (B) thereto.

## VIII

The Ottoman and Persian Governments will distribute among the officials on the frontier a sufficient number of copies of the delimitation map drawn up by the Commission, together with copies of translations of the statement provided for in Article XV of the Commission's Rules of Procedure. It is understood, however, that the French text alone shall be regarded as authentic.

LOUIS MALLET
EHTECHAMOS-SALTANEH MAHMUD
MICHEL DE FIERS
SAID HALIM

# APPENDIX
# VII

## MEMORANDUM ADDRESSED BY THE CHIEFS OF THE TRIBES OF ARABISTAN TO THE COUNCIL OF THE LEAGUE OF ARAB STATES (FEBRUARY 7, 1946)

We have the honor as chiefs of the tribes of the Emirate of Arabistan, to address this memorandum to your respectable assembly, in the hope of receiving from our Arab brothers represented in the Council of the League the support and assistance that every Arab people should expect.

During the one hundred and twenty-five years of our modern history, Arabistan had enjoyed an autonomous regime. The Persians exercised a merely nominal power in our region, that was assured by a delegate sent by Teheran and who resided outside of the region. This situation was maintained until the takeover by the dictator Reza Shah Pahlavi in Teheran. The latter destroyed the Arab entity of Arabistan. He emprisoned our Emir, the regretted Sheikh Khazaal, Emir of al-Mohammarah, who has been dragged off to Teheran where he was strangled in prison in 1936. The government erected in our region is a regime of military dictatorship imposed by Teheran.

We, Arab inhabitants, making up the overwhelming majority of the population, were forbidden the use of the Arabic language, language of our ancestors. The military government has done nothing to improve the educational system. The region of Arabistan does not even benefit from the same favors and attentions as the rest of Iran, because in their hearts the Persian leaders consider Arabistan like a foreign country, despite their assertions. Contrary to the facts of history and geography, they pretend that Arabistan is an integral part of Iran. Arabistan is prosperous, but it does not benefit from the fruit of its riches, which are diverted to the advantage of other regions in Iran. We do not have the same rights as the Persian population. We are not allowed to elect representatives to the Iranian Parliament. The Iranian civil servants present in our region look down on us and behave as petty tyrants. The Arabs are treated like slaves. These state employees are completely ignorant of democratic principles, the rights of peoples and minorities as defined by the Treaty of Versailles, the Pact of the League of Nations and the declarations made during the last World War by the presidents of recognized democracies.

In raising our voices in protest to the League of Arab States, to which we are connected by language, race, customs and history, we ask the independent Arab countries who are members of the League to wield their influence within the international organizations in order to support our struggle for our legitimate national rights.

It is not just that we Arabs, whose numbers attain 1.5 million persons, are deprived of rights that have been recognized to other minorities in Iran. We solicit the support of 60 million Arabs represented in the Arab League so that we can be freed from oppression. The

Arab League, in giving its aid and support to Arab countries, ought not forget our region which has suffered for twenty years. Even so, during these past twenty years the population of Arabistan has been forgotten by the Arab peoples and governments.

The danger hanging over the Arab entity of Arabistan is even more serious than that represented by the Zionist colonialism in Palestine. The aim of Zionism is to throw the Arabs out of their homes, but it cannot succeed in eliminating the Arab character of Palestine, even if only one Arab family were to remain in Palestine. The Persians belong to the same religion as the Arabs, which is not the case in Palestine. Therefore, differing from the Zionists who do not dispose of this arm, the confessional community is used by the Persians with efficiency, so that the Arab national identity of both the individual and the region of Arabistan is threatened.

His Excellency Sheikh Abdallah, son of our beloved Sheikh Khazaal, Emir d'al-Mohammarah, in whom we have placed our confidence, our support and our encouragement, and who speaks in our name, has recently undertaken a mission of peace to the Iranian government in order to obtain recognition of the legitimate rights of his people and his region. The Iranian government has ignored this gesture and has launched a military offensive against Emir Abdallah, obliging him to leave our region. Throughout this ordeal Emir Abdallah has received no moral or political aid from the Arab leaders.

In the name of Arab nationalism and solidarity, we ask the Arab League to help its brothers who share the same history, the same civilization and the same culture. We hope that our Arab brothers delegated to the League will take our present situation into consideration and that God will guide you for the good of our Nation.

May peace be with you as well as the mercy of God.

February 7, 1946.
Signatures.

## FRONTIER TREATY BETWEEN THE KINGDOM OF IRAQ AND THE EMPIRE OF IRAN WITH THE ANNEXED PROTOCOL SIGNED ON JULY 4, 1937 IN TEHERAN

His Majesty the King of Iraq, of the one part, His Imperial Majesty the Shahinshah of Iran of the other part,

Sincerely desirous of consolidating the bonds of brotherly friendship and good understanding between the two States, and in order to definitely settle the frontier question between their two countries, have decided to conclude the present Treaty and for this purpose have appointed as their Plenipotentiaries:

His Majesty the King of Iraq: His Excellency Dr. Naji Al-Asil, Minister of Foreign Affairs.

His Imperial Majesty the Shahinshah of Iran: His Excellency Enayatollah Samiy, Minister of Foreign Affairs, who, having exchanged their full powers, found in good and due form, have agreed on the following:

### ARTICLE 1

The High Contracting Parties agree that the following documents, with the exception of the modification specified in Article 2 of the present Treaty, are considered valid and that They are bound to observe them:

a) The Protocol relating to the Turko-Persian Delimitation signed at Constantinople on November 4, 1913;

b) The Proceedings of the Commission of Delimitation of the frontier of 1914.

Having regard to the provisions of this Article and with the exception of the provisions made in the following Article, the boundary between the two States is that defined and traced by the above-mentioned Commission.

## ARTICLE 2

The boundary on reaching the furthest point of Shoteit Island (approximately latitude 30° 17' 25" North, longitude 48° 19' 28" East) rejoins, in a line drawn perpendicular to the low-water mark, the Thalweg of Shatt-al-Arab and follows it as far as a point situated opposite the existing jetty N° 1 of Abadan (approximately latitude 30° 20' 8.4" North, longitude 48° 16' 13" East). From this point the boundary rejoins the line of low-water and follows the tracing of the frontier as described in the Proceedings of 1914.

## ARTICLE 3

Immediately after the signature of the present Treaty the High Contracting Parties shall appoint a commission for the purpose of erecting the frontier pillars the location of which has been fixed by the Commission mentioned in paragraph (b) of Article 1 of the present Treaty and of fixing additional pillars, which it considers useful to erect.

The composition of the Commission and the program of its work shall be fixed by a special arrangement between the two High Contracting Parties.

## ARTICLE 4

The following provisions shall apply to the Shatt-al-Arab from the point where the land frontier of the two States descends into the said river as far as the open sea:

a) The Shatt-al-Arab shall remain open to merchant ships of all countries equally. All dues levied shall be in the nature of payment for services rendered and intended solely to cover in an equitable manner the expenses of maintaining the navigability, and improving the navigable channel and the approach of the Shatt-al-Arab from the seaward side, or to meet expenditures incurred in the interest of navigation. The said dues shall be calculated on the basis of the official tonnage of ships or their draught, or both together.

b) The Shatt-al-Arab shall remain open to the passage of warships and other vessels belonging to the two High Contracting Parties used for non-commercial purposes.

c) The fact that in the Shatt-al-Arab the boundary sometimes follows the low-water mark and sometimes the Thalweg or the medium filum aquae does not prejudice in any way the right of user of the two High Contracting Parties in the whole course of the river.

## ARTICLE 5

The two High Contracting Parties, having a common interest in the navigation of the Shatt-al-Arab as defined in Article 4 of the present Treaty, undertake to conclude a convention concerning the maintenance and improvement of the navigable channel, dredging, pilotage, dues to be levied, sanitary measures, measures to be taken for the prevention of smuggling and all other matters relating to the navigation in the Shatt-al-Arab as defined in Article 4 of the present Treaty.

## ARTICLE 6

The present treaty shall be ratified and the instruments of ratification shall be exchanged at Baghdad as soon as possible. It shall come into force as from the day when this exchange takes place.

In witness whereof the Plenipotentiaries of the two High Contracting Parties have signed the present Treaty.

Done at Teheran, in Arabic, Persian and French, of which in case of difference the French text shall prevail, the fourth day of July, one thousand nine hundred and thirty-seven.

Signed *Naji Al-Asil*
Signed *Samiy.*

## *PROTOCOL*

At the time of proceeding to the signature of the Treaty concerning the delimitation of the boundaries between Iraq and Iran, the two High Contracting Parties have agreed as follows:

1 - The geographical coordinates shown approximately in Article 2 of the above-mentioned Treaty shall be definitely fixed by a Commission of experts composed of an equal number of members nominated by each of the High Contracting Parties.

The definite geographical coordinates so determined within the limits fixed in the above-mentioned Article shall be recorded in a procès-verbal which, after having been signed by the members of the above-mentioned Commission, shall be an integral part of the Boundary Treaty.

2 - The High Contracting Parties undertake to

conclude the convention mentioned in Article 5 of the Treaty in the course of one year from the entry into force of the Treaty.

If, not withstanding the efforts exerted by Them, this convention is not concluded in the course of the year, this period may be extended by common agreement of the High Contracting Parties.

The Imperial Government of Iran agrees that during the period of one year mentioned in the first paragraph of this article and during the extension of this period, if this extension takes place, the Royal Government of Iraq shall undertake on the bases now in force all matters which are to be dealt with by this Convention. The Royal Government of Iraq shall, by means of biannual communications, keep the Imperial Government of Iran informed of the works carried out, the dues levied, the expenses incurred and of all other measures taken.

3 - The authorization given by one of the High Contracting Parties to a warship or other public vessel used for non-commercial purposes belonging to a third State to enter ports belonging to the said High Contracting Party and situated on the Shatt-al-Arab shall be regarded as having been given by the other High Contracting Party in order that such vessel may make use of its waters when passing through the Shatt-al-Arab.

Nevertheless, that High Contracting Party who has given such an authorization must inform the other Party thereof immediately.

4 - It is understood that subject to the rights of Iran in Shatt-al-Arab, nothing in this Treaty prejudices the rights of Iraq and its obligations undertaken towards the British Government regarding the Shatt-al-Arab in accordance with Article 4 of the Treaty dated June 30, 1930, and paragraph 7 of its Annexure, signed on the same date.

5 - The present Protocol shall be ratified at the same time as the Treaty concerning the delimitation of the frontiers of which it shall form, as an Annexure, an integral part. It shall come into force at the same time as this Treaty.

The present Protocol is made in Arabic, Persian and French. In case of difference the French text shall prevail.

Done at Teheran in duplicate, on the fourth day of July, one thousand nine hundred and thirty-seven.

Signed *Naji Al-Asil*
Signed *Samiy*.

# APPENDIX
## IX

## MEMORANDUM ADDRESSED BY THE IRAQI MINISTRY OF FOREIGN AFFAIRS TO THE EMBASSY OF THE IRANIAN ISLAMIC REPUBLIC IN BAGHDAD (SEPTEMBER 11, 1980)

The Ministry of Foreign Affairs presents its compliments to the Embassy of the Islamic Republic of Iran and has the honor to point out that:

1. While observing the Iranian behavior we have made several conclusions concerning this matter, in the forefront of which is that owing to the confusion inside Iran and the defects of the machinery of the state and its miscalculations, we say that the Iranian leadership may not be aware of the fact that Iran has really encroached upon Iraqi territories, thus violating international law and the conventions that were signed between the two countries, including the Algiers Agreement of 1975.

If the matter were true, then we advise the Iranian leadership to ask its responsible organs about the frontiers and agreements in order to be sure of what we have said and to behave accordingly, on the basis of knowledge and not illusion.

2. The Iranian leadership should realize the fact that raiding towns inhabited by civilians, as it did to the two

Qadhas of Khanaqin and Mandali, is not an easy matter nor is it a political or violent game which the Iranian officials may enjoy now and then inside Iran. It should also be aware of the fact that such an act is a serious matter in the Iraqi view, a matter which must be avoided if you do not want relations to deteriorate greatly or else you will be answerable for this to God, the Iranian peoples and world public opinion.

3 We have no covetous designs concerning Iranian territories, thus, if our military units partly encroached upon Iranian territories, their acts should not be understood as an expansion at the expense of Iranian territory, but mainly as an arrangement in these territories for the safety of our units and the defense of the Iraqi Zein-al-Qaws.

The Ministry avails itself of this opportunity to renew the assurances of its highest consideration.

To: The Embassy of the Islamic Republic of Iran, Baghdad.

# APPENDIX
## X

## MESSAGE FROM DR. SAADOUN HAMMADI
## TO MR. ADAM KOJO,
## SECRETARY GENERAL OF THE AFRICAN UNITY
## ORGANIZATION
## (MAY 16th, 1980)

Mr. Adam Kojo, Secretary General of the Organization of African Unity (OAU),

I would like to put before you and, through you, before the members of your esteemed Organization, the following information regarding the statements and behavior of the Iranian Government and officials which prove that Iran is still pursuing the same path and the same racist expansionist policy pursued and practiced by the deposed Shah's regime. The Iranian Government is still set on occupying the three Arab islands which the Shah occupied by force in violation of all international law and international custom. Furthermore, it interferes in the internal affairs of other countries in an attempt to export the so-called Iranian Revolution and threatens to resort to using force.

We would like to refer here to statements made by Abul Hassan Bani Sadr, the Iranian President, on 3-23-1980 to "An-Nahar Arab and International" newspaper, to the effect that Iran will never evacuate or return the

219

three Arab islands, and that the Arab countries, namely, Abu Dhabi, Qatar, Oman, Dubai, Kuwait and Saudi Arabia, are not independent countries according to Iran.

Furthermore, the Commander of the Iranian infantry forces stated after a meeting he held with Khomeiny and Bani Sadr on 4-7-1980 that Iraq is a Persian territory. Ghotbzadeh, the Iranian Foreign Minister, stated on 4-9-1980 that "Aden and Baghdad belong to us."

Al-Khomeiny has stated that Iran will demand the exercise of its sovereignty over Baghdad if Iraq insists upon demanding the Arab islands. Moreover, Khomeiny addressed an appeal to the Iraqi people and the Iraqi armed forces, urging them to revolt and topple the Government of Iraq. On 4-9-1980, Ghotbzadeh, the Iranian Minister of Foreign Affairs, announced that his government had decided to overthrow the Government of Iraq.

In addition, the Iranian authorities have committed many acts of aggression against the Iraqi Embassy in Teheran and the two Iraqi Consulates in Khorramshahr and Kermanshah, as well as against the Iraqi schools, institutions and communities in Teheran. The Government of Iran has made attempts on the lives of Iraqi officials, and has committed many terrorist actions, causing many casualties, dead and wounded, among whom innocent people including women and children.

These Iranian aggressive actions constitute a flagrant violation of international law and custom and the United Nations Charter, as well as the principles and objectives of the Nonalignment Movement in which Iraq was one of the first supporters of admitting Iran as a member.

The Government of the Republic of Iraq had hoped that the new regime of Iran would clear the remnants of the racist and expansionist policies which the Shah had pursued and would devote its efforts to solving the problems of the Iranian peoples. On many occasions, the Iraqi Republic has expressed to the Government of Iran at the highest levels, its good intentions and readiness to establish strong relations based on good neighborliness and non-interference in the internal affairs of others, but the Iranian Government has given evidence by its behavior that it is resolved to play the same role as the deposed Shah's regime, a matter which threatens the Arab sovereignty and interests and increases the tension and conflict in the area. It has given a pretext to imperialist countries, in particular, the United States, for military intervention in the area.

While the Government of the Republic of Iraq will endeavor to protect its sovereignty and territorial integrity and maintain its security and to protect the sovereignty and national interests of the Arab nation, it holds the Iranian Government responsible for the acts that would jeopardize world peace and security.

I would be grateful if you will kindly circulate the contents of this document to the members of your organization.

Please accept, Excellency, the assurances of my highest consideration.

Dr. Saadoun Hammadi
Minister of Foreign Affairs

221

# APPENDIX
## XI

## SPEECH DELIVERED
## BY PRESIDENT SADDAM HUSSEIN
## ON SEPTEMBER 17, 1980

Dear Brothers, Members of the National Assembly,

In accordance with the decision of the Revolution Command Council, we asked you for this extraordinary session to acquaint you with very crucial issues concerning the Homeland and the Nation, thus reflecting the belief of the Leadership of the Party and Revolution in your effective role in reinforcing the national will and defending the rights of the people and the sovereignty of the Homeland. This step also affirms the democratic practice that we are proud of, and expresses the solid relationship between the masses on one hand and the Revolution and the leading national institutions on the other.

Dear Brothers!

Our national and pan-Arab issues and questions are not separate from our national and pan-Arab history, both old and modern. Hence, we should study our history and derive essential lessons from it in order to get acquainted with the present basic facts.

Over the past ages, colonial powers used all available means to devitalize the Arab Nation and subjugate it to other hegemonies and to exploit its territories and sources.

The most serious act committed against the Arab Nation by the British and the French colonialists and by the American and all other imperialists in this age was the creation of the Zionist entity under well-known historical circumstances with the aim of maintaining the fragmentation of the Arab Nation, and debilitating it so that the task of exploiting and dominating it may be lightened.

After the creation of the Zionist entity in occupied Palestine, some certain interests, covetous intentions and policies of its own started to take shape, some of which met with those of imperialism on a wide scale, while the others maintain their own particularity.

Since its foundation, the Zionist entity has not been protected only by world imperialism. International Zionism, whose dangerous influence is widespread in many countries, serves this entity and renders to it all means of power to smooth the way for its aggressive and expansionist designs against the Arab Nation.

This entity is not a frontline outpost for imperialism only, but also for world racist Zionism with all its covetous designs and aggressive and expansionist interests in this vitally important region.

Throughout the last three decades of its existence, the Zionist entity had achieved its task in backing the fragmentation of the Arab homeland and devitalizing the Arab Nation's capabilities of advancement and progress. Whenever it had the opportunity, this entity committed aggressive and expansionist acts against Arab territories.

The enlightened vanguards of the Nation, which follow with great concern and high consciousness the designs of world Zionism, have now become well aware

224

that imperialist and Zionist forces are no longer satisfied with the division of the Arab Nation achieved earlier this century, but started the refragmentation of the Arab countries so that one or two united parts, each constituting a strategic depth to the other and adjacent to the Zionist, may not be able to pose a threat to that entity or check its expansionist and covetous designs against the Arab homeland.

Iraq is in the forefront of those countries which have become a target for this vicious imperialist-Zionist machination. It was placed as a target for various geographical, political, economic and historical reasons. It was also singled out because of the fighting nature of its people and their role in defending the dignity and sovereignty of the Arab nation throughout the ages, on one hand, and because of its capability of advancement and forward movement when appropriate requisites are made available, on the other.

Imperialists and Zionists strove to fragment Iraq by stirring up contradictions between patriotic particularities and the country's pan-Arab affiliation, that is, by instigating chauvinistic and isolationist trends during various periods in its modern history. They sought to create conflict between the Iraqis' affiliation to religions and communities, and their affiliation to the Homeland and the Nation.

Prior to the Revolution of July 17, 1968, Iraq had been made ready for division. World imperialist and Zionist forces had applied various malicious means to divide Iraq into small inconsiderable entities which if they had been set up (God forbid) they would have been incapable of safeguarding freedom, independence and honor, and would have prevented Iraq from carrying out effectively and earnestly its duty in defense of the Nation's sovereignty and dignity, in recovering its rights and in contributing to its humanitarian message. They would have obstructed Iraq's path of struggle against the Zionist entity with its extensions and with the imperialist powers backing it up and rendering it all means of substance.

Although we realize that the Iraqi people were born to struggle valiantly against all forms of conspiracy and imperialist-Zionist machinations before the July Revolution, historical facts give evidence that without this Revolution, with the successes it scored in enhancing national unity and carrying out the task of national construction in various fields, the dismemberment of Iraq would have been highly probable because of the conditions of weakness, disintegration and penetration by imperialist-Zionist forces and espionage networks that it suffered from before the Revolution.

Within the framework of this design, these forces endeavored, before the inception of the Revolution and after its inception in particular, to supply the reactionary puppet leadership in northern Iraq with huge quantities of modern weapons and big financial aid, giving these puppets the power to pose a serious threat at the time to Iraq's integrity, its future and its national and pan-Arab mission.

Actually, Iran carried out this direct role of helping the puppet leadership with the support and encouragement of American imperialism and world Zionism, which had mobilized all their military information, political and advanced intelligence resources for this plan.

With the help of its virtuous sons from all ethnic and religious communities, Iraq waged a valiant battle against this puppet gang and those who are behind them.

Inspired by the honor of Iraq, the duty of defending the integrity of the Homeland and the glory and message of the Arab nation, the Iraqi Army performed its task, valiantly offering the dearest sacrifices of courage and steadfastness.

Our people offered all sacrifices needed in the battle which lasted twelve months, that is, from March 1974 to March 1975. The casualties of the Iraqi Army in that battle exceeded 16 thousand martyrs and wounded soldiers, while the total figure of the casualties of the people in general was more than 60 thousand killed and wounded.

Despite the valiant performance of our Army in fighting the puppets and those who have been backed up by the American-Zionist and Iranian forces, and despite the high morale of our men, it was impossible to ignore the material and objective requirements of the battle. Those requirements are sometimes of supreme significance in determining a lot of political and military outcomes.

The main problems in our fighting against the turmoil of the collaborators was the continuity of the flow of arms, and ammunition in particular, in a way that matched the unlimited quantities of arms, ammunition and supplies put at the disposal of these collaborators on behalf of American imperialism and Zionism.

The situation reached a serious phase when the Iranian regime amassed all the best modern weapons against our valiant forces and put forces into action to fight our own directly. Iranian forces carried out maneuvers, movements and deployments along our eastern borders for the purpose of engaging our army on different fronts, thus strengthening the military situation of the collaborating gang. This attitude was aimed at defeating our army or reducing its capacity to face any suspected insurgency when our army would be short of ammunition and its provisions exhausted. Hence, the imperialist-Zionist conspiracy of dismembering, weakening and liquidating its pan-Arab role could be implemented.

The question reached a very crucial point when our supplies and essential ammunition began to run out and three heavy shells were all that remained for the Air Force.

We know quite well that arms sales today, at high levels in particular, are not subject to purely commercial considerations. They are often subject to merely political considerations and the strategy of the country itself.

The armament of our army mainly depends on the Soviet Union which supplied us with sophisticated arms over the last few years, but that was the fact then, during our struggle and fight against the collaborating gangs in the north of the homeland. We blame no one and make no justification in disclosing this historical fact. We rather want to replace it in the proper context. We hid the fact of the acute shortage of our ammunition then and kept this information in a very limited circle at the Leadership level. We did this so that the secret would not leak out to the enemy who would make use of it by escalating their conspiracies and aggression, and so that the morale of our forces, who were fighting valiantly and honorably with all other available types of arms, be kept high. But this fact had its significant reflection on our political decision-making in the conflict existing then between Iran and us.

This is one aspect of the question, the other is the conditions of the battle Iraq participated in during the 1973 October War against the Zionist enemy. The War broke out with the Zionist entity without Iraq being informed, and without giving it time enough for the preparation of its armed forces. Nevertheless, Iraq had to take part in the fight, and the decision was taken in keeping with Iraq's stand and its pan-Arab responsibilities, regardless of the motives and nature of those who planned it and of Iraq's relations with the regimes participating in the war.

228

Iraqi forces were, at the time, deployed along the eastern front in full readiness for any Iranian aggression on the national soil. In order to provide proper conditions for moving the Iraqi forces to the battle with the Zionist enemy, the Revolution Command Council issued a statement on October 7,1973 in which it reaffirmed Iraq's readiness to settle the problems with Iran peacefully. So, Iraq sent its striking forces to Syria where they had the honor of taking an effective role in protecting Damascus from falling and checking the Zionist advance over the Syrian soil.

From the realistic point of view, issuing that statement implies Iraq's readiness to consider the claims of Iran in Shatt-al-Arab. When the late President Boumediene approached Iraq and Iran in 1975, suggesting that direct negotiation be held in Algiers between the two sides on questions of dispute, we accepted the initiative, considering it as an opportunity to safeguard Iraq's security, national integrity and its army's safety.

On this basis, the Leadership of the Party and State decided to accept negotiations with Iran and to accept the Thalweg Line as a border line in the Shatt-al-Arab area, in return for Iran's evacuation of Iraqi territories previously usurped, in violation of the Constantinople Protocol of 1913 and the supplementary proceedings of the 1914 meetings of Border Commissioners for the demarcation of borders between the two countries. These territories include the Zein al-Qaws and Saif Saad areas, liberated a few days ago by our armed forces. Iran was also to refrain from extending military and other types of aid to the collaborating gang in the northern part of the country. On these bases, negotiations with Iran were held and so the accord of March 6, 1975 was signed.

The agreement was, at the time, an event of significance. Immediately following its announcement, the collaborators collapsed and surrendered. The army gained 152 thousand pieces of arms, although the Iranians took back large quantities of arms during the two-week period given them to withdraw, but they were obliged to leave behind great quantities of weapons and ammunition which were taken by our forces.

The Algiers accord was, at the time, a daring, wise, patriotic and national decision. Courage is expressed not only by the capable use of gun and sword on the frontline of battle with the enemy, whether in defense or attack. Courage could also be expressed by the courageous political decision, at the Leadership level, to defend the people and the nation and safeguard its sovereignty. This is true, especially when these aims cannot be attained only by the edge of the sword and by gun.

In light of these circumstances, the decision saved Iraq from serious dangers which were threatening its integrity, security and prospects in the future. It offered our people an opportunity to carry on its Revolution, and with the process of construction and progress, to attain higher levels of power, progress and prosperity, matters which keep up Iraq's honor and sovereignty and which place the powerful and strong Iraq at the disposal of the Arab nation and its glorious mission.

Such a decision, however, was not a surrender to bitter realities, despite the fact that realities were bitter and serious. Instead, it was a sort of mastering of realities in a capable act of leadership that was balanced between all calculations of conditions and resources.

The March Accord was an outcome of the prevailing circumstances. Our people understood that accord well and considered it, under those circumstances, as a great victory. Hence, they received it with great joy.

Although our army was valiantly fighting the traitors

and dealing them telling blows, and unaware of the shortage in vital ammunition, it received the Accord with great joy, because it grasped its implications with regard to the country's integrity and future, and appreciated the objective conditions of the Accord.

Following the signing of the Accord, negotiation and contacts were held in view of enforcing its clauses, especially those concerning demarcation, fixing border pillars and other technicalities. Three basic protocols were signed on the basis of the Accord, namely, the protocol of delineation of river borders, the protocol of redemarcation of land borders and the protocol on border security.

The Iranian side benefitted at an early stage from the protocol of delineation of the river borders in Shatt-al-Arab, whereas additional time was normally required for the implementation of the protocol of land-borders. The measures of returning these territories to Iraq were delayed owing to the conditions of the former Iranian regime in 1979 and 1980. The new regime assumed office while our territories were still under the other party's control. We then understood the new regime's need for some time to honor its commitments under the Accord. But since the first day of the assumption of power by this ruling group in Iran, we noticed an aggressive stand and a breach of neighborly relations on their part. They also started to announce subsequently their non-adherence to the March Accord. At a very early stage, the ruling clique in Iran violated an essential clause of the Accord when they called back from America the individuals who had been leading collaborators. The puppet Barazani and some of his sons were ready to go back to Iran and resume their aggressive activities against Iraq; but he died there in the country of his American masters. His sons and heads of the collaborating insurgency came to Iran, using it, with the explicit support of the ruling authorities in Iran, as a springboard for threatening the sovereignty of Iraq and its national security.

The Iranian rulers' attitude, since they had assumed office, has confirmed their violation of the relations of good neighborliness and their non-commitment to the clauses of the March Accord. They, therefore, fully bear the legal and de facto responsibility of rendering this accord null and void.

At the time it was signed, this accord, despite the difficult conditions besetting Iraq, was based on balanced factors, the breach of any of which was to be a breach of the entire Accord.

Since the rulers of Iran have violated this accord from the very beginning of their assumption of power through unmasked and deliberate interference in the domestic affairs of Iraq and by supporting and arming, exactly as the Shah did, the American-Zionist backed collaborating insurgents, and by refusing to return the Iraqi territories that we were obliged to liberate by force, for these reasons, I hereby announce before you that the Accord of March 6, 1975 is terminated on our part too. (The Revolution Command Council issued a decree to this effect).

Therefore, the legal relationship in Shatt-al-Arab must return to what it was prior to March 6, 1975. This river must restore its Iraqi Arab identity as it had been throughout history in name and in reality, with all the disposal rights emanating from full sovereignty over the river. Iraq has proved through its relations with the world at large that it respects all its commitments, and that it cannot accept any threat, aggression or encroachment upon its sovereignty and dignity. The people and the army of Iraq are ready to fight courageous battles, however great the sacrifices may be, in order to safeguard honor and sovereignty.

We took this historic decision to recover full sovereignty over our lands and waters, and we shall act with power and with capability against anyone who tries to challenge this legitimate decision.

We affirm to you, as we did before, that we seek good relations with neighboring countries, including Iran; that Iraq has no designs on Iranian territories and that we did not have any intention to wage war against Iran or expand the area of conflict beyond defending our rights and sovereignty.

We declare to those in Iran who have been blinded by vanity and urged by suspect motives and to all those imperialists, Zionists and opportunists behind them, we say that they have recently had to learn lessons when our valiant army wrested the areas of Zein-al-Qaws and Saif Saad together with our border outposts in a manner suited to courageous and faithful men. We want them to respond to the voice of right and reason which calls for maintaining good neighborly relations with Iraq and the Arab nation, and to relinquish every inch of territory they usurped from Iraq and the Arab nation. Only by this they may serve their people and prove that they are revolutionaries, not agents of imperialist and Zionist forces and backward racists harboring hatred and enmity toward the Arab nation and seeking to incite dissension among its ranks to fragment and devitalize it, thus implementing the Zionist designs or consequently being in line with it.

We say before you, the Arab nation and the world at large, that we have exposed the false guise under which this ruling clique assumed office in Iran. This clique utilized religion in a false manner to expand at the expense of Arab sovereignty and Arab higher interests. The ruling clique in Iran created feuds and divisions amidst the Nation notwithstanding the crucial circumstances through which the Nation is passing, and its struggle against Zionist aggression and imperialist powers.

The false mask of the religious cause is merely a cover for Persian racialism and deep-rooted hatred of the Arabs. This mask is utilized by the Iranian clique to incite trends of chauvinism, hatred and schism among the peoples of the region, thus serving world Zionism whether consciously or unconsciously.

There are some that are driven by many motives which we will not mention now, who said: "Khomeiny is different from the Shah, why are you treating him like this?" Our answer is that we had sincerely hoped that Khomeiny was different from the Shah with regard to our patriotic and national causes, and to the occupation of Arab territories in particular. We gave him time enough to prove whether he was really different from the Shah. But he, together with those who are in office in Iran, proved that they are not different from the Shah in their expansionist designs and ambitions and their racial attitude towards the Arabs. Contrary to justice, they hang on to all territories the Shah had usurped from Iraq and to the occupation of the Arab islands of Greater Tumb, Lesser Tumb and Abu Musa. They also repeated even those expansionist claims the Shah had given up under the pressure of the Arab will. As regards Iraq, they refused even to return the territories that the Shah agreed to return according to the clauses of the Agreement of 1975.

When we talk sorrowfully about the racism of the Iranian regime and its aggressive attitudes, we do not forget to mention the stands of the Iranian peoples, including the Persians, with appreciation. We harbor for them feelings of sympathy and wish to establish with them friendly relations, and we wish them salvation from the plight they are now undergoing.

234

We warmly greet our brothers the Arabs of Ahwaz who are suffering oppressive conditions under the Khomeiny regime, more than they suffered under the Shah's regime. We hail the honest fighting Kurds in Iran and all friendly Iranian people, assuring them all that we do not harbor any designs on a single inch of their land, and that we have only sympathy and friendliness for them.

We hope that our neighbor Iran will be free and independent and play a positive role in the region, within the Nonalignment Movement and within the people's struggle for freedom, independence and progress. We assure the world that Iraq which had been managing navigation affairs in the Shatt-al-Arab prior to March 6, 1975, in conformity with its full rights of sovereignty, had shown genuine capability, efficiency and a high sense of responsibility in achieving this task. Iraq today is even more capable of performing its duties in this respect. We hope that all parties concerned, including the Iranian side, will respect the sovereignty of Iraq over Shatt-al-Arab and conduct themselves accordingly.

A comrade asked me at a Party meeting about the potential reserve we maintain for facing the suspicious racist enmity shown by the new regime in Iran. I told him that the Leadership has habituated the Iraqi people to having always some potential reserve to use in historic crucial times. But I tell you and all Iraqis and the honest Arab nation that the main reserve, whether potential or not, with which we surprised the machinations of the puppets in Iran who are incited by rotten mentalities and racialist motives and with which we will face all aggressive imperialist-Zionist and racist designs, is the great Iraqi people. It is our people who are characterized by seriousness and endowed with unlimited preparedness for sacrifice, and who strongly adhere to their legitimate rights and draw inspiration from their great historical heritage, the heritage of the great Islamic message, and from the history of the great Arab nation and the glories of the great Iraq.

This reserve is our valiant Iraqi Army which is endowed with the same spirit and is living up to the principles of the Revolution while following the examples set in the bright history of the Arab nation and that of glorious Iraq.

# APPENDIX
## XII

## ALGIERS DECLARATION OF MARCH 6, 1975.

During the convocation of the OPEC Summit Conference in the Algerian capital and upon the initiative of President Houari Boumediene, the Shah of Iran and Mr. Saddam Hussein, Vice-Chairman of the Revolution Command Council, met twice and conducted lengthy talks on the relations between Iraq and Iran. These talks, attended by President Houari Boumediene, were characterized by complete frankness and the sincere will of both parties to reach a final and permanent solution to all problems existing between their two countries, in accordance with the principles of territorial integrity, border inviolability and non-interference in the internal affairs of others.

The two High Contracting Parties have decided to:

First: Carry out a final delineation of their land boundaries in accordance with the Constantinople Protocol of 1913 and the Proceedings of the Border Delimitation Commission of 1914.

Second: Demarcate their river boundaries according to the Thalweg line.

Third: Accordingly, the two parties shall restore security and mutual confidence along their joint borders. They shall also commit themselves to carrying out a strict and effective observation of their joint borders so as to put a final end to all infiltrations of a subversive nature wherever they may come from.

Fourth: The two parties have also agreed to consider the aforesaid arrangements as inseparable elements of a comprehensive solution. Consequently, any infringement of one of its components shall naturally contradict the spirit of the Algiers Accord. The two parties shall remain in constant contact with President Houari Boumediene, who shall provide Algeria's brotherly assistance whenever needed in order to apply these resolutions.

The two parties have decided to restore the traditional ties of neighborliness and friendship, in particular by eliminating all negative factors in their relations, through a constant exchange of views on issues of mutual interest and through the promotion of a balanced cooperation.

The two parties officially declare that the region ought to be secure from any foreign interference.

The Foreign Ministers of Iraq and Iran shall meet in the presence of Algeria's Foreign Minister on March 15, 1975 in Teheran in order to make working arrangements for the Iraqi-Iranian joint commission which was set up to apply the resolutions taken by mutual agreement as specified above. And in accordance with the desire of the two parties, Algeria shall be invited to the meetings of the Iraqi-Iranian joint commission. The commission shall determine its agenda, working procedures and hold meetings, if necessary. The meetings shall be alternately held in Baghdad and Teheran.

His Majesty The Shah of Iran accepted with pleasure the invitation extended to him by His Excellency President Ahmed Hassan al-Bakr to pay a state visit to Iraq. The date of the visit shall be fixed by mutual agreement.

On the other hand, Mr. Saddam Hussein agreed to visit Iran officially at a date to be fixed by the two parties.

H.M. The Shah of Iran and Mr. Saddam Hussein have both expressed their deep gratitude to President Houari Boumediene who, motivated by brotherly sentiments and a spirit of disinterestedness, has worked for the establishment of a direct contact between the leaders of the two countries and consequently contributed to reviving a new era in the Iraqi-Iranian relations, with a view to the higher interest of the future of the region in question.

# APPENDIX
# XIII

## TREATY CONCERNING THE STATE FRONTIER AND NEIGHBORLY RELATIONS BETWEEN IRAQ AND IRAN SIGNED ON JUNE 13, 1975 AND THE PROTOCOLS ANNEXED THERETO*

His Imperial Majesty the Shahinshah of Iran,
His Excellency the President of the Republic of Iraq,

Considering the sincere desire of the two Parties, as expressed in the Algiers Agreement of March 6, 1975, to achieve a final and lasting solution to all the problems pending between the two countries,

Considering that the two Parties have carried out the definitive redemarcation of their land frontiers on the basis of the Constantinople Protocol of 1913 and the minutes of the meetings of the Frontier Delimitation Commission of 1914, and have delimited their river frontiers along the Thalweg,

Considering their desire to restore security and mutual trust throughout the length of their common frontier,

Considering the ties of geographical proximity, history, religion, culture and civilization which bind the peoples of Iran and Iraq,

---

* This text is taken from that deposited with the United Nations under Article 102 of the Charter under reference Nos 14903 to 14907.

Desirous of strengthening their bonds of friendship and neighborliness, expanding their economic and cultural relations and promoting exchanges and human relations between their peoples on the basis of the principles of territorial integrity, the inviolability of frontiers and non-interference in the internal affairs of others,

Resolved to work towards the introduction of a new era of friendly relations between Iran and Iraq based on the full respect for the national independence and sovereign equality of States,

Convinced that they are helping thereby to implement the principles and to achieve the purposes and objectives of the Charter of the United Nations,

Have decided to conclude this Treaty and have appointed as their plenipotentiaries:

*His Imperial Majesty the Shahinshah of Iran:*
His Excellency Abbas Ali Khalatbary,
Minister of Foreign Affairs of Iran.

*His Excellency the President of the Republic of Iraq:*
His Excellency Saadoun Hammadi,
Minister of Foreign Affairs of Iraq.

Who, having exchanged their full powers, found to be in good and due form, have agreed as follows:

ARTICLE ONE

The High Contracting Parties confirm that the State land frontier between Iraq and Iran shall be that which has been redemarcated on the basis of and in accordance with the provisions of the Protocol concerning the redemarcation of the land frontier and the annexes thereto, attached to this Treaty.

242

## ART. 2

The High Contracting Parties confirm that the State frontier in the Shatt-al-Arab shall be that which has been delimited on the basis of and in accordance with the provisions of the Protocol concerning the delimitation of the river frontier, and the annexes thereto, attached to this Treaty.

## ART. 3

The High Contracting Parties undertake to exercise a strict and effective permanent control over the frontier in order to put an end to any infiltration of a subversive nature from any source, on the basis of and in accordance with the provisions of the Protocol concerning frontier security, and the annex thereto, attached to this Treaty.

## ART. 4

The High Contracting Parties confirm that the provisions of the three Protocols, and the annexes thereto, referred to in Articles 1, 2 and 3 above and attached to this Treaty as an integral part thereof, shall be final and permanent. They shall not be infringed upon under any circumstances and shall constitute the indivisible elements of an overall settlement. Accordingly, a breach of any of the components of this overall settlement shall clearly be incompatible with the spirit of the Algiers Agreement.

## ART. 5

In keeping with the inviolability of the frontiers of the two States and the strict respect for their territorial integrity, the High Contracting Parties confirm that the course of their land and river frontiers shall be inviolable, permanent and final.

## ART. 6

1. In the event of a dispute regarding the interpretation or implementation of this Treaty, the three Protocols or the annexes thereto, any solution to such a dispute shall strictly respect the course of the Iraqi-Iranian frontier referred to in Articles 1 and 2 above, and shall take into account the need to maintain security on the Iraqi-Iranian frontier in accordance with Article 3 above.

2. Such disputes shall be resolved in the first instance by the High Contracting Parties, by means of direct bilateral negotiations to be held within two months after the date on which one of the Parties so requested.

3. If no agreement is reached, the High Contracting Parties shall have recourse, within a three-month period, to the good offices of a friendly Third State.

4. Should one of the two Parties refuse to have recourse to good offices or should the good offices procedure fail, the dispute shall be settled by arbitration within a period of not more than one month after the date of such refusal or failure.

5. Should the High Contracting Parties disagree as to the arbitration procedure, one of the High Contracting Parties may have recourse, within 15 days after such disagreement was recorded, to a court of arbitration.

With a view to establishing such a court of arbitration, each of the High Contracting Parties shall, in respect to each dispute to be resolved, appoint one of its citizens as arbitrator and the two arbitrators shall choose an umpire. Should the High Contracting Parties fail to appoint their arbitrators within one month after the date on which one of the Parties received a request for arbitration from the other Party, or should the arbitrators fail to reach an agreement on the choice of the umpire before that time limit expires, the High Contracting Party which requested arbitration shall be entitled to request the President of the International Court of Justice to appoint the arbitrators or the umpire, in accordance with the procedures of the Permanent Court of Arbitration.

6. The decision of the court of arbitration shall be binding and enforceable by the High Contracting Parties.

7. The High Contracting Parties shall each defray half the costs of arbitration.

## Art. 7

This Treaty, the three Protocols and the Annexes thereto, shall be registered in accordance with Article 102 of the Charter of the United Nations.

## Art. 8

This Treaty, the three Protocols and the Annexes thereto, shall be ratified by each of the High Contracting Parties in accordance with its domestic law.

This Treaty, the three Protocols and the Annexes thereto, shall enter into force on the date of exchange of the instruments of ratification in Teheran.

In witness whereof the Plenipotentiaries of the High Contracting Parties have signed this Treaty, the three Protocols and the Annexes thereto.

Done in Baghdad, on June 13, 1975.

<table>
<tr><td>(Signed)</td><td>(Signed)</td></tr>
<tr><td>Abbas Ali Khalatbary</td><td>Saadoun Hammadi</td></tr>
<tr><td>Minister of Foreign Affairs<br>of Iran</td><td>Minister of Foreign Affairs<br>of Iraq</td></tr>
</table>

This Treaty, the three Protocols and the Annexes thereto, were signed in the presence of His Excellency Abdel-Aziz Bouteflika, Member of the Council of the Revolution and Minister of Foreign Affairs of Algeria.

## PROTOCOL CONCERNING THE REDEMARCATION OF THE LAND FRONTIER BETWEEN IRAN AND IRAQ

Pursuant to the provisions of the Algiers communiqué of March 6, 1975, the two Contracting Parties have agreed to the following:

### ARTICLE ONE

A. The Two Contracting Parties affirm and recognize that the redemarcation of the State land frontier between Iran and Iraq was a field operation performed by the mixed Iraqi-Iranian-Algerian Committee on the basis of the following:

1. The Constantinople Protocol of 1913 and the minutes of the meetings of the 1914 Commission to delimit the Turco-Persian frontier;

2. The Teheran Protocol dated March 17, 1975;

3. The record of the meeting of Ministers of Foreign Affairs, signed at Baghdad on April 20, 1975 and approving, *inter alia,* the report of the Committee to Demarcate the Land Frontier, signed at Teheran on March 30, 1975;

4. The record of the meeting of Ministers of Foreign Affairs, signed at Algiers on May 20, 1975;

5. The descriptive record of operations in the demarcation of the land frontier between Iran and Iraq, prepared by the Committee to Demarcate the Land Frontier and dated June 13, 1975. The record constitutes Annex 1 and is an integral part of this Protocol;

6. Maps on the scale 1:50,000 indicating the land frontier line and the position of the old and new frontier marks. The maps constitute Annex 2 and are an integral part of this Protocol.

7. Record cards of the old and new frontier marks;

8. A document giving the coordinates of the frontier marks;

9. Aerial photographs of the Iraqi-Iranian frontier strip indicating the positions of the old and new frontier marks.

B. The two Parties undertake to complete the demarcation of the frontier between frontier marks No. 14 A and No. 15 within two months.

C. The two Contracting Parties shall cooperate in producing aerial photographs of the Iranian-Iraqi land frontier with a view to using them in plotting the frontier on maps scaled 1:25,000, indicating the position of the frontier marks. This work shall be completed within a period not exceeding one year taking effect May 20, 1975, and shall be without prejudice to the entry into force of the Treaty of which this Protocol is an integral part.

The descriptive record relating to the land frontier and referred to in paragraph 5 above shall be amended accordingly.

The maps produced pursuant to the present section C shall supersede all existing maps.

## ART. 2

The State land frontier between Iraq and Iran shall follow the line indicated in the descriptive record and the maps referred to respectively in paragraphs 5 and 6 of Article 1 above, with due regard to the provisions of section C of that Article.

## ART. 3

The frontier line defined in Articles 1 and 2 of this Protocol shall also divide the air space and the subsoil vertically.

## ART. 4

The two Contracting Parties shall establish a Mixed Iraqi-Iranian Commission to settle, in a neighborly and cooperative spirit, the status of landed property, constructions, or technical or other installations whose national character may be changed by the redemarcation of the land frontier between Iraq and Iran. Such settlement shall be by means of repurchase compensation or any other appropriate formula, with a view to eliminating any source of litigation.

The Commission shall settle the status of State property within two months. Claims concerning private property shall be submitted to it within two months. The status of this private property shall be settled within the following three months.

## ART. 5

1. A Mixed Commission composed of representatives of the competent authorities of the two States shall be established to inspect the frontier marks and determine their condition.

The Commission shall make this inspection annually, in September, in accordance with a timetable which it shall prepare beforehand within an appropriate period of time.

2. Either Contracting Party may request the other in writing to have the Commission carry out, at any time, an additional inspection of the frontier marks. In the event of such a request, the inspection shall be made within a period not exceeding 30 days after the date of the request.

3. Whenever an inspection is made, the Mixed Commission shall prepare the relevant reports and submit them under its signature to the competent authorities of each of the two States. The Commission may, if need be, call for the construction of new frontier marks according to the specifications of the existing ones, provided that the course of the frontier line is not thereby altered. Where new frontier marks are constructed, the competent authorities of the two States shall check the frontier marks and their coordinates against the relevant maps and documents referred to in Article 1 of this Protocol. The authorities shall then position the frontier-marks under the supervision of the Mixed Commission, which shall prepare a record of the operation and submit it to the competent authorities of each of the two States so that it may be annexed to the documents referred to in Article 1 of this Protocol.

4. The two Contracting Parties shall be jointly responsible for the maintenance of the frontier marks.

5. The Mixed Commission shall be responsible for replacing displaced frontier marks and reconstructing destroyed or missing marks, on the basis of the maps and documents referred to in Article 1 of this Protocol, taking care not to alter the position of the marks, under any circumstances. In such cases, the Mixed Commission

shall prepare a record of the operation and submit it to the competent authorities of each of the two States.

6. The competent authorities of each of the two States shall exchange information on the condition of the frontier marks with a view to finding the best ways and means of protecting and maintaining them.

7. The two Contracting Parties undertake to take all necessary steps to protect the frontier marks and prosecute individuals who have moved, damaged or destroyed them.

## ART. 6

The two Contracting Parties have agreed that the provisions of this Protocol, signed without any reservation, shall henceforth govern any matter relating to the frontier between Iran and Iraq. On this basis, they solemnly undertake to respect their common and definitive frontier.

Done in Baghdad, on June 13, 1975.

<table>
<tr><td>(Signed)</td><td>(Signed)</td></tr>
<tr><td>Abbas Ali Khalatbary</td><td>Saadoun Hammadi</td></tr>
<tr><td>Minister of Foreign Affairs<br>of Iran</td><td>Minister of Foreign Affairs<br>of Iraq</td></tr>
</table>

Signed in the presence of His Excellency Abdel-Aziz Bouteflika, Member of the Council of the Revolution, Minister of Foreign Affairs of Algeria.

## *PROTOCOL CONCERNING THE DELIMITATION OF THE RIVER FRONTIER BETWEEN IRAN AND IRAQ*

Pursuant to the decisions taken in the Algiers communiqué of March 6, 1975,

The two Contracting Parties have agreed as follows:

### ARTICLE ONE

The two Contracting Parties hereby declare and recognize that the State river frontier between Iran and Iraq in the Shatt-al-Arab has been delimited along the Thalweg by the Mixed Iraqi-Iranian-Algerian Committee on the basis of the following:

1. The Teheran Protocol of March 17, 1975;

2. The record of the Meeting of Ministers of Foreign Affairs, signed at Baghdad on April 20, 1975, approving, *inter alia*, the report of the Committee to Delimit the River Frontier, signed on April 16, 1975 on board the Iraqi ship *El Thawra* in the Shatt-al-Arab;

3. Common hydrographic charts, which have been verified on the spot and corrected and on which the geographical coordinates of the 1975 frontier crossing points have been indicated; these charts have been signed by the hydrographic experts of the Mixed Technical Commission and countersigned by the heads of the Iranian, Iraqi and Algerian delegations to the Committee. The said charts, listed hereafter, are annexed to this Protocol and form an integral part thereof:

Chart No. 1: Entrance to Shatt-al-Arab, No. 3842, published by the British Admiralty;

Chart No. 2: Inner Bar to Kabda Point, No. 3843, published by the British Admiralty;

Chart No. 3: Kabda Point to Abadan, No. 3844, published by the British Admiralty;

Chart No. 4: Abadan to Jazirat Ummat Tuwaylah, No. 3845, published by the British Admiralty.

ART. 2

1. The frontier line in the Shatt-al-Arab shall follow the Thalweg, i.e. the median line of the main navigable channel at the lowest navigable level, starting from the point at which the land frontier between Iran and Iraq enters the Shatt-al-Arab and continuing to the sea.

2. The frontier line, as defined in paragraph 1 above, shall vary with changes brought about by natural causes in the main navigable channel. The frontier line shall not be affected by other changes unless the two Contracting Parties conclude a special agreement to that effect.

3. The occurrence of any of the changes referred to in paragraph 2 above shall be attested jointly by the competent technical authorities of the two Contracting Parties.

4. Any change in the bed of the Shatt-al-Arab brought about by natural causes which would involve a change in the national character of the two States' respective territories or of landed property, constructions, or technical or other installations, shall not change the course of the frontier line which shall continue to follow the Thalweg in accordance with the provisions of paragraph 1 above.

5. Unless an agreement is reached between the two Contracting Parties concerning the transfer of the frontier line to the new bed, the water shall be re-directed at the joint expense of both Parties to the bed existing in 1975 as marked on the four common charts listed in Article 1, paragraph 3, above — should one of the Parties so request within two years after the date on which the occurrence of the change was attested by either of the two Parties. Until such time, both Parties shall retain their previous rights of navigation and of user over the water of the new bed.

## ART. 3

1. The river frontier between Iran and Iraq in the Shatt-al-Arab, as defined in Article 2 above, is represented by the relevant line drawn on the common charts referred to in Article 1, paragraph 3, above.

2. The two Contracting Parties have agreed to consider that the river frontier shall end at the straight line connecting the two banks of the Shatt-al-Arab, at its mouth, at the astronomical lowest low-water mark. This straight line has been indicated on the common hydrographic charts referred to in Article 1, paragraph 3, above.

## ART. 4

The frontier line as defined in Articles 1, 2 and 3 of this Protocol shall also divide the air space and the subsoil vertically.

## ART. 5

With a view to eliminating any source of controversy, the two Contracting Parties shall establish a Mixed Iraqi-Iranian Commission to settle within two months any questions concerning the status of landed property, constructions, or technical or other installations, the national character of which may be affected by the delimitation of the Iranian-Iraqi river frontier, either through repurchase or compensation or any other suitable arrangement.

## ART. 6

Since the task of surveying the Shatt-al-Arab has been completed and the common hydrographic chart referred to in Article 1, paragraph 3 above has been drawn up, the two Contracting Parties have agreed that a new survey of the Shatt-al-Arab shall be carried out jointly, once every 10 years, with effect from the date of signature of this Protocol. However, each of the two Parties shall have the right to request new surveys, to be carried out jointly, before the expiry of the 10 year period.

The two Contracting Parties shall each defray half the cost of such surveys.

## ART. 7

1. Merchant vessels, State vessels and warships of the two Contracting Parties shall enjoy freedom of navigation in the Shatt-al-Arab and in any part of the navigable chan-

nels in the territorial sea which lead to the mouth of the Shatt-al-Arab, irrespective of the line delimiting the territorial sea of each of the two countries.

2. Vessels of third countries used for purposes of trade shall enjoy freedom of navigation, on an equal and non-discriminatory basis, in the Shatt-al-Arab and in any part of the navigable channels in the territorial sea which lead to the mouth of the Shatt-al-Arab, irrespective of the line delimiting the territorial seas of each of the two countries.

3. Either of the two Contracting Parties may authorize foreign warships visiting its ports to enter the Shatt-al-Arab, provided such vessels do not belong to a country in a state of belligerency, armed conflict or war with either of the two Contracting Parties, and provided the other Party is so notified no less than 72 hours in advance.

4. The two Contracting Parties shall in every case refrain from authorizing the entry to the Shatt-al-Arab of merchant vessels belonging to a country in a state of belligerency, armed conflict or war with either of the two parties.

## Art. 8

1. Rules governing navigation in the Shatt-al-Arab shall be drawn up by a mixed Iranian-Iraqi Commission, in accordance with the principle of equal rights of navigation for both States.

2. The two Contracting Parties shall establish a Commission to draw up rules governing the prevention and control of pollution in the Shatt-al-Arab.

3. The two Contracting Parties undertake to conclude subsequent agreements on the questions referred to in paragraphs 1 and 2 of this Article.

## ART 9

The two Contracting Parties recognize that the Shatt-al-Arab is primarily an international waterway, and undertake to refrain from any operation that might hinder navigation in the Shatt-al-Arab or in any part of those navigable channels in the territorial sea of either of the two countries that lead to the mouth of the Shatt-al-Arab.

Done in Baghdad, on June 13, 1975.

| (Signed) | (Signed) |
|---|---|
| **Abbas Ali Khalatbary** | **Saadoun Hammadi** |
| Minister of Foreign Affairs of Iran | Minister of Foreign Affairs of Iraq |

Signed in the presence of His Excellency Abdel-Aziz Bouteflika, Member of the Council of the Revolution and Minister of Foreign Affairs of Algeria.

## PROTOCOL CONCERNING SECURITY ON THE FRONTIER BETWEEN IRAN AND IRAQ

In accordance with the decisions contained in the Algiers·Agreement of March 6, 1975,

Anxious to re-establish mutual security and trust throughout the length of their common frontier,

Resolved to exercise strict and effective control over that frontier in order to put an end to any infiltration of a subversive nature, and, to that end, to establish close cooperation between themselves and to prevent any infiltration or illegal movement across their common frontier for the purpose of causing subversion, insubordination or rebellion,

Referring to the Teheran Protocol of March 15, 1975, the record of the meeting of Ministers of Foreign Affairs, signed in Baghdad on April 20, 1975, and the record of the meeting of Ministers of Foreign Affairs, signed in Algiers on May 20, 1975,

The two Contracting Parties have agreed as follows:

### ARTICLE ONE

1. The two Contracting Parties shall exchange information on any movement by subversive elements which may attempt to infiltrate one of the two countries with a view to committing acts of subversion, insubordination or rebellion.

2. The two Contracting Parties shall take the necessary steps with regard to the movements of the elements referred to in paragraph 1 above.

They shall inform each other immediately of the identity of such persons, on the understanding that they shall do their utmost to prevent those persons from committing acts of subversion.

The same steps shall be taken with regard to any persons who may assemble within the territory of one of the two Contracting Parties with the intention of committing acts of subversion or sabotage in the territory of the other Party.

## ART. 2

The many forms of cooperation established between the competent authorities of the two Contracting Parties relating to the closing of frontiers to prevent infiltration by subversive elements shall be instituted by the frontier authorities of the two countries, and shall be pursued up to the highest levels in the Ministries of Defense, Foreign Affairs and the Interior of each of the two Parties.

## ART. 3

The infiltration points likely to be used by subversive elements are as follows:

1. *Northern frontier zone*
From the point of intersection of the Iranian, Turkish and Iraqi frontiers to (and including) Khanaqin - Qasr-e-Shirin: 21 points.

2. *Southern frontier zone*
From (but not including) Khanaqin - Qasr-e-Shirin to the end of the Iranian-Iraqi frontier: 17 points.

3. The above infiltration points are named in the annex.

4. The points specified above shall be supplemented by any other infiltration point which may be discovered and will have to be closed and controlled.

5. All frontier crossing points except those currently controlled by the customs authorities shall be closed.

6. In the interest of promoting relations of all kinds between the two neighboring countries, the two Contracting Parties have agreed that, in the future, other crossing points controlled by the customs authorities shall be created by common consent.

### ART. 4

1. The two Contracting Parties undertake to provide the necessary human and material resources to ensure the effective closure and control of their frontiers, so as to prevent any infiltration by subversive elements through the crossing points mentioned in Article 3 above.

2. If, in the light of experience gained in this matter, experts should decide that more effective measures must be taken, the corresponding procedures shall be established at monthly meetings of the frontier authorities of the two countries, or at meetings between those authorities, should the need arise.

The conclusions and records of such meetings shall be communicated to the higher authorities of each of the two Parties. Should there be disagreement between the frontier authorities, the heads of the administrations concerned shall meet in either Baghdad or Teheran to reconcile the points of view and draw up a record of the outcome of their meetings.

### ART. 5

1. Any subversive persons who may be arrested shall be handed over to the competent authorities of the Party in whose territory they were arrested and shall be subject to the legislation in force.

2. The two Contracting Parties shall inform one another of the measures taken against persons referred to in paragraph 1 above.

3. Should subversive persons cross the frontier in an attempt to escape, the authorities of the other country shall be informed immediately and shall take all necessary steps to apprehend such persons.

## Art. 6

In case of need and where the two Contracting Parties so agree, entry to certain areas may be declared prohibited in order to prevent subversive persons from carrying out their intentions.

## Art. 7

In order to establish and promote cooperation which is mutually beneficial to both Parties, a permanent Mixed Committee comprising the heads of the frontier authorities and representatives of the Ministers of Foreign Affairs of the two countries shall be established and shall hold two sessions a year (at the beginning of each half of the calendar year).

At the request of one of the two Parties, however, special meetings may be held to consider how intellectual and material resources might be better used for the closure and control of the frontiers and to review the effectiveness and proper implementation of the basic provisions governing cooperation as provided for in this Protocol.

## Art. 8

The provisions of this Protocol relating to the closure and control of the frontier shall be without prejudice to the provisions of specific agreements between Iran and Iraq concerning grazing rights and frontier commissioners.

## ART. 9

With a view to guaranteeing the security of the common river frontier in the Shatt-al-Arab and preventing the infiltration of subversive elements from either side, the two Contracting Parties shall take such appropriate steps as the installation of lookout posts and the detachment of patrol boats.

Done in Baghdad, on June 13, 1975.

<table>
<tr><td>(Signed)</td><td>(Signed)</td></tr>
<tr><td>Abbas Ali Khalatbary</td><td>Saadoun Hammadi</td></tr>
<tr><td>Minister of Foreign Affairs<br>of Iran</td><td>Minister of Foreign Affairs<br>of Iraq</td></tr>
</table>

Signed in the presence of H.E. A.A. Bouteflika Minister of Foreign Affairs of Algeria.

## *RECORD*

In connection with the description of the Iranian-Iraqi land frontier annexed to the Protocol concerning the redemarcation of the land frontier between Iran and Iraq of June 13, 1975, the undersigned representatives of Iran and Iraq, duly empowered, have reached agreement on the following arrangements:

1. With regard to the description of the course of the frontier between mark No. 101 and mark No. 101/1, it has been agreed that the frontier line shall run between two springs bearing the same name "Chiftekan."

Accordingly, the description set out in Annex 1 to the Protocol concerning the redemarcation of the land frontier, which reads:

> It shall go in a straight line to a point situated between two springs bearing the same name "Chiftekan," whence it shall ascend in a straight line to the crest of Sour Kuh mountain,

signifies that the frontier line shall run between the two springs, which lie approximately 5 meters apart.

The existing arrangements for sharing the waters of the two springs (12 hours for Iran and 12 hours for Iraq in any 24-hour period) shall continue to apply.

The representatives of the two Parties deem it desirable to erect one or two additional marks between mark No. 101 and mark No. 101/1, in order to delineate more clearly the course of the frontier.

2. The description of the frontier between mark No. 81 and mark No. 82 set out in Annex 1 to the Protocol concerning the redemarcation of the land frontier between Iran and Iraq, which reads:

> It shall then climb the Dere-i-Tekkiyeh ravine, skirting the orchards situated therein in such a way as to leave them in Persian territory. From the point where these orchards end, 'it shall follow the Thalweg of the ravine...

specifically provides that the frontier shall skirt all existing orchards, thus leaving them in Iranian territory. The representatives of the two Parties have agreed on the erection of six additional marks in order to delineate more clearly the course of the frontier.

3. The erection of the additional marks referred to in paragraphs 1 and 2 above shall be effected *in situ* by the duly authorized representatives of the two countries. The marks shall be constructed as soon as weather conditions permit.

Done in Baghdad, on December 26, 1975.

<table>
<tr><td>For Iran:</td><td>For Iraq:</td></tr>
<tr><td>(Signed)</td><td>(Signed)</td></tr>
<tr><td>General Ebrahim Khalvati</td><td>Alladin Al-Sakkal</td></tr>
</table>

# APPENDIX
## XIV

## REPLY OF PRESIDENT SADDAM HUSSEIN TO DR. KURT WALDHEIM, SECRETARY GENERAL OF THE U.N. (SEPTEMBER 29, 1980)

I received your letter dated September 28, 1980, and on this occasion I wish to reaffirm to you that shortly before the Security Council meeting on 9/28/1980, I announced in an official speech broadcast on Iraqi radio and TV the readiness of Iraq to observe an immediate cease-fire between Iran and Iraq, provided that the other side abides by the cease-fire and resorts to direct negotiation or through a third party, or through any international organization or party we respect and trust in view of achieving a just and honorable solution ensuring our rights and sovereignty.

Our decision is fully aligned with the spirit of Resolution No. 479 taken by the Security Council later on at its meeting No. 2248 on 9/28/1980. Hence, it is only natural that we accept the aforesaid resolution of the Security Council and we declare that we are ready to abide by it on condition that the Iranian side abides by it. We hope that the Security Council will take the appropriate measures to urge the Iranian side to abide by this Resolution.

On this occasion, the Government of the Republic of Iraq wishes to express its appreciation of the efforts exerted personally by you and by the Security Council for the sake of maintaining security and stability in our region in a manner which serves the aims of humanity for a just peace.

Saddam Hussein
President of the Republic of Iraq

# APPENDIX
# XV

## SHLOMO ARONSON:
## THE NUCLEAR FACTOR IN THE MIDDLE EAST (1)

The full-scale efforts exerted by Iraq in the nuclear realm have obviously caused serious misgivings in Israel. Tel Aviv's criticisms are especially aimed at the construction of two generators. The smallest, called "Isis", seems to have started operating, whereas the other, which is much larger, was damaged during an attack even before its delivery to Iraq. The name of this generator, "Osiris", has been modified by the manufacturer to become "Osirak" in honor of the buyer. Even before the present war with Iran, the Iraq led by Saddam Hussein was preparing itself to become an active, preponderant power in the Middle East. American experts have reported the successes of the Iraqi regime in the areas of civil organization as well as the numerical growth of the army, which now contains ten divisions, several of which are tank forces. The same experts point out the ambitious aims of Saddam Hussein, for whom Iraq is a modern Arab Babylonia. This enterprise of modernization achieved by means of resources derived from the exploitation of oil, is intimately tied to a radical "Arabization" which nevertheless rejects any subservience to fanatic Islamic doctrines, the effects of which would hold up the modernizing process, as abundantly demonstrated in both the Western countries and in Israel. Iraq thus appears like a potential great power, whose influence stretches throughout the "Fertile Crescent" to the Gulf region as

(1) Taken from "As-Safir", (Beirut), January 27, 1981.

the chief candidate for hegemony over the Arab world and as a dangerous enemy for Israel.

Furthermore, Iraq has till now never signed an agreement for a truce with us and involved itself on the "eastern front" during the Kippur War, before joining the "rejection front". Iraq is also mixed up in the politics of the Palestinian organizations, among which it upholds the most extremist, notably those whose responsibility was proven in several woeful crimes committed inside Israel. It indeed seems natural that Iraq is trying to add an authentic atomic alternative to its great power by way of its oil resources and France's Machiavellian aid which nothing can stop. The nuclear option serves the purposes and ambitions of modern Iraq... Iraq has no other need for it other than accomplishing the traditional ambition of the Ba'ath Party and giving the Arabs an international weight which will allow them to act as a "third power" between the two Supers. The Iraqi nuclear ace will strengthen the force of the Arabs, and Baghdad will become the principle stronghold in the conflict with Israel.

In the war it is leading against Iran in a vital region, Iraq has demonstrated extreme prudence and has carefully assured the preservation of its army. Hence, why would Saddam Hussein, who is relatively distrustful and pragmatic, need nuclear dissuasion? It seems that the reasons for this choice are both political and psychological: it involves the strengthening of his position in the Gulf and among the other Arab countries, making things swing over to his advantage. Saddam maybe believes that his choice neutralizes that of the Israelis, to the point of letting him declare a permanent state of war against us and to back up terrorist attacks without risking a nuclear catastrophe. According to Haytham Al-Ayoubi, military spokesman for the Palestinians, an infinite number of stabs in the back, strategically supported by Iraq, will without open warfare wind up in the ultimate collapse of the Zionist entity.

It is not yet known whether the sabotage of the "Osirak" generator in France last year and the air raid against the "Isis" generator and the building assumed to house "Osirak", have been successful in seriously delaying the nuclear plans of Baghdad. It is known that France delivered 13 kg of enriched uranium (out of the 72 kg promised by France) which suffice to produce an atomic bomb with the help of a special apparatus that Iraq has already ordered, among other items, from Italy. We cannot say whether the Italian apparatus arrived at its destination. The French specialists working on the preliminary operations of the "Isis" and "Osirak" generators were not present at the time. Thus, the Iraqis are free to use the uranium they received and to make any use of it they wish.

We can suppose — and this supposition is just as correct as it is incorrect — that the Iraqi nuclear project was postponed because of the war. But the mere existence of that plan justifies all of the attempts made by Israel to delay its functioning for as long as possible. We must continue to look toward the United States and Europe for help — as far as this is possible — but at the same time it is important that we conceal our own nuclear option.

Yitzhak Shamir, Minister of Foreign Affairs, acted wisely when, like his predecessors at that ministry, he suggested the denuclearization of the Middle East region provided that negotiations be opened on the subject with the Arab states. In parallel to these diplomatic talks, the Iraqi-Iranian war and the arms race, so traditionally striking in the region and in which Israel is involved, demand a time of meditation along with a new examination of the situation.

# APPENDIX
## XVI

## STATEMENT BY DR. SAADOUN HAMMADI, MINISTER OF FOREIGN AFFAIRS OF THE REPUBLIC OF IRAQ, BEFORE THE U.N. SECURITY COUNCIL (OCTOBER 15, 1980)

Mr. President,

Allow me first to extend to you and to the distinguished members of the Council my sincere thanks for having given me the opportunity to participate in this meeting.

Mr. President,

As one of the founding members of the United Nations, Iraq has strongly adhered in its international relations to the purposes, principles, and rules of the Charter of the United Nations. As a member of the Non-Aligned movement, the principles of nonalignment constitute the cornerstone of our foreign policy. We have not only dedicated ourselves to those principles, but also translated them into action in our international relations. Whether in our region, or in the world arena, our policy has always been the preservation of international peace and security as well as the avoidance of a world economic catastrophe. But this policy absolutely rejects any form of interference from any quarter and irrespective of its pretext. Hence, we cannot agree with any attempt or action to interfere in the internal affairs of our country that is contrary to the legally established norms of State conduct.

Having said this, permit me to state that the problem with which the Council is seized should be looked upon in its proper perspective. Otherwise, we are liable to overlook some of its important dimensions, and consequently, no viable solution is likely to emerge. The problem is neither new nor simple. It goes back over four hundred and sixty years of history. It is not a mere border problem nor a minor conflict over navigational rights. It is much wider than that. Historically, it is established that since 1520, eighteen treaties have been concluded by the "Persian State" with its western neighbors on its relations therewith including the question of borders, only to be terminated by the said state, whether by word or by deed. We are neighbors of Iran and have shared with the Iranian peoples cultural, religious and humanitarian ties. We have become convinced since sometime that the policies and actions of the successive regimes in Iran are clearly that of territorial expansion. I shall not bother the Council with a detailed historical account. I need only recall one fact from very recent history. All of us witnessed visions of power and domination of the Shah, which were not confined to the Arab Gulf area, but extended also to the Indian Ocean and beyond. And all of us note today President Bani Sadr of Iran declaring that between Muslim countries there are no borders. This was not meant to indicate a policy for free and open relations among Islamic States, because the Iranian Government claims many Islamic countries as belonging to Iran such as Bahrain, Yemen, Oman and even the capital of my country.

272

Mr. President,

The Iranian Government and its representatives claim that since the Islamic Republic was established in Iran, my Government has adopted a hostile attitude toward the new regime. This allegation is utterly baseless. Khomeiny was given refuge in Iraq for about fifteen years and was given full scale moral and material support for over seven years. Iraq welcomed the new regime from the very early days in every sense.

The president of the Republic of Iraq addressed a telegram of congratulations to Khomeiny on April 5, 1979, on the occasion of the declaration of the Islamic Republic. In that telegram, our President expressed on behalf of the people and Government of Iraq and on his own behalf, the "sincerest congratulations" to Khomeiny and the "neighborly and friendly peoples of Iran, hoping that the new republican regime would open wider opportunities to serve the friendly Iranian peoples in a manner that promotes Iran's role in the service of peace and justice in the world and forges the strongest relations of friendship with the Arab countries in general and Iraq in particular."

To that telegram, we received two answers from Khomeiny, a nice one through the Ministry of Foreign Affairs and another published by the Pars New Agency and other newspapers, on April 19-21, 1980, containing an entirely different attitude, a hostile tone and improper language. So we pursued the matter through the diplomatic channel to seek clarification. We were told by Prime Minister Bazargan and Foreign Minister Yazdi that the former was the official one, and that an investigation shall be carried out to know how the second version appeared. We considered the matter settled, although neither the outcome of that investigation was communicated to us, nor did we see any official correction in the Iranian press later.

273

Despite that unhappy incident, we continued with our official contacts. My Government addressed to the Bazargan Government a note in which it expressed its earnest intention to establish the closest fraternal ties and cooperative relations with neighboring peoples and countries, especially with Iran, on the basis of respect for sovereignty, non-interference in internal affairs and respect for the legitimate aspirations of peoples in accordance with the principles they choose through their own free will. The note also expressed the view that Iraq has a special view on the relations between the people of Iraq and the neighboring peoples of Iran and Turkey, for these peoples are not merely neighbors, but also brothers, with whom the Arab nation in general and the Iraqi people in particular are related by old Islamic ties and common history since hundreds of years. In addition, the people of Iraq, who have struggled for years against colonial domination, the corrupt monarchy and exploitation, achieved their victory through the revolution of July 17, 1968 led by the Arab Ba'ath Socialist Party. Hence, the people of Iraq look with sympathy and support upon the struggle waged by the friendly and neighborly Iranian peoples for freedom, justice and progress. It feels joy and pride when the Iranian people achieve victory in those respects. In the same tone, a similar satisfaction was expressed in the note regarding the statements and positions of Prime Minister Bazargan which emphasized the Islamic character of some of the popular trends in Iran, because such has been the principle and the practical position of the Arab Ba'ath Socialist Party. Such a trend was considered by Iraq as an important positive transformation in the region, one which would contribute to promote its independence and development. Finally, the note went on to express Iraq's sincere hope for prosperity to the friendly and neighborly Iranian people, and for strong relations of fruitful cooperation between Iraq and

274

Iran in a manner promoting common bonds, serving the mutual interests of both countries and strengthening freedom, peace, and stability in the region. Later on, my Government extended an invitation to Prime Minister Bazargan to visit Iraq and discuss bilateral relations on the basis of mutual cooperation. The same invitation was renewed by the Iraqi Vice-President of the Revolution Command Council during the Month of Ramadhan, i.e. July-August 1979, in a telegram on that religious occasion. I should say for the record that Mr. Bazargan was also cooperative and tried to strengthen the relations between the two countries. Ever after our relations became tense with Iran the President of the Republic of Iraq in two meetings with Mr. Yazdi in Havana last year clearly expressed his willingness to meet with the Iranian leaders at the highest level to resolve our differences peacefully. I reaffirmed the same thing to Minister Yazdi when I met with him last year here at the United Nations. Minister Yazdi said that they will consider the matter in Teheran, but nothing materialized.

Now let us ask: what was the outcome of all these efforts, which surely by any criterion cannot be considered as hostile?

Prime Minister Bazargan resigned, and with him went Foreign Minister Yazdi. So, the arena was left free for Khomeiny and his followers. At this time, Khomeiny reached the point of unmasking the true intentions of his Islamic revolution, by deciding to export it to Iraq and the Arab Gulf region. Under his auspices and with his blessings, a meeting was held at Qom for the leaders of the reactionary and sectarian al-Daawat party (meaning «The Call» party). The decision was reached to overthrow our Government, through subversion, sabotage and terrorism by the so-called "Jondi el Imam", i.e. the Imam's Soldiers, which meant the militants of the said party. The

275

idea was, after making terror reign in Iraq, to destabilize its Government, then a popular uprising would bring it down. Here, Khomeiny was obviously thinking that what he achieved in Iran could be secured in Iraq as well.

The task of the so-called Imam's soldiers was carried out by Iranian infiltrators and residents in Iraq as well as first generation Iraqis of Iranian origin. We witnessed all over our country, and particularly in the central and southern parts, acts of sabotage and terrorism of increasing magnitude. Those acts were committed at al-Thawra and Kadhumain in Baghdad, and cities like Karbala, Najaf, Amarah, Basra, An-Nasiriyah. They consisted in hurling explosive materials on the masses during religious and national occasions, throwing nitric acid on the faces of people attending prayers at mosques, poisoning food and water prepared for the pilgrims of the holy shrines in Karbala, Najaf, Khadhumain and the like. At al-Thawra in Baghdad, a heavily populated working class area, the terrorist attack claimed many lives and a number of Iranian terrorists were caught. The Iranian Ambassador, Mr. Doa'i, met me personally later to plead for the release of the terrorists, and we responded positively. All these acts were directed from Qom, as daily instructions were issued to al-Daawat agents through Khomeiny's broadcasting stations from Teheran, Qasr-e-Shirin, Ahwaz, Abadan and Kurdistan. Those stations also issued instructions to manufacture local bombs for use in killing innocent citizens. The Iraqi security forces seized considerable amounts of money, arms, bombs, poisons and explosive materials in the hideouts of the said criminal group.

The most cruel terrorist act was the throwing of bombs at a huge student's gathering at al-Mustansiriyah University in Baghdad on April 1, 1980, where an attempt to assassinate Mr. Tareq Aziz, member of the Revolution

Command Council and Deputy Premier, in which lives were lost and many were injured. Similarly, the throwing of bombs from the Iranian school at Wazriya Street onto the funeral procession of those innocent who were murdered in the former incident, on April 5, 1980, in which some Iranian diplomats took part. In addition, an attempt on the life of the Minister of Culture and Information was carried out on April 12, 1980 before his ministry. In all these incidents, Iranians were caught which followed the description of Jondi el Imam, which I mentioned earlier.

We reacted to those acts of terrorism by expelling Iranian residents from our country. Our action was prompted by reasons of internal security, as no state in the world could be expected to condone acts against its internal security from foreigners residing within it.

It is worthy to note that parallel to the acts I have just described, the Barazani followers, now harbored and supported in Iran, began to commit similar acts of terrorism in the northern part of our country.

In addition, the Khomeiny authorities started to prevent the return of Iraqi Kurds from Iran to Iraq and to persecute any remnants of families when some of their members had succeeded in returning to the homeland.

All these acts were accompanied by a formidable public media propaganda campaign, unprecedented in its fanatical and sectarian religious overtones. Iraq, in fact, was not alone in witnessing those acts. Similar actions were attempted in Kuwait, Saudi Arabia, Bahrain, and the United Arab Emirates.

Mr. President,

Khomeiny's scheme through the so-called Islamic Revolution was to destabilize the region through inciting religious sectarian strife. We in Iraq refuse such a medieval ideology. Our concept is secular, and we do not mingle affairs of state and religion. Revolutions cannot be imposed from the outside against the free will of the people. We are bound to stand against Khomeiny's theories and practices in defense of our security, well-being and independence. The Khomeiny authorities accuse us of fomenting civil strife in Iran amongst the national minorities. The said authorities have lost sight of the fact that the Arabs, Kurds, Turkomans, Baluchi and the other national minorities in Iran, contributed in the national struggle which brought the downfall of the Shah. It was natural, therefore, that those minorities expected the so-called Islamic revolution to grant them their national rights. Iraq has nothing to do with their renewed struggle to achieve national aspirations. Why should we? What inherent hostility could we possibly have against Iran, the Iranian peoples or Khomeiny, for that matter, had it not been for the most dangerous of all forms of interference in our internal affairs?

Mr. President,

Iraq has put before the Council in Document S/9323 dated July 11, 1969, some historical facts and details regarding the legal status of the Iraqi-Iranian border up to 1969. This document will be brought up to date and presented to you in order to show that the policy of territorial expansion is a cardinal policy of successive Iranian Governments. That policy has always followed the same pattern: first, an Iranian allegation, then denial of legal obligations, to be followed by a new legal instrument designed to secure a territorial gain for Iran, and then the same sequence repeating itself.

The Algiers Agreement of March 6, 1975 was no exception to this pattern. The political situation in our

278

region during the period preceding that date witnessed the emergence of the Shah in Iran as the policeman of the region. The expansion plans and pretentions of the Shah were met by us with firm adherence to sovereignty, full independence and non-interference in internal affairs of States. Neither ideologically nor pragmatically did we fit into the picture. Hence, the reactionary rebellion of Barazani was adopted as the means for the solution.

The idea was to disrupt our national unity in order to overcome our resistance. The Shah provided huge quantities of sophisticated armaments to Barazani. The Iranian army gave important logistical support to the rebellion. Israel in turn armed and trained Kurdish rebels under Barazani from 1965 to 1975, as well as providing them with instructors. This was reported by the New York Times of September 29, 1980, which published a report on the disclosure of what it termed the "tightly suppressed secret" by Menachem Begin on the date just mentioned. The said report indicates that the Israeli assistance started under Eshkol and grew under Golda Meir and Rabin, and that the last Israeli instructor left when Barazani was evacuated in 1975. While our people were valiantly fighting against the rebellion, a new factor emerged in relation to the balance of the military situation, that is, the October 1973 War. With a view to creating the appropriate conditions which would enable us to participate with our Arab brethren in that battle, my Government decided to seek a political settlement through peaceful means with Iran. Consequently, when the late President of Algeria Houari Boumediene offered to mediate, we accepted.

Against this political background, the Algiers Agreement was negotiated and concluded in the form of a package deal. It had both political and juridical aspects. The spirit of the agreement was that the parties decided "in all sincerity" to conclude it with a view to reaching "a final and permanent solution to all the problems existing between their two countries", and that the arrangements agreed upon were "in application of the principles of territorial integrity and inviolability of borders and non-interference in internal affairs." The elements of the package deal were the definitive demarcation of land frontiers on the basis of legal agreements between the two countries, delimitation of water frontiers in the Shatt-al-Arab according to the Thalweg line, the restoration of security and mutual trust along the common boundaries and the commitment to exercise strict and effective control over them with a view to putting an end to all acts of infiltration of a subversive character, no matter where they originate from. The most fundamental obligation which the two parties assumed, and which indicated the package deal nature of the Agreement, was Paragraph 4 thereof in which the Parties considered the three elements just mentioned as "integral elements of a comprehensive solution, and, hence, any impairment of any of their components shall naturally be contrary to the spirit of the Agreement."

In order to translate these arrangements into more concrete instruments, a Joint Iraqi-Iranian Ministerial Commission was established in which Algeria participated and a Treaty on International Frontiers and Good Neighborliness, along with three Protocols and Annexes, were signed in Baghdad on June 13, 1975. In this connection, it is worthy noting that Article 4 of the Treaty on International Frontiers and Good Neighborliness explicitly consecrated the nature of the package deal of the Algiers Agreement.

Mr. President,

Upon the entry into force of the Frontiers Treaty, Iran acquired sovereignty over half of the Shatt-al-Arab; hence, securing an early advantage. In return, Iraq did not receive the land areas that Iran had trespassed, contrary to its international obligations. This was the situation when the Shah toppled from power. Upon the installation of the new regime in Teheran, the Government of Iraq saw fit to allow the new government a period of grace before pressing for the completion of the process of returning the areas which belong to Iraq.

Notwithstanding Iraq's positive attitude towards the changes in Iran, Teheran's new rulers soon revealed their enmity towards Iraq through their official pronoucements and information media. They started to display Iran's renewed intentions of territorial ambitions and aggressive expansionism.

I should like to quote here a few examples of the scores of statements made by high Iranian officials and directed against Iraq and the Arab countries:

On March 21, 1980 in a statement delivered by Khomeiny's son on behalf of his father, he declared that, and I quote, "We must do our utmost to export our revolution to other parts of the world and renounce the concept of keeping the revolution within our own boundaries."

On April 3, 1980, Ghotbzadeh, then Foreign Minister of Iran, declared that Aden and Baghdad belong to Iran; on April 9th, he further added that his government had decided to overthrow the Iraqi Government. Bani Sadr, the President of Iran, in an interview with "An Nahar Al-Arabi Wal Dawli" in its issue no. 151 of March 24, 1980, stated that Iran would not evacuate nor return the

281

three Arab islands Iran had occupied by force in 1971; and that the Arab countries of United Arab Emirates, Qatar, Oman, Kuwait and Saudi Arabia are not independent states. Khomeiny was quoted in the "Joumhuri Islami" dated April 19, 1980 as saying that "the Iraqi people should liberate itself from the claws of the enemy; it is the duty of the Iraqi people and army to turn against this un-Islamic party in Iraq." In an interview with Radio Monte Carlo on April 30, Ghotbzadeh denied the Arabs the right to reclaim the three islands of Abu Musa and the Greater and Lesser Tumbs in the Gulf, because he said all the countries around the Gulf are historically part of Iranian territory. In an interview with "Al Khaleej" newspaper of May 1st, Ghotbzadeh was asked whether he did not consider Khomeiny's statement to the effect that if Iraq continued in its policies he, Khomeiny, would go to Baghdad to liberate the Iraqi people, as interference in the internal affairs of Iraq; Ghotbzadeh replied: "This could not be considered as interference in Iraq's affairs since we consider the Islamic nation as one, and the Imam (Khomeiny) is a religious leader, he is thus a leader for the Iraqi people and all Islamic peoples, as he feels responsible for Iran, so he feels responsibility towards Iraq."

In addition, the present Iranian government committed another grave violation of the Algiers Agreement. While the said Agreement enjoined Iran to restore security and trust along its common boundaries with Iraq, and to exercise strict and effective control for the purpose of putting an end to all infiltrations of a subversive character it openly violated this fundamental obligation. It brought over and offered refuge in Iran to the remnants of the former rebellion against Iraq, namely, the sons of Barazani and his followers.

With the explicit support of the ruling authorities in Iran, those groups used Iranian territory as a base for hreatening and interfering in the internal security and national integrity of Iraq. Repeated Iraqi demands for the eturn of Iraqi lands not only were frustrated, but also vere met with new territorial claims as I have indicated.

Unlike the Ayatollah Khomeiny, Mr. President, Iraq till has faith in this international organization. Iraq has n fact twice brought complaints against Iran before this Council. The first was in 1971 when Iran occupied, by orce, the three strategic Arab islands in the Arabian Gulf, and that complaint was brought on behalf of the Sheikhdom of Ras al-Khaimah. It is sad to state that the ailure of the Security Council to effect Iranian withdrawal from the occupied islands served to encourage the Shah and his successors to pursue their dream of establishng Persian hegemony over the whole of the Arabian Gulf.

Iraq's second complaint before this Council was made n 1974 after Iranian acts of aggression committed across he same borders which are the cause of the present conflict. Again United Nations mediation failed to stop ranian expansionist ambitions and Iran engaged, as I have already stated, in blatant military interference in Northern Iraq.

Mr. President, the prelude to the present conflict was not limited to what I have mentioned so far. There were not less than fifty-seven violations of Iraqi airspace by Iranian military aircraft between the period from February 23, 1979 to May 28, 1980. In addition to the repeated Iranian artillery fire on Iraqi territories and border police posts, there were more than fifteen intensive Iranian bombardments between August 26, 1979 and June 3, 1980. Most of the bombardments originated from the Iraqi lands withheld by Iran, namely, Zein-al-Qaws, Saif-Saad and Maimak. Iraqi and foreign vessels navigating the Shatt-al-Arab were often subjected to attacks by Iran.

All these incidents and violations were the subject of numerous official notes delivered to the Iranian Foreign Ministry and the Iranian Embassy in Baghdad, and to which no Iranian replies were received.


Mr. President,

Declarations were made by official circles in Iran that it no longer considered itself bound by the Algiers Agreement. On June 19, 1979, Mr. Sadiq Tabtabai, the political assistant of the Iranian Ministry of the Interior said that Iran did not implement the Algiers Agreement. In a statement broadcast from Iran's television network on September 15, 1980, General Falahi, Deputy Joint Chief of Staff of the Iranian Army, said that Iran does not recognize the Algiers Agreement, and that the areas of Zein-al Qaws and Saif-Saad are Iranian as well as the Shatt-al Arab. The latest was that of President Bani Sadr himself. He was reported by Teheran Radio on September 17, 1980 to have said, inter alia, the following to the French News Agency: "On the political plane, Iran has not fulfilled the Algiers Agreement signed with Iraq in 1975... The Shah's regime itself did not fulfill it." All our persistent efforts through diplomatic and political channels to have Iran keep its obligations were in vain. Consequently, we were left with no choice but to re-assert our rights under international law by taking possession of our lands. In response to the position of the Iranian Government, which it has clearly stated through word and deed to terminate the Algiers Agreement of March 6, 1975, my Government decided to consider the said Agreement as terminated on the grounds of the provisions of Paragraph 4 thereof to which I referred earlier.

In pronouncing that decision, we strongly emphasized

284

that we have no territorial ambitions in Iran. Furthermore, we openly declared that we have no intention whatsoever of waging war with Iran, or extending the scope of the conflict beyond the limits of defending our sovereignty and legitimate rights.

The response of the Government of Iran to this legitimate position was to escalate the situation to total war through indiscriminate hostile acts involving the use of force against Iraqi and foreign vessels in the Shatt-al-Arab. Iran started bombing civilian centers and economic establishments inside our country. Consequently, my Government was left with no choice but to direct preventive strikes against military targets in Iran. There was, to borrow from a well-known case, "a necessity of self-defense, instant, overwhelming, leaving no choice of means and no moment of deliberation" (The Caroline, 1837). In taking those actions, my Government clearly and openly declared that Iranian civilian targets shall not be the object of military strikes unless Iran continues to strike at such targets in Iraq. Thus, our actions involve "nothing unreasonable or excessive, since the act justified by the necessity of self-defense must be limited by that necessity and kept clearly within it" (ibid).


Mr. President,

Iraq does not stand for war, nor does it believe in the use of force in international relations. Iraq, as its record proves, and particularly so in its frontier relations with Iran, has always adhered strictly and honorably to the letter and spirit of its international commitments. But at the same time, Iraq does not accept any form of threat or aggression against its sovereignty and dignity, and we are ready to make all the sacrifices necessary for the preservation of our legitimate rights and vital interests.

Concern has been expressed regarding the repercussions of the recent events on the world economic interests which might be adversely affected. Let me point out at once that Iraq is keen to protect the economic interests of other nations, within its ability. So any attempt to widen the character and scope of our problem with Iran would endanger the situation. Such an attitude would invite further foreign intervention in our part of the world which we earnestly want to keep outside the sphere of influence and rivalry of the Big Powers in the interest of international peace and security and world economic prosperity.

Mr. President,

It is well known to the Council and the international community as a whole, that Iraq has responded favorably and positively to the various calls addressed to it and the efforts made to stop the fighting and move towards a peaceful settlement of the present conflict. We have cooperated with the Security Council from the outset and have participated in its deliberations. Our response to this Council's resolution N° 479 of September 28, 1980 was prompt and positive; our President informed the Secretary General (document S/14203 of September 20, 1980) that... "we naturally accept the above-mentioned resolution... and declare our readiness to abide by it if the Iranian side does likewise", and that "we hope that the Security Council will take the necessary measures to urge the Iranian side to abide by that resolution."

Iran, Mr. President, officially rejected the call of the Council. Moreover, in response to the good-will mission undertaken by the President of Pakistan and the Secretary General of the Islamic Conference, we offered a unilateral cease-fire from October 5-8, which actually went into effect at dawn on October 5th. Iran's response was a large-scale attack on land, sea and in the air.

Mr. President,

I should finally like to reaffirm before the Council that Iraq does not stand for the use of force in international relations. We firmly believe in the peaceful settlement of disputes. We fully realize that as a developing country we need to utilize all our energies and resources for social and economic development. But at the same time we cannot stand idle against any encroachment upon our legitimate sovereign rights in our total territories, our security, peace or well-being.

Thank you.

# APPENDIX
# XVII

## STATEMENT OF MR. SADDAM HUSSEIN, PRESIDENT OF THE REPUBLIC OF IRAQ, ON THE IRAQ-IRAN CONFLICT BEFORE THE THIRD SUMMIT MEETING ON THE ISLAMIC CONFERENCE
## 19-22 RABI'L-AL AWAL, 1401, JANUARY 25-28, 1981
## TAIF, SAUDI ARABIA

In the name of God, the Merciful and the Compassionate
Brother President
Your Highness Prince Fahd
Brothers

I should like at the outset to express on behalf of the Delegation of Iraq and on my own behalf our sincere thanks and gratitude to his Majesty King Khalid bin Abdul-Aziz, to His Highness Prince Fahd for all the untiring efforts in organizing this August Conference and ensuring all means of its success. We pray to God Almighty now that the leaders of the Islamic States are gathered in the holy city of Mecca in the land of divine revelation and the starting point of the great message of Islam to inspire us with determination, strength and reason for the purpose of achieving the great goals for which we are gathered here, and of realizing positive results in the service of our holy religion and our believing people.

Iraq has embarked upon the initiative of requesting the convening of a special meeting to discuss its conflict with Iran in order to present in detail all the dimensions and the historical background of the conflict. This is in order to explain to Their Majesties and Excellencies the Kings and Presidents of the Islamic States and their representatives the present war going on in our region and which was imposed upon us by Iran.

Any problem cannot be divorced from its historical framework and direct causes. The efforts to solve the present outstanding conflict in a just and honorable manner require a precise understanding of the nature of the conflict and the light of its correct historical background.

The problem between Iraq and Iran goes back to more than 450 years in history. If we want to trace it chronologically, it is not a mere boundary problem, nor is it a minor conflict over navigational rights. It is much wider than that, as the problem signifies Iran's expansionist ambitions in the neighboring and adjacent Arab areas.

Historically, and since 1520, eighteen Treaties have been concluded between the Persian State and its western neighbor regarding its relations therewith, including the question of borders. On all occasions, the Persian State chose the opportunity to violate the said Treaties whether by word or deed.

The Persian and Ottoman States concluded the first Treaty in 1520 after Iran had occupied and annexed some areas of Iraq, which was then part of the Ottoman State. The Persian State was forced by that Treaty to withdraw from the territories it had occupied. That Treaty was followed by others, notably the Treaty of 1639 which was concluded at Zehab, and which included for the first time the basis for the delimitation of boundaries between the two States. The said Treaty was affirmed by the Treaty concluded at Kurdan in 1746, which provided that the boundaries between the two States were those provided for in the Treaty of 1639.

It is worth noting that in both of those Treaties, the Persian State was forced to withdraw from Arab lands within the Ottoman State against which, due to reasons of geography, the Persian State used to trespass.

Subsequent to the war that took place between the Ottoman and Persian States, the First Treaty of Erzeroum was concluded in 1823. This Treaty confirmed the previous treaties concluded in relation to frontiers, especially that of 1746, and considered them binding and still in force. In this new Treaty, the two Parties especially emphasized the prevention of interference by the Persian State in whatever manner in the affairs of Iraq, which was at the time part of the Ottoman State. But the boundary problems between the two states continued because of the continuation of Persian territorial encroachments and despite the Treaty already referred to. Due to the emergence of competition between Tzarist Russia and Britain to control the area, the Ottoman and Persian States considered reaching final and firm borders between themselves. In this connection, Tzarist Russia and Britain performed the role of mediators, and the Second Treaty of Erzeroum was concluded in 1847. In that Treaty, the Persian State obtained its first territorial expansion at the expense of Arab rights. The boundaries before 1847 were to the east of the Island of Abadan in the area of Shatt-al-Arab, as is shown on Map No. 1 of the Maps Pamphlet distributed to you, and they were to run along the eastern bank of Shatt-al-Arab as is also shown on Map No. 2.

In this connection, although Shatt-al-Arab with all its waters remained in the hands of the Ottoman State, as well as a part of Iraq which was then part of the Ottoman State, the Persian State still secured a territorial gain over the lands on the eastern bank in the form of recognizing Persian sovereignty over the port and anchorage of Mohammarah in front of al-Haffar Canal in Karun River, and the Island of Khizr, now called Abadan. The rest of the lands, towns, and ports on the said bank remained in the hands of the Ottoman State.

It is worth noting that the Treaty of 1847 explicitly provided that each Party renounced all its territorial claims in the lands of the other and undertook not to interfere in its internal affairs.

Accordingly, a joint commission was set up to mark the frontiers on the maps in accordance with the frontiers description provided for in the Treaty. That task was not achieved because of the wars which took place in the area, namely, the Crimean War between the Ottoman State and Russia (1854-1856), the British-Persian War (1856-1857), and the Balkan War (1876-1878). So, the situation remained stagnant until 1911 when a difference arose regarding the implementation of the Treaty of Erzeroum as a result of the refusal of the Persian State to abide by it.

Consequently, the Protocol of Teheran was concluded in 1911, and contained the agreement of the Ottoman and Persian States to set up a joint commission to meet in Istanbul to decide upon and fix the frontier line between the two countries in a detached and neutral spirit. Afterwards, a technical commission was to apply the description of the boundaries on land according to the provisions of the Treaty of Erzeroum of 1847.

After the Parties had met in Istanbul in 1912, they could not agree on the plan of work. As a result of the mediation of Russia and Britain again, the Istanbul Protocol of 1913 was concluded and signed by representatives of both parties and the mediating powers. The said Protocol provided a clear description of the frontier line between the two countries, which was similar to that of the Treaty of Erzeroum, 1847. The Protocol provided for demarcating the frontier line on land and constructing the necessary pillars by a commission the tasks of which were specifically determined. The Protocol also provided that any sector of the frontiers demarcated on land were to be considered as finally determined and were not to be subject to any amendment or revision thereafter.

In this Protocol, the Persian State once again secured a territorial gain at the expense of Arab rights. The Ottoman State ceded part of the Arab territory in the Shatt-al-Arab in front of Mohammarah Port and for a distance of four miles. Hence, the frontier line in this area was to run in the mid-channel for the said distance and to revert back to following the eastern bank of the river until it reached the sea, leaving under Persian control a number of islands, as shown on Map No. 3 of the Maps Pamphlet, already distributed to you.

Consequently, a joint commission was set up according to the Protocol, and composed of representatives of Russia, Britain, the Ottoman State and Iran. The commission demarcated the frontier line on land in accordance with the description mentioned in the Protocol from the point of confluence of Shatt-al-Arab with the Arab Gulf in the south till Ararat in the north. The commission completed its work in October 1914, along with the records of its meetings, decisions, maps, and the construction of 126 frontier pillars. These are the documents known as "The Proceedings of the Meetings of the Commission for the Delimitation of the Turco-Persian Frontiers, 1914". Thus, one should assume that the boundaries became final and recognized by the two Parties.

When Iraq became independent from the Ottoman Empire after the First World War, it succeeded the said Empire, in accordance with the rules of International

Laws, in the Turkish Treaties relating to the Iraqi territory, the last of which were the 1913 Protocol and the Proceedings of the Frontier Delimitation Commission of 1914. It was therefore to be expected that Iran should not pose any problem to Iraq in this respect. But, in fact, in the early days of Iraq's independence, and particularly in 1932, Iran committed a number of encroachments against Iraq's territory, and declared its non-adherence to the 1913 Protocol and the 1914 Proceedings. It started to commit a series of acts of armed intervention in the Shatt-al-Arab and territorial encroachments by constructing border posts guarded by military forces inside Iraq. These encroachments were the subject of the complaint launched by Iraq in the League of Nations in 1934. The League recommended that the dispute be settled through direct negotiations.

The said conflict came to an end by the conclusion of the Border Treaty between Iraq and Iran on July 4, 1937. Article 1 of that Treaty considered the 1913 Protocol and the Proceedings of the Meetings of the Frontier Delimitation Commission of 1914 as vaild and that the two Parties were bound to observe them, and provided, accordingly, that the boundary line between the two States was that defined and traced by the above-mentioned Commission of 1914.

As regards the Shatt-al-Arab, Iran expanded again in accordance with this treaty, at the expense of Iraq's territorial sovereignty, and obtained a new territorial gain in addition to what it had already gained in accordance with the 1913 treaty, namely, Iraq ceded a small part of the Shatt-al-Arab in front of Abadan to Iran, wherein the frontier line runs along the Thalweg for a distance of about four miles.

With the exception of that, the boundary line between Iraq and Iran remained at the low water level at the eastern bank of the Shatt-al-Arab according to the delimitation of the frontiers described in the Proceedings of the Meetings of the Frontier Delimitation Commission of 1914. This is shown on Map No. 4 of the Maps Pamphlet, also distributed to you.

Article 3 of the 1937 Treaty provided for the appointment of a commission for erecting the frontier pillars the location of which had been fixed and constructed by the 1914 Commission and for fixing additional pillars which it considered useful to erect. The purpose was, as declared in the preamble of the Treaty, to definitely settle the frontier question between the two countries. The Frontier Pillars Commission was constituted in 1938 and proceeded with its work until it was interrupted in 1940 because of Iran's withdrawal from it when it realized that it had committed a large territorial encroachment on Iraqi lands in the area of Um Sheer in the Governorate of Missan in southeastern Iraq. Shortly afterwards, Iran reverted to causing the same boundary problems to Iraq which it used to raise before the conclusion of the 1937 Treaty. It started again to encroach upon Iraqi lands in numerous areas by constructing armed border posts and committed acts of armed intervention in the Shatt-al-Arab, calling for the navigation therein to be entrusted to the competence of a joint commission with legislative, executive and judicial powers, despite the fact that it is a national river subject to full Iraqi sovereignty, as its name indicates.

Iran continued to raise these problems to Iraq during the era of both the monarchical and the republican regimes. It escalated its position, despite the fact that Iraq continued to seek through diplomatic channels to settle the dispute and forge normal relations with Iran according to the legal obligations in force of both countries.

Despite all that, Iran followed anew the same path which it used to pursue in the past. It declared unilaterally on April 19, 1969 the termination of the Border Treaty of 1937.

Accordingly, Iran continued to deny its international obligations and violation of Iraqi sovereignty over land and in the Shatt-al-Arab. It persisted in its flagrant interference in the internal affairs of Iraq through all means. The situation became critical, to the extent of committing an armed aggression against Iraq in certain border areas, which prompted Iraq to launch a complaint against Iran in the Security Council in 1974.

Iraq sought all means to settle the dispute with Shahinshahi Iran in accordance with the rules of international law. But Iraq's efforts were met at times with refusal and with procrastination at others.

Iran is used to choosing every given opportunity to call for the re-delimitation of the boundaries in Shatt-al-Arab on the basis of the Thalweg, i.e. the line of the deep navigable channel. The aim is clear, naturally, to achieve a new territorial gain at the expense of Iraq by obtaining half of Shatt-al-Arab for a long distance in the river.

This situation continued from 1969 after the Revolution, until 1975 when the Algiers Agreement of that year came about.


Mr. President,
Brothers,

Before we deal in detail with the Algiers Agreement, we should like to explain to you its immediate background, for that would shed an enormous light on its paragraphs and fundamental objectives.

Since the Revolution of July 17, 1968, Iraq was and still is one of the firm adherents to the policy of non-alignment, which is based on the principles of non-interference in others' internal affairs, respect of national sovereignty of all States, and ensuring peace and security in the world.

In addition, our foreign policy does not tolerate any interference in the independence of Iraq and the Arab countries, our sovereignty, territorial integrity in any form, from any side or on any pretext whatsoever. We have adhered to this policy and these principles in our foreign policy, proceeding from a profound need and a long national and Pan-Arab experience in this regard. For, as you are no doubt aware, any disequilibrium in the basis of State relations would certainly lead to impairing the rights and sovereignty of one side in favor of another.

In order to avoid this phenomenon, which has often led to tension and crisis, it is imperative to base international cooperation on rules that aim at the achievement of joint interests within the framework of non-interference in internal affairs. That is particularly true in the case of neighboring States, because the geographical reality imposes upon them a policy of good neighborliness, and non-intervention in each other's internal affairs.

In its relations with Iran, Iraq has firmly adhered to that policy, an approach which is based on a number of realities that arise from the geographical proximity and the historical ties between the people of Iraq and Iranian peoples.

Our relations with Iran have witnessed grave crises because of the policies of successive regimes in Iran which have considered Iraq and the Arab homeland, particularly the Arab Gulf area, as a sphere for domination and influence.

297

The said policies have been expressed in different forms appropriate to the particular exigencies of the time. During the rule of the Shah, arrogance, aggression, territorial expansion at the expense of the Arabs and attempts to harm Iraq's national sovereignty and the rights of the Arab nation were a constant pattern. Iraq and the Arab nation were regarded as a sphere of influence for the expansionist plans of Iranian interests. That policy has been followed throughout history by the State of Persia against its neighbors to the west, as we have shown.

When the Revolution of July 17, 1968 took place in Iraq, and at the time when Iraq was occupied with building a new society on the basis of justice and welfare, struggling to liberate its national wealth from the exploitation of colonial monopolies, adding its efforts to those of its Arab brothers in the struggle against the Zionist aggression, in that particular time, the regime of the Shah in Iran was acquiring arms at a very exceptional level. That regime was preparing itself to exercise the role of policeman in the region with the full support of, and in coordination with, the United States of America and the colonial forces in the world. That suspect policy drove the Shah to provoking independent Iraq, constantly seeking to weaken and harass the national regime brought about by the Revolution. The beginning was a propaganda campaign and numerous attempts at plotting, creating political crises, supporting the rebellious and mutinous movement in northern Iraq, openly and unabatingly, continuing with their territorial encroachments, ignoring international agreements, and committing armed aggression, in actual fact.

Then in order to achieve his ambitions, the Shah began to exert military pressure directly or indirectly, believing that military means would ensure the achievement of his expansionist aims and ambitions.

The Shah began to support the reactionary secessionist rebellion in northern Iraq on a large scale and hence started to exercise a direct role in the field in order to dismember Iraq.

The Shah's support for the secessionist rebellion was limitless. He provided the reactionary leadership of the rebellion with huge quantities of modern and sophisticated armaments and put at its disposal all his material, military, political and media facilities, including the services of his advanced intelligence apparatus. He presented it with direct military support by sending contingents of his army to the areas of fighting, and amassed his troops along all the borders with Iraq. All that took place under the care and with the encouragement of the United States, and the participation of the Zionist entity through its representatives, whose Prime Minister declared on September 29, 1980 that the Zionist entity had provided Barazani with weapons, equipment, instructors, and provided the rebels with training from 1965 to 1975.

Iraq fought a bitter conflict against that agent clique and the aggressive policies of the Shah, in order to defend its sovereignty and national unity. Iraq suffered sixty-thousand casualties between martyrs and wounded of the armed forces, personnel and civil population, aside from enormous material losses. The military situation reached a dangerous point when the Shah advanced his troops on numerous occasions to fight directly against our forces on various fronts in view of supporting the military position of the agent rebellion.

These were the conditions which dictated upon us, and indeed forced us, to work towards a political solution. Hence, when the late President of Algeria, Houari Boumediene, may God rest his soul in peace, took the initiative of communicating with us and Iran, we agreed to that initiative, and the Algiers Agreement was concluded on March 6, 1975, under these circumstances.

The spirit of the Algiers Agreement appears in its Preamble, which provided that the Parties had reached the Agreement in order to arrive at a final and permanent solution to all existing problems between the two countries, in application of the principles of territorial integrity, inviolability of frontiers and non-interference in internal affairs. The four Paragraphs of the Agreement provided the following:

1. Carrying out a definitive demarcation of terrestrial frontiers on the basis of the Istanbul Protocol of 1913 and the Proceedings of the Meetings of the Delimitation Commission of the Turco-Persian Frontiers of 1914.

2. The delimitation of the fluvial frontiers in Shatt-al-Arab according to the Thalweg line. We have already explained that the Thalweg line runs in the middle of the deep, navigable waters.

3. The undertaking of the two Parties to restore security and confidence along the common frontiers and the obligation to exercise a strict and effective control over the said frontiers for the purpose of cessation of all acts of infiltrations of a subversive character.

4. The agreement to consider all the above-mentioned arrangements as indivisible elements of a comprehensive solution, and that hence any violation of which shall naturally be considered as against the spirit of the Algiers Agreement. That is to say, that any violation of any of the three interconnected paragraphs will be considered a violation of the paragraphs as a whole. This is the Algiers Agreement and these are its circumstances.

In order to put these arrangements into the form of a document containing the technical details, a joint ministerial Iraqi-Iranian Commission was established with the participation of Algeria. The Treaty on State Frontiers and Good Neighborliness, its three Protocols and annexes were signed at Baghdad on June 13, 1973.

It is evident from what we have said that the Algiers Agreement represented a package deal in which the political and juridical aspects were balanced in a manner which made the violation of any of its constituent elements a violation of the balance and a reason for the collapse of the Agreement. By the same token, it follows logically that in the implementation of the settlement referred to, the two Parties should be able to achieve the balanced gains which they have agreed upon at the time and in accordance with the circumstances to which we have already referred. But what happened in fact was that Iran scored an instant and direct gain as soon as the Algiers agreement entered into force, for its position in the Shatt-al-Arab became that of a partner in sovereignty over a large part of it. This was because of the redelimitation of the frontiers in the Shatt-al-Arab on the basis of the Thalweg. As for the Iraqi lands upon which Iran had encroached, they were not delivered to Iraq before the fall of the regime of the Shah. We were in the process of receiving them when the Revolution in Iran began; their delivery was in fact delayed and when the new rulers took over they did not return these lands to us. Iran thus continued to occupy Iraqi lands dear to us. Also, they have not been delivered since the fall of the Shah's regime as shown in Maps Nos. 6 and 7 of the Maps Pamphlet, already distributed to you.


Mr President,

The new regime in Iran came to power after the fall of the Shah's regime, and the situation regarding the implementation of the Algiers Agreement was as I explained.

Iran has achieved a new territorial gain which it benefitted from at the expense of Iraq, but Iraq has not obtained what was due to it according to all the international agreements concluded before 1975, and the 1975 Agreement itself.

Despite that, we expected or hoped that the new rulers would open a new page in their relations with Iraq and the Arab nation. On this basis, Iraq, on its part, took numerous positive initiatives towards achieving that goal.

We addressed an official Note to the Iranian government on February 13, 1979, in which we explained Iraq's established policy of forging the closest fraternal ties and relations of cooperation with the peoples neighboring Iraq, and particulary with Iran, on the basis of respect of sovereignty, and non-interference in internal affairs. We also expressed our sympathy and support for the struggle being waged by the Iranian peoples for freedom, justice and progress, pointing out Iraq's appreciation of the victory achieved by the Iranian peoples.

The President of the Republic of Iraq also addressed on April 5, 1979, a telegram to Khomeiny on the occasion of the declaration of the Islamic Republic, in which he expressed his congratulations, and Iraq's desire that the new republican regime would open wider opportunities to serve the friendly Iranian peoples in a manner that promotes Iran's role in the service of peace and justice in the world, and forges the strongest relations of friendship and neighborliness with the Arab countries in general and Iraq in particular. Khomeiny, however, replied to that telegram in a manner contrary to the courtesy due to Heads of State, and particularly that between Muslim leaders.

Despite that we sent an invitation to Mr. Mehdi Bazargan, the head of the interim Iranian government, to visit Iraq and conduct negotiations regarding bilateral relations and the bases of joint cooperation. On August 2, 1979, the Vice-Chairman of the Revolution Command Council renewed the invitation in a letter to Mr. Bazargan on the occasion of the month of Ramadan.

In the ministerial Meeting of the Coordinating Bureau of Nonaligned Countries which was held in Colombo in 1979, Iraq was behind the inclusion of a paragraph in the final declaration welcoming Iran's withdrawal from CENTO. Iraq also welcomed Iran's application to join the Movement of Nonaligned Countries and the adoption of a recommendation to that effect at the Summit Conference in Havana.

In my statement to the Sixth Summit Conference of Nonaligned States held in Havana, I welcomed Iran's membership in the Movement. I personally emphasized in two meetings with the former Foreign Minister of Iran, Mr. Ibrahim Yazdi, in Havana during the Nonaligned Summit Conference of 1979, Iraq's desire to establish relations of cooperation and good neighborliness with Iran. We have expressed our readiness to meet with Iranian leaders in order to deal with the problems of bilateral relations by peaceful means. Our Foreign Minister also emphasized this approach in his meeting with the Foreign Minister of Iran in September 1979 at the United Nations Headquarters in New York. When the President of the Republic of Iran, Mr. Bani Sadr, assumed his office, our Ambassador in Teheran visited him upon my personal instructions, on February 20, 1980, to convey to him personal congratulations on that occasion.

We have taken all these steps in order to put our relations with Iran on correct and positive bases. Our starting point was the policy of good neighborliness, and the desire to establish normal relations with Iran. But in their well-known arrogance, the new rulers of Iran turned away from all these initiatives. They were determined with full intention to abuse Iraq, to expand at its expense, and to go along the same hostile and expansionist path taken by the Shah of Iran. This appeared from the statements made by them, and their deeds and practices, regarding which we have distributed to the distinguished delegations dossiers containing ample and documented information.

The basic motive behind the hostile position adopted by the new regime in Iran is the desire to expand at the expense of Iraq and the Arab countries in the Arab Gulf region and to interfere in its internal affairs. This has now taken a new cover, which is what the Iranian high officials term as the exportation of the revolution to the neighboring countries.

You all know that this is the policy of the new rulers of Iran which tries to export what is known as their new revolution and its principles to all Islamic countries. There is no one amongst you who does not know that they are interfering in the internal affairs of all Islamic countries.

Iran's new rulers have behaved on this basis, and declared that explicitly on various occasions.

Mr. President,
Brothers,

The attitude and intentions of the Iranian regime in the so-called exportation of the revolution did not stop at making statements, but passed that limit in endeavors to transform it into actual reality against Iraq and other Islamic countries. This took place under the direct supervision of the regime's leaders. In Qom and Teheran, specialized institutions and quarters were established to plot against Iraq and the neighboring states.

The plotting against Iraq was escalated through the commission of acts of terrorism and sabotage by Iranians, which the Iranian authorities helped to infiltrate inside Iraq, assisted by Iranian residents in Iraq and individuals of Iranian descent. In fact, these groups committed during the first half of 1980 ugly terrorist acts, from which not even the Muslim praying masses in the mosques escaped. All these terrorist acts were directed from Qom, as has been established by the instructions issued and broadcast daily to the agents of the Iranian regime from the official Iranian broadcasting stations, which even included instructions as to manufacturing local bombs. This is in addition to the official statements emanating from the responsible Iranian officials which instigated murder, terrorism, and sabotage. The most cruel act of terrorism was the hurling of bombs at a huge student gathering held at al-Mustansiriyah University in Baghdad on April 1, 1980, which resulted in the killing and wounding of a large number of students. A similar act was the hurling of bombs on April 5, 1980 from the Iranian school in Waziriyah onto the funeral procession of the martyrs who were killed at the al-Mustansiriyah incident. In this second operation, some Iranian officials of the Iranian School's teachers participated.

In all these incidents, Iranian agents were caught, and the security forces seized large quantities of arms, ammunition and money, which were given by the ruling authorities in Teheran for the disposal of those agents. It is worth noting that the objectives and organization of this agent organ, connected with Qom, were uncovered for us by one of its leaders whose confessions were broadcast by Iraqi Radio and Television at the time.

The Embassy of the Republic of Iraq in Teheran was the target of numerous acts of aggression, provocation, and threats of burning and occupation. Hundreds of demonstrations were organized against Iraq with the full knowledge of the Iranian authorities. The Iraqi Ministry of Foreign Affairs and the Iraqi Embassy in Teheran sent numerous notes of protest to the Iranian government regarding these acts. The Iraqi Ambassador in Teheran called on the Vice-Prime Minister of Information, the Prime Minister, and the responsible officials of the Iranian Foreign Ministry in connection therewith. All this in addition to calling in the Iranian Ambassador in Baghdad by the Iraqi Foreign Ministry on numerous occasions to deliver protests to him against those attacks and to request that the necessary measures be taken to stop them; copies of these notes have been distributed to you.

The Consulate of the Republic of Iraq at Mohammarah was subject to the ugliest kind of aggression. It was attacked on October 11 and 26, and November 1 and 7, 1979. Its doors and windows were destroyed, its officials and guards beaten, and its records abused. All those acts were committed in order to have the Consulate closed, and it was actually closed by the Iranian side.

The Iraqi Ministry of Foreign Affairs protested against those acts on December 5, 1979, and the Iranian authorities deported the staff of the Consulate on January 11, 1980, after it had treated them very harshly; this was done before the date agreed upon by both countries for the closure of the Consulate.

It is also worth noting that the Iranian authorities have abused of the privileges of the Iraqi schools in Teheran, closed them all, and deported their staff. None escaped the Iranian attacks, not even the Iraqi Airways office in Teheran.

All these acts undoubtedly constitute a flagrant violation of neighborly relations and the principle of non-interference in the internal affairs of others and the prevention of infiltration of a subversive character regulated by the Algiers Agreement.

The rulers of Iran did not stop at that; they started, in parallel with their sabotaging activities, to renew the life of the rebellious movement in Northern Iraq. The Iranian government recalled the leaders of that movement, already defeated in 1975, from the United States of America to Iran and gave them a new support, as the Shah did formerly, and the means to threaten Iraq's security and national unity. The Iranian government has also put a special broadcasting station at the disposal of that clique which cooperated with the Zionist entity between 1965 and 1975, as has been recognized by Begin in his above-mentioned speech.

I have referred a while ago to the question of the Iraqi lands which Iran did not deliver to Iraq despite its long encroachment thereupon, as provided by the Algiers Agreement, and how the fall of the Shah's regime led to a standstill in their delivery. The new regime came to power and we granted it the opportunity to implement Iran's obligations. But what happened with the advent of the era of the new regime is that instead of delivering them back to Iraq, with the beginning of tension, the Iranian military presence in those Iraqi lands increased. Those very areas themselves, being areas of Iraq, became the source of armed attacks on the Iraqi border region. The attacks were coupled with persistent violations of Iraqi airspace by the Iranian Air Force. For example, we should like to mention to you that the number of violations of Iraqi airspace by the Iranian Air Force reached 249 for the period from February 1979 to September 1980. This is recorded in the official notes sent by Iraq to Iran through the Iraqi Ministry of Foreign Affairs. The number of incidents of firing across the frontiers and on the border posts and attacks thereon, artillery shelling, obstructing navigation in the Shatt-al-Arab, and shelling of civilian targets, reached 244 for the period of June 1979 to September 1980. This is also recorded in official Notes. Civilian aircraft were fired at three times and one airplane was forced by the Iranian Air Force inside Iraqi airspace, to land in Iran during the period of August to September 1980. The bombardment of economic installations including petroleum installations took place seven times during the period of January to September 1980. All these violations which flagrantly contravene the Algiers Agreement, and any principle of normal relations with Iran, have been documented in official Notes forwarded to the Iranian government, hoping that it would abide by law and reason. The number of official Notes forwarded to the Iranian government reached 293, which you will find amongst the documents distributed.

On September 4, 1980, a dangerous turning point in the chain of those violations occurred. The Iranian military forces used American-made heavy artillery of 175 mm caliber to bombard peaceful Iraqi towns. Thus, the towns of Khanaqin, Mandali, Zurbatiyah and the oil region known as Naft-khaneh, where the savage bombardment started, were all exposed to heavy shelling which resulted in severe loss in lives and damage to property. It is worth mentioning that concentrated savage bombardment was carried out from the areas of Zein al-Qaws, Saif Saad and Maimak, which are part of Iraqi lands usurped by Iran, and which are recognized as such and documented in all international treaties concluded between Iraq and Iran including the 1975 Agreement.

At noon on September 7, 1980, savage bombardment again occurred in the same manner. In turn, we called the Chargé d'Affaires of the Iranian Embassy in Baghdad to the Foreign Ministry on that date and delivered a Note to him. In it we stated that Iranian military units had encroached upon numerous areas of Iraqi territory as was the case with, inter alia, Zein al-Qaws, and that the said encroachments had continued. We requested him to convey to his government that it should immediately end those encroachments by withdrawing the Iranian military forces from areas encroached upon. But the Iranian forces continued their bombardments until nightfall of that day.

On the following day, September 8, 1980, the Iranian Chargé d'Affaires was again called in to the Foreign Ministry and we handed him another Note. In that Note we stated that the Iraqi military forces, in the exercise of our legitimate right of self-defense, were forced to end the Iranian occupation of Zein al-Qaws and regain the occupied Iraqi territories.

In the Note we expressed the hope that the Iranians would learn from that event and give back the Iraqi lands which Iran had encroached upon in previous times, as was agreed upon in the 1975 Treaty, hence avoiding the possibility of wider confrontation between the two countries. But the following days again witnessed concentrated military activities by the Iranian military forces inside the Iraqi territories that had been encroached upon. Our government found it necessary once again to call in the Iranian Chargé d'Affaires to the Foreign Ministry on September 11, 1980. He was handed a detailed Note, this time stating the following points:

First, from our observation of Iranian conduct and reactions, we have reached various conclusions, the first of which is that, because of the confusion in Iran and the disordered structure and information sources of the Iranian State, the Iranian leadership might not be aware of the fact that Iran had encroached upon Iraqi territories in contravention of International Law and past agreements between the two countries, including the Algiers Agreement of 1975. If this is so, we advise the Iranian leadership to ask the Iranian authorities responsible for frontier matters and agreements in order to ascertain our point of view and henceforth to base its action on knowledge rather than illusion.

Secondly, the Iranian leadership should realize that striking at cities populated by civilians, as it did in bombarding Khanaqin and Mandali, is neither a light matter nor a game of violence of the sort with which the Iranian officials entertain themselves at times inside Iran. Striking at Iraqi cities is considered a grave matter which should be avoided by Iran, if it does not wish relations between the two countries to deteriorate dangerously. The rulers of Iran alone will bear the responsibility of those aggressive actions before God, the Iranian peoples and world public opinion.

Thirdly, Iraq has no ambitions with regard to Iranian territories.

You will observe from the end of this note that in spite of continued aggression culminating in shelling towns and the use of Iranian Air Force against our Armed Forces, the Note was nevertheless prudent and reasonable in trying to guide Iran into knowing the historical and legal background of the problem and to avoid any misjudgment.

All these diplomatic Notes encountered deaf ears, as we did not receive any reply to them from the rulers of Iran, except one full of vituperation and threats, delivered before September 22nd.

Iran has persisted in its hostile attitude, and has not shown any respect for the 1975 Agreement. On the contrary, the Iranian officials stated publicly more than once that they do not recognize that Agreement, describing it as against the interests of Iran. They even described 'it as dead, saying — and some of you present at this session know this — that it was suspicious, and concluded under the auspices of the U.S.A. by Saddam Hussein and the Shah. These declarations were made before and after the rulers of Iran assumed power. In particular, they did not reply to the Iraqi official written Note of June 27, 1980, in which we specifically asked them whether they considered that Agreement as still valid between the two countries.

In view of all this clear evidence, it was established by the Government of the Republic of Iraq that the Iranian Government had violated the elements of the comprehensive settlement contained in the 1975 Agreement and that it had terminated it unilaterally. Consequently, the Iraqi Government decided on September 17 to consider the said Agreement and those following it and based upon it as terminated on the part of Iraq, after Iran had terminated them by word and deed. This was done in accordance with Paragraph (4) of that Agreement and Article (4) of the Treaty on State Frontiers and Good Neighborliness which was based upon it.

On that occasion, Iraq called upon the Iranian authorities to accept the new situation and act rationally and wisely in view of the exercise by Iraq of its legitimate rights and full sovereignty over all its terrestrial territories and fluvial territory in the Shatt-al-Arab.

I personally declared on that occasion that we do not desire any war with Iran, nor do we aim at widening the area of conflict with it outside the restoration of Iraq's legitimate rights of territorial sovereignty, and that Iraq has no territorial ambitions in Iran. Yet, the Iranian government escalated the conflict. It began from September 19th to shell with heavy artillery and bombard with planes densely populated areas and vital economic installations in Iraq, Iraqi and foreign incoming and outgoing commercial vessels in the Shatt-al-Arab and the navigational channels in the river as well as its approaches in the Arab Gulf, aiming meanwhile at Iraqi military forces. In addition, the Iranian authorities declared the closure of its airspace to civil aviation, and the closure of the Strait of Hormuz to Iraqi navigation, contrary to international law. It also declared public mobilization and amassed its military forces along the whole border in great concentration, and started widespread military operations. The Iranian military forces issued four military communiqués, broadcast over Radio Teheran, relative to its activities from September 18, 1980. In its third communiqué issued on September 19, 1980, Iran stated that it had used the air force in its military operations. In the same communiqué, the Iranian authorities boasted that it had set on fire the Naft-khaneh field in Iraq. All this happened before September 22, 1980, which is considered by some to be the beginning of the war between Iraq and Iran, while the war really began on September 4th, 1980, as explained by all these accidents and confirmed by military communiqués broadcast with impunity and boasting.

In face of these acts, we issued a statement on September 22, 1980, warning the ruling authorities in Iran of the consequences of that escalation and the indiscriminate strikes which they had committed, putting the full responsibility in connection therewith upon the said authorities. The Iraqi government also explained in that statement that the acts committed by Iran made it necessary to direct preventive strikes against Iranian military targets inside Iran with a view to protecting the safety, security, and vital interests of Iraq. Thus, once again Iraq was forced to exercise its right of preventive self-defense in accordance with international law in order to repel aggression.

If the war was meant to start on Iraqi territory, then let it start on Iranian territory; and when we declare that we will not withdraw our forces from Iranian territory until they put an end to the state of war, and recognize our rights as fixed in treaties concluded between us and them, this is because we want to ensure the security of Iraq, and will not withdraw without guarantees of these principles; otherwise Iran will push forth and the war will take place on Iraqi territory, destroying Iraqi economic installations and Iraqi towns. This we shall not allow.

Brothers,

It is clear from what I have said that it was Iran which started the war against Iraq on September 4, 1980, and expanded it during the following days. Iraq has not encroached upon Iran's borders or rights, when it was forced to liberate Iraqi lands in Zein al-Qaws, Saif Saad, Maimak and other Iraqi territories from the illegal Iranian occupation during the period from September 8 to September 11, 1980. Despite the Iranian escalation and widening of military operations, Iraq was patient throughout the whole period of September 11 to September 22, 1980, without crossing the frontier line into Iran. Iraq's patience came to an end when Iran widened its aggression to the extent of closing the Shatt-al-Arab, our sole national fluvial outlet to the sea, striking at our vital economic interests and peaceful cities including oil installations and the closing of the Hormuz Straits; we gained ample evidence as to the wider aggressive intention of Iran when the totality of Iraq became exposed to a wide military action from Iran. We were again forced on that date to defend ourselves by pushing the Iranian military forces deep inside the Iranian land mass in order that our towns, population, and interests remain secure from aggression.

All these acts and practices committed by the rulers of Iran left nothing of the provisions of the Algiers Agreement. The Agreement was demolished by Iran in word and deed. And it is surprising that after a month from the beginning of war on September 4, 1980, the Iranians raised the question of applying the provisions of the 1975 Treaty relating to the settlement of disputes contained in Article (6) of the said Treaty. That Article is related to the settlement of differences between the two Parties regarding the interpretation and application of the Treaty, and this presupposes the existence of the Treaty through the adherence of both parties to it. It is untenable logically and legally to have Iran allowing for itself the termination of the Treaty by word, deed, and aggression, and then come to apply a provision which presupposes, at the time of its application, the adherence of Iran to the Treaty that contains it. Any argument to the contrary would be dangerous from the viewpoint of substance, namely, that there is a contradiction between the provisions regarding this question and those contained in Article (4) of the Treaty, which incarnated the provisions of Paragraph (4) of the Algiers Agreement which I explained to you earlier. The meaning of this would be to divorce the Algiers Agreement and the Treaty from being a comprehensive settlement composed of indivisible politico-juridical elements.

Brothers,

This is how the war started between us and Iran. Despite all these bitter facts, Iraq cooperated with all international efforts to settle the conflict and end the fighting. We offered Iran peace on September 28,

314

1980, and declared that what we seek is to regain our legitimate national rights over our lands and waters. We have also declared our full readiness to withdraw from the Iranian territories and establish normal relations with Iran on the basis of respect of sovereignty and non-interference in internal affairs. We have accepted the Security Council Resolution (479) of September 28, 1980 and declared on our part a unilateral cease-fire from October 5-8, 1980, in response to the request of H.E. President Mohammed Zia-ul-Haq of Pakistan, who was undertaking a good-offices mission in his capacity as the Chairman of the Islamic Conference at the time. His Excellency did not touch upon this in his address. Do you realize, Gentlemen, how dangerous it is for one side to take the initiative of ceasing fire unilaterally while the two armies are locked in battle? The Iraqi Army was locked in battle with the Iranian Army but when President Zia-ul-Haq asked Iraq to take the initiative as a brotherly, face-saving gesture towards Iran, we responded because we do not want to humiliate the Iranian people or army; but we do not allow anyone to humiliate our people and army, nor to violate our sovereignty and security. Thus, we accepted a cease fire in spite of objections at first by a number of brothers in the leadership to this serious matter. We declared our acceptance of this step three days earlier, although Iran rejected it. We adhered to the date and time decided upon to cease fire; but Iran tried to exploit it to launch a counterattack. It is then natural that such a cease-fire is impractical and incorrect. But Iran only met these sincere intentions by its persistence in aggression, arrogance, and hostile statements. Moreover, some have misinterpreted this gesture of good will on the part of Iraq, its readiness to establish peace and the cease-fire as a weak point, in the hope that Iran, through a military solution, may impose a new *fait accompli* upon Iraq, contrary to its sovereignty, security and the interests of its people.

We have emphasized to all those who have sought to stop the war and the achievement of a peaceful settlement that we have fought in response to the Iranian aggression and for legitimate rights, and that we aim at restoring those rights and achieving a just and honorable settlement to the conflict in pushing away the evil from our sovereignty and people. We have also emphasized the necessity for the prevalence of the principle of non-acquisition by force in the relations between Iraq and the Arab Nation, on the one hand, and Iran on the other. The lands and rights which Iran has usurped by force should be restored to its lawful owners. This is one of your constant principles as well as being a principle of international law, a divine as well as a mundane law; Iraq is fully ready to restore the Iranian lands occupied in the war. By all this, a just and honorable settlement will be achieved. Hence, the appropriate climate for the establishment of normal relations between Iran, the Arabs and Iraq, away from expansionist inclinations and acts of aggression, would be achieved, as well as the appropriate conditions for all the countries in the area for evolution, development, stability, and real independence.

We emphasized these bases from a position of strength, and not a position of weakness; it is a position of strength based upon just principles, and not upon aggression, and we state once again our full desire and readiness to cooperate with all the international organizations, including the Organization of the Islamic Conference, to reach that honorable goal. Iraq did not start this war, neither did it desire its continuation. The rulers of Iran bear the full responsibility for triggering the war and its continuation, with all the disaster that it will have brought to Iran and the Islamic peoples.

Mr. President,
Brothers,

Islam does not ordain disunity and strife.  It does not allow breach of pledges and violation of agreements, for although the Algiers Agreement was imposed on us, in the conditions I have already described, yet had the new rulers of Iran adhered to it, we would have done the same, not because we believe the Algiers Agreement to be correct, but because we signed it, for we do honor agreements, whereas the new rulers of Iran violated the 1975 Agreement and therefore there can be no return to it. Moreover, Islam does not accept the denial of the rights of others.  It does not approve of fanning conflicts, enmities, the use of force and violence against Muslims without a legitimate reason.

It is not part of Islam to divide the unity of the Muslims and separate them from each other.

The noble religion of Islam orders us to do good deeds and not abuse, to give everyone his due rights, and that none of us should violate the other.  Islam orders us to protect our neighbors, respect his rights and assist him, and not to usurp his lands, nor spill the blood of his sons illegally.

The Great Prophet, Mohammed, Peace be unto Him, is the last prophet and the Seal of Messengers, the Book of God is clear, and the Sunna of His Prophet and His Companions is as clear as the sun.  There is no new prophesy, or trusteeship over Muslims, and there is nothing between the Muslim and his God except the Book of God and the Sunna of His Prophet.

The opportunity for peace still exists, and the possibility for the unity of Muslims is still real if we adhere to right, away from grudges, and return to reason, away from fanaticism and greed.

Brothers,

After all this, I am but part of you and of this honorable Conference. Whatever the Conference decides upon, we shall be party thereunto. And as we have already clearly declared over and over again, we are willing to achieve peace, not out of weakness or fear, but out of a sincere desire reflecting good will and humanity, and expressing divine principles leading in that direction.

May Allah help us all to follow His Commands and lead us to wisdom and the correct path.

Peace be upon you all.

# BIBLIOGRAPHY

ABED (S.A.): *The Role of al-Kawassem in the Arabian Gulf.* Baghdad, 1976.

ABOUL-FIDA: *Takwim-al-Bouldan,* Baghdad.

AKKAD (Salah): *Political Currents in the Arabian Gulf,* Cairo, 1965, (Arabic).

AL-AZZAWI (Abbas): *History of Iraq between Two Occupations,* VIII, Baghdad, 1956, (Arabic).

BAGHDADI (Safi-el-Din): *Observation Posts of Places and their Names,* I, Cairo, 1954, (Arabic).

BAKER (Taha): *Introduction to the History of Ancient Civilizations,* I, Baghdad, 1955, (Arabic).

BERREBY (Jean-Jacques): *The Arabian Gulf,* Beirut, 1959, (Arabic).

BERRYNE (Jacqueline): *The Discovery of the Arabian Peninsula,* Beirut, 1963, (Arabic).

BRIERE (Claire) and BLANCHET (Pierre): *Iran, la Révolution au Nom de Dieu,* Paris, Le Seuil, 1979.

BROKLMAN (Karl): *History of the Muslim Peoples* (translated into Arabic by Mounir Baalbaki and Nabih Faris), Beirut, 1955.

BUTTEN (M.): *Babylone,* Paris, 1948.

CURZON (George N.): *Persia and the Persian Question,* II, London, 1892.

Daïrat-al-Maarif al-Islamiyah: *Encyclopedia of Islam,* I, article « Khuzestan », IX, chap. I.

DARWICH (Bacha): *Report on the Outline of Turco-Iranian Borders,* Baghdad, 1953, (Arabic).

DELLA VALLE (Pietro): *The Travels of Sig. Pietro della Valle into the East-Indies and the Arabian Desert,* Hakluyt Society, 1902.

DHORME (Edouard): *Les Religions de Babylone et d'Assyrie,* Paris, PUF, 1949.

GARABIYYA (Abdul-Karim): *Introduction to Modern Arab History,* I, Damascus, 1960, (Arabic).

HAIDARY (F.): *The Title of Glory: Baghdad, Basra et Najd,* Baghdad, 1962, (Arabic).

HACHIMI (Mohammad): *The Three Heroes,* Baghdad, 1937, (Arabic).

HAMAWY (Yakout): *Mojamul Bouldan,* (Encyclopedia of the World), I, Cairo, 1906.

HITTI (Philip K.): *History of the Arabs,* Macmillan Student Editions, London, 10th edition, 1979, (see also Arabic edition, 1976).

HOURANI (Georges): *The Arabs and Navigation in the Indian Ocean,* Cairo, 1958, (Arabic).

HUSNI (Abdul-Razzak): *Modern Political History of Iraq,* III, Sidon, 1957, (Arabic).

IBN HAWKAL: *Image of the Earth,* al-Hayatt Books, Beirut, 1968, (Arabic).

INTAKI (Abdul Massih): *The Voyage of King Hussein through the Nile Valley,* Cairo, 1917, (Arabic).

AL-ISTIKHRI (M.): *Al-Masalek Walmamalek,* (Roads and Kingdoms), I, Cairo, 1961, (Arabic).

JAMES (Felix Jones): *Narrative of a Journey to the Frontier of Turkey and Persia, through a Part of Kurdistan,* Submitted to the Government on August 16, 1848. Selections from the records of the Bombay Government, nº XLIII, New series.

AL-KALKASHANDI (Abdul-Abbas Ahmed): *Nihayat-al-Arb fi maarifat ansiba' al-Arab,* Cairo, 1959.

KHAZAAL (H.K.): *Political History of Kuwait,* I and III, Beirut, 1963, (Arabic).

LE STRANGE (Guy): *The Land of the Eastern Caliphate,* Cambridge, 1905.

LONGRIGG (H. Stephen): *Four Centuries of Modern Iran,* Oxford, 1925.

LORIMER (J.G.): *Gazette of the Persian Gulf, Oman and Central Arabia,* 2 vol. Calcutta, 1908.

MOHAMMAD (Abdul Amir): *Maritime Forces in the Arabian Gulf during the XVIIIth Century*, Baghdad, 1961, (Arabic).

AN-NABHANI (M.): *At-tuhfat An-Nabhaniyya*, IX, Cairo, 1342 H.

NAJJAR (M.A.): *Political History of Arabistan 1897-1925*, Dar al-Ma'aref, Cairo, 1971, (Arabic).

NAWAR (Abdul Aziz): Modern History of Iraq, Cairo, 1968, (Arabic).

PARROT (A.): *Archéologie Mésopotamienne, les Etapes*, Paris, 1946.

ROWLINSON (H.): *England and Russia in the East*, London, 1875.

REZA Shah: *Memoirs*, translated by Ali al-Basri, Baghdad, 1950.

AR-RIHANI (Amin): *Moulouk al-Arab*, II, Beirut, 1951.

ROBERTS (J.M.): *The Hutchinson History of the World*, Hutchinson Publishing Group, London, 1976.

RODINSON (Maxime): *Les Arabes*, Paris, PUF, 1979.

SARKIS (Yaakoub): *Geographical Research*, I, Baghdad, 1948, (Arabic).

SHIBR (J.B.): *History of the al-Moucha'chi'in*, Baghdad, 1965, (Arabic).

SYKES (Sir Percy); *A History of Persia*, II, London, 1921.

TESKEIRA (Pedro): *The Travels of Pedro Teskeira*, « Kings of Harmuz » and extracts from « Kings of Persia », Hakluyt Society, 1902.

WILBER (Donald N.): *Iran: Past and Present*, Princeton University Press, 1956.

WILSON (Sir Arnold): *South West Persia, a Political Officer's Diary, 1907-1914*, Oxford, 1941.

ZABET (Chaker): *International Relations and Border Agreements between Iraq and Iran*, Baghdad, 1966, (Arabic).

AZ-ZARKALI: « *Al-A'lam* », Cairo, 1954.

## NEWSPAPERS and REVIEWS

AL-ANBA', January 19, 1981.
AL-ANWAR, January 29, 1981.
BAGHDAD OBSERVER, March 15, 1981.

L'EXPRESS, October 4, 1980.

GÉOPOLITIQUE DU PÉTROLE, December 31, 1979.

AL-HAWADESS, n° 1271, March 13, 1981.

HERALD TRIBUNE, September 26, 1980.

JOURNAL OFFICIEL DE LA RÉPUBLIQUE FRANÇAISE, September 24, 1980.

KAYHAN, Teheran, April 28, 1979.

LE MATIN, September 26, 1980.

LE MONDE, July 21-22, August 29, September 19-26, 29-30, October 1, 3-4, 7, 15, 17, 30, 1980, January 6, 1981.

AL-MOSTAKBAL, September 15, 1979 and n° 123, June 20, 1980.

AN-NAHAR, September 23, 25, 26, 28, 29; October 1, 3, 15, 1980.

AN-NAHAR ARABE ET INTERNATIONALE, March 24, 1980.

LE POINT, n° 419, September 24, 29, 1980.

REVUE DE LA POLITIQUE INTERNATIONALE, Cairo, n° 8, April 1967.

REVUE DU MONDE MUSULMAN, Belgium, n° 11, November 1980.

AS-SAFIR, September 28, 1980.

ATH-THAWRA, September 28, 1980.

AL-WATAN AL-ARABI, January 22, 1981.

## DOCUMENTS

IRAQ-IRAN CONFLICT, documentary file, Baghdad, 1980.

U.N. S.P.V.2251.

U.N. S 14203.

# INDEX*

## A

Abadan: 50, 70, 75, 77, 79, 96, 113, 115, 135, 139, 140, 142, 145, 152.
Abbasids: 15, 60.
Abdallah (Sheikh): 81, 96.
Abdel Karim: 86.
Abdul-Ilah: 97.
Abdul-Majid: 75.
Abi Waqqas (Sa'ad bin): 15.
Abu Dhabi: 30.
Abul-'Abbas Al-Muqtadir: 59.
Abu Musa: 29, 30, 35, 38, 42, 44, 45, 47, 117, 127.
Aden: 31.
Ahwaz: 49, 51, 59, 68, 79, 86, 87, 97, 122, 127, 132, 135, 138, 139, 145.
al-Ali (Salah Omar): 118.
Alexander the Great: 49.
Algiers (Agreement of): 35, 101, 103, 109, 111, 113, 121.
Amer Bani Sa'sa'a: 68.
Amin (Abdel Fattah Mohammed): 138.
Amir Achraf (treaty): 74.
Amman: 128, 151.
Aqrawi (Hachem Hassan): 138.
Arab League: 96, 97, 98, 107.
Arabian Gulf: 38, 39, 48, 56, 62, 63.
Arabistan: 29, 33, 40, 48, 54, 58-62, 85-88, 91, 92, 94, 97, 98, 101, 102, 151, 152-153.

Arabistan Liberation Front: 97, 98.
Arabistan National Liberation Front: 98.
Arafat (Yasser): 155, 156.
Arab Nationalism: 30, 147.
Arbil: 122.
Ard Roum (treaty): 74.
Ashtar: 133.
az-Ze'baq (Mohieddine): 95.
Azerbaidjan: 33, 157.
Aziz (Tareq): 19, 20, 120, 121, 153.

## B

Ba'ath (party): 21, 23, 26, 121.
Bab-al-Mandab: 38.
Babylonia: 55, 56.
Bachtakwa: 85.
Baghdad: 22, 31, 60, 76, 79, 115, 125, 133.
Baha'ud-Dawla: 60.
Bahrain: 29, 35, 41, 45.
Bakr: 59.
al-Bakr (Ahmed Hassan): 27.
Baluchistan: 33, 157.
Bandar Abbas: 42, 66.
Bani Al-'Am: 55.
Bani Bridi: 59, 60.

* This index does not include the appendices.

324

Khairallah (Adnan): 122, 123, 147.

Khalaf (Kassem Mohammed): 138.

Khalkhali (Sadegh): 34, 100.

Khanaqin: 108.

al-Khaqani (Sheikh Abdel Mohsen): 95.

al-Khaqani (Sheikh Mohammed): 99, 100.

Kharijites: 59.

Kharj: 122.

Khazaal (Sheikh): 78, 79, 81, 82-88, 95, 96.

Khodr: 50, 75, 77.

Khomeiny: 25, 26, 27, 31, 34, 38, 99, 100, 105, 121, 128, 132, 136, 148, 150, 155, 157, 161.

Khorramshahr (see Mohammarah).

Khosrowabad: 113.

Khuzestan: 49, 91, 94.

Kirkuk: 122, 132.

Kouteiba: 108.

Kurdistan: 33, 113, 131, 152, 157.

al-Kut: 122.

Kuwait: 30, 41, 45, 71, 96, 98.

# L

Larak: 44.

League of Nations: 95.

Lanja: 47.

Luristan: 85.

# M

Madani: 100.

Mahmoud (Abdel Wahab): 138.

Malmairca (Isidoro): 125.

Masjed Soleyman: 50.

Masirah: 38.

Mecca: 92.

Mehran: 108, 127, 145.

Mesopotamia: 40, 53, 56, 59.

Missan: 48, 52, 93.

Miza'al: 81, 82.

Modar: 60.

Mohammarah: 28, 39, 50, 51, 52, 68, 71, 72, 75, 76, 79, 80, 82, 87, 95, 113, 114, 115, 122, 127, 132, 135, 138, 140, 141, 142, 145.

al-Mohseniyah: 61.

Mokri (Mohammed): 130.

Mongols: 60.

Mosul: 59, 122, 132.

Moucha'chi'i (Mubarak Ben Abdul-Muttaleb): 61.

Moucha'chi'ins: 52, 61.

Moujahed Khan: 85.

Mourad IV: 73.

Movement of the Arab Revolution for the Liberation of Arabistan: 98.

Movement of the Mujahidin of the Arab Muslim People: 101.

Movement of Nonaligned Countries: 22, 107, 125, 129, 155, 156.

Mubârak (Abdul Muttaleb): 61.

Muskie (Edmund): 118.

al-Mustansiriyah: 19, 20, 21, 23, 24.

Mustapha Lwand: 108.

Muzayriah: 108.

# N

Nader Chah (treaty): 74.

Naft Chaabiyah: 122.

Naft Khaneh: 108.

Nafud: 40.

Nahr Abul-Arabid: 77.
Najib Pacha: 75.
National 'Congress of Arabistan: 98.
an-Nasiriyah: 53.
Nasser Eddine Chah: 79.
Niniveh: 115.

Qarmatians: 59.
Qasr-e-Shirin: 73, 107, 108, 115, 122, 127, 142.
Qata' Mandali: 108.
Qatar: 30, 41, 44, 45, 71.
Qom: 22, 25, 100.
al-Qurnah: 39.

# O

Omassiyah: 73.
Oman: 30, 41, 44, 46, 47, 70, 71.
Organization for African Unity: 107.
Ottoman (Empire): 16, 41, 65, 67, 68, 69, 70, 72, 73, 74, 75, 77, 83, 92.

# P

Pahlavi (dynasty): 34, 95.
Palme (Olaf): 154.
Perim: 38.
Persia: 13, 14, 15, 36, 37, 41, 49, 56, 57, 62, 65, 66, 67, 69, 73, 74, 75, 77, 84-86, 160.
Peter the Great: 66.
Political Organization of the Arab People of Arabistan: 97, 101.
Popular Army: 141, 153, 157.
Popular Movement of Arabistan: 101.
Portugal: 41, 63, 65.

# Q

Qadisiyah: 15, 72.
Qadjar (dynasty): 82, 84.

# R

Rabi'ah (tribe): 60, 61, 79.
Rachidoun: 60.
Radjai (Mohammed Ali): 126, 129, 146, 147.
Ramadan (Taha Yassin): 141.
Ras-al-Khaimah: 44, 46.
Ras-Sinai: 38.
Reconciliation Committee: 154.
Red Sea: 38.
Reza Khan: 13, 84-89.
Riyadh: 35.
Rouhani (Sadegh): 35.
Rouleau (Eric): 94.
Russia: 66, 67, 83, 84, 130.
Rustam: 15.

# S

as-Sa'adah (Coalition): 97.
as-Sa'adah (party): 97.
Safawid: 16, 50, 61, 73.
as-Safawi (Ismail): 16, 61, 65.
Saljuq: 60.
Sanandaj: 115.
Sarbil: 127.
Sasanid: 55, 56
Saudi Arabia: 30, 41, 45, 50, 92, 154.

# MAPS

# Mesopotamia

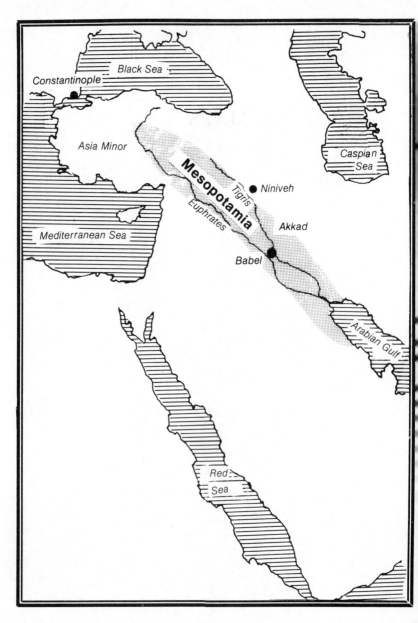

# IRAQ - IRAN - Middle East

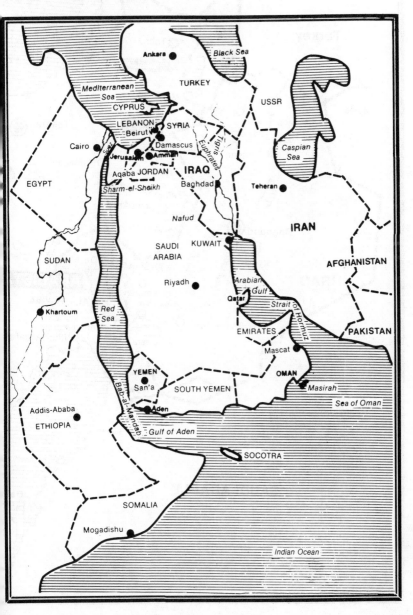

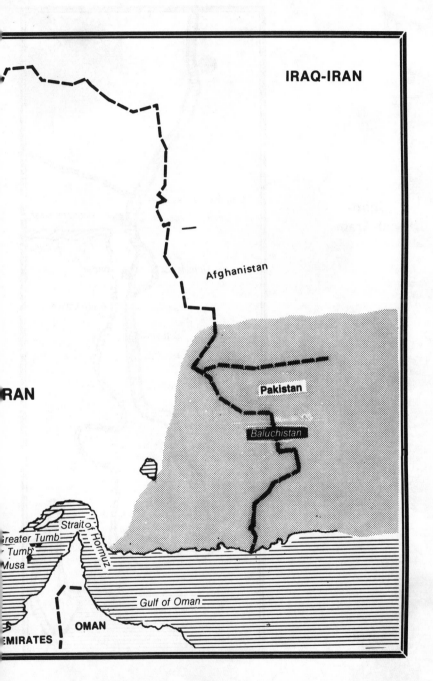

IRAQ-IRAN

Afghanistan

RAN

Pakistan

Baluchistan

Strait

Hormuz

Greater Tumb

Tumb

Musa

Gulf of Oman

OMAN

EMIRATES

**Shatt-
al-Arab**

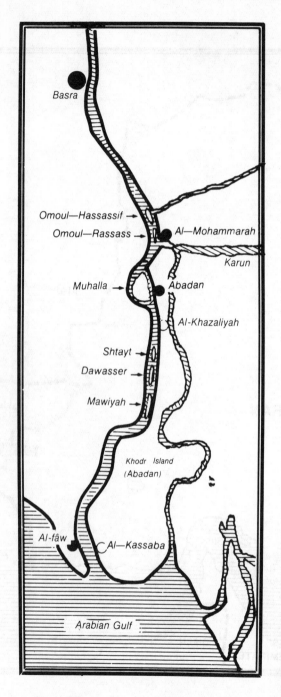

Basra

Omoul—Hassassif →

Omoul—Rassass →

Al—Mohammarah

Karun

Muhalla →

Abadan

Al-Khazaliyah

Shtayt →

Dawasser →

Mawiyah →

Khodr Island
(Abadan)

Al-fâw

Al—Kassaba

Arabian Gulf

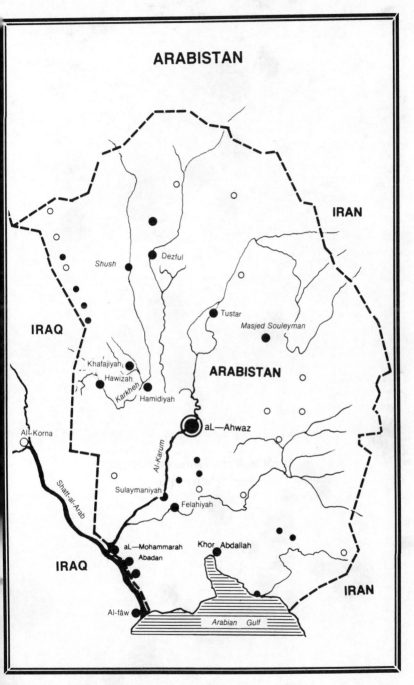

# ARABISTAN

IRAN

Shush

Dezful

IRAQ

Tustar

Masjed Souleyman

Khafajiyah

Hawizah

Karkheh

Hamidiyah

ARABISTAN

Al-Korna

aL—Ahwaz

Al-Karum

Shatt-al-Arab

Sulaymaniyah

Felahiyah

aL—Mohammarah

Abadan

Khor Abdallah

IRAQ

IRAN

Al-fâw

Arabian Gulf

Dépôt légal 2ᵉ trimestre 1981 - 23284
Imp. Schiffer - Paris